Victorian Patchwork

Books by Cyril Pearl

The Girl with the Swansdown Seat
Wild Men of Sydney
Always Morning
Pantaloons & Antics
Morrison of Peking
Bawdy Burns
Dublin in Bloomtime
Rebel Down Under
Victorian Patchwork

Victorian Patchwork

Cyril Pearl

HEINEMANN : LONDON

William Heinemann Ltd
15 Queen Street, Mayfair, London W1X 8BE

LONDON   MELBOURNE   TORONTO
JOHANNESBURG   AUCKLAND

Printed in Great Britain by
Cox & Wyman Ltd, London, Fakenham and Reading

'The history of the Victorian Age will never be written; we know too much about it'

Lytton Strachey

Contents

Victorian Patchwork

I

Every age is a patchwork, but the Victorian is unique for its complexity and its contrasts. It was a brutal age, but it produced notable humanitarians. It was a callous age, but it produced notable reformers. It was a conformist age, but it produced notable rebels. It was a materialist age, but it produced poets as well as stockbrokers, philosophers as well as factory-owners. It preached a morality which is still, pejoratively, called 'Victorian', but it had its playboys as well as its puritans, its triumphant whores as well as its downtrodden wives. It was an age of faith and an age of doubt, of flaunted wealth and frightful poverty. Whatever else it was, certainly it was not humdrum. It had a vitality, an exuberance, and a curiosity that subsequent ages have lost. And despite the pharisaical code of its middle class, it was a remarkably tolerant age. We tend to overlook this. 'In one respect,' says Bertrand Russell, 'the Victorian age was more tolerant than our own because it was less democratic. There was a respect for eminence of whatever kind, and a toleration for the eccentricities of the eminent which was not extended to the vulgar herd. Darwin and Huxley were unmolested when they proclaimed opinions which would have been intolerable in a village blacksmith, George Eliot was widely received, although a village girl who indulged in similar conduct would have been an outcast.'

An American, Howard Mumford Jones, writes of the Victorians in similar terms:

> They made a Jewish novelist prime minister of England, despite his curls and his waistcoats; and I need not comment on the chances of either a Jew or a novelist, much less both, being elected President of this enlightened Republic. They elected an atheist to Parliament, and when Parliament threw him out they continued to elect him until not atheism, but Parliament, gave way; and I hardly need mention the possibility of electing a Charles Bradlaugh to the Senate of the United States. They suffered a group of aliens to tie up the business of the House of Commons night after night under the leadership of Parnell and his followers; and I cannot imagine delegates from the Hawaiian Islands or Puerto Rico enjoying the same liberty in the House of Representatives. Huxley told the bishop to his face in a public meeting that he was a liar; yet Huxley served on more public commissions . . . than any other

British scientist. Would an American professor in a state university be similarly honoured?

I think we talk too much about Victorian moral conformity.

We talk too much about Victorian conformity because the middle class was conformist and we talk too much about Victorian prosperity because the middle class was prosperous. A common error of historians is to reconstruct the past in terms of a small minority. 'What reader of general history knows how nine people out of ten lived in Rome or Athens or Thebes?' Joseph McCabe asks in his *Social Record of Christianity*. What reader of general history knows how nine people out of ten lived in mid-Victorian London or Manchester or Glasgow? 'The mid-Victorians were pre-eminently a Bible-reading, church-going, sabbatarian generation,' says Mr David Thomson. But they also were pre-eminently a smut-reading, brothel-going, sceptical generation. It depends on which mid-Victorians you mean.

G. M. Trevelyan is perhaps the most persuasive of that numerous band of historians for whom the story of nineteenth-century England means the story of, at most, 10 per cent of its population. It was 'a century of peace, security and wealth', he told listeners to a BBC broadcast in 1948. 'In the nineteenth century', he said, 'our fortunate ancestors were not precluded by national poverty from obtaining the books they wanted to study, or buying beautiful things, or from travelling to see them.' In the same mood of myopic nostalgia, Mr Derek Hudson writes of the 'happy, prosperous eighteen-fifties', and Mr G. M. Young says: 'Of all decades in our history a wise man would choose the eighteen-fifties to be young in.'

Mr Young does not say whether this is true of all wise men, irrespective of their station in life. It is doubtful whether the young man who in 1850 was transported for life for stealing a few carpenters' tools would have agreed with him, nor the fourteen-year-old boy who was sentenced to twelve months' hard labour, with two whippings, for stealing a few handkerchiefs. Such sentences were common in the 'happy, prosperous eighteen-fifties'. How happy and prosperous were they, in fact?

Here is an item from *The Times* report of the Middlesex Sessions of April 1853:

Thomas Smith, 14, James Cook, 10, charged with stealing 12 wine glasses. The judge said that the history of the younger boy, Cook, would illustrate the operation of summary punishments.

During the last 12 months, he had undergone seven sentences of imprisonment and six whippings, yet here he was again. He had no home, and no means of subsistence. The Court could not, as the law stood at the present, send him to Parkhurst, where he would have received an education which would have enabled him to have earned his future livelihood; and there was no other course than to send him to a common prison. The sentence, therefore, was that each prisoner should undergo imprisonment and hard labour for six months.

And here, in the happy 1850s, Henry Mayhew, the indefatigable chronicler of the London poor, reports in the *Morning Chronicle* a talk with three young girls who earn their living by 'needle and slop work':

1. 'I make moleskin trowsers. I get 7d or 8d a pair. I can do a pair in a day and twelve, when there is full employment, in a week. When I am fully employed I get from 7/- to 8/- a week. My expenses out of that for twist, thread and candles are about 1/6 a week, leaving me 6/- a week clear. But I have coals to pay for – at least 6d a week more, so 5/6 is the very outside of what I earn in full work. Taking one week with another, all the year round, I don't make above 3/- clear money a week. The trowsers work is held to be the best paid of all. I give 1/- a week rent.'
2. 'I work at slop trowsers, moleskin and cord – no cloth. We make about 4/- a week but we must work till nine or ten o'clock every night for that. I earn clear just upon 3/- a week.'
3. I do the shirt work – the fine full-fronted white shirts. I get 2¼d each for 'em. There were six button-holes, four rows of stitching in the front, and the collars and waistbands stitched as well. By working from 5 o'clock in the morning till midnight each night, I be able to do seven in the week. This would bring me in 17½d for my whole week's labour – out of that the cotton would be taken, that came to 2d every week, so that left me 15½d to pay rent, living, and buy candles with.

Or let us glimpse through the windows of a typical London house in Mr Derek Hudson's 'happy, prosperous eighteen-fifties'. The quotation is from Charles Dickens's *Household Narrative of Current Events* for April 1852:

A case occurred at Bow Street on the 3rd, showing the urgent need for *Sanitary Regulations as to the Dwellings of the Poor*. Eight men were summoned for non-compliance with the provisions of the Common Lodging-houses Act. They rent rooms at No. 214 Church Lane, St. Giles's; the proceedings were for the sake of the lodgers, whose health and lives must be endangered by the present state of things. Charles Reeves, a surveyor under the act, gave this evidence. On the night of the 8th March, he went to the house in order to inspect it.

In the room No. 1, belonging to the defendant Collins, the size of which was 15 feet 6 inches by 14 feet 6 inches, which ought to have contained only nine persons, he found five families. In one bed, a man, his wife, and three children; in a second, a boy and a girl; in a third, a man and his wife; in a fourth, a man, his wife, and three children; and the same in a fifth, making in all twenty. There were no partitions, nor was the act in any way complied with.

In the second room, belonging to Calman, there were ten people, the regulations allowing three; in the third room, in which Leary was the landlord, there were twelve persons, the proper number being eight. In the fourth room, 11 feet 8 inches by 10 feet 8 inches, there were fourteen occupants, the regulation number being four. In the fifth room there were eight lodgers instead of three; in the sixth room, which ought to have contained only seven, there were twenty-two men, women and children; in the seventh room, there were twelve, six being the authorized number; in the eighth room, there were nine instead of seven; making altogether one hundred and seven people sleeping in a house which was adapted to accommodate only forty-seven. The whole of the rooms were in a most filthy and pestilential condition. There were very few bedsteads, and the occupants slept all together without any regard to decency. There was no water laid on, nor was there any means by which these unfortunate creatures could cleanse their persons.

The defendants, several of whom could only speak Irish pleaded ignorance of the act, and promised to do all that was requisite.

Mr. Henry remarked upon the miserable condition of the unhappy creatures, who were obliged to resort to such filthy abodes; and said the evil was attributable in a great measure to the owners of the houses, who let them to such persons as the defendants, and extorted from them rents so high that they were obliged to overcrowd their rooms in order to pay them, or even get their own living.

Conditions were little better when a Royal Commission into the Housing of the Poor sat in 1884–5. The forty-three-year-old Prince of Wales was a member of the Commission and dutifully attended the first four sessions. But during the spring and summer of 1884, when the Commissioners were hearing evidence about the housing of the London poor, His Royal Highness was fulfilling other social obligations in Paris, La Bourbole, Baden and Koeningstein, or attending the races at Newmarket ('which,' said *The Times*, 'calls for very slight comment') and at Goodwood, or sailing his yacht at Cowes. Unfortunately he thus missed the evidence of Lord William Compton, a younger son of the Marquess of Northampton. The Marquess owned a castle and 23,600 acres in Northampton, and a large area of Clerkenwell, in London. Lord William visited some of the six hundred tenements of his father's property, some leased from the estate directly, others through a complex of sub-leases. Lord William mentioned 'families of six, seven, eight and nine all living in one room; six families living in six rooms, with one W.C. between them; a family of nine adults living in two rooms, one without windows or ventilation'. The principal housefarmer on the estate was a Mr Decimus Alfred Ball, who, with another housefarmer, Mr Ross, ran the Clerkenwell Vestry. Messrs Ball and Ross made sure that no property – from which they extracted up to 150 per cent profits – would ever be condemned by sanitary inspectors who depended on the Vestry for their jobs.

When Inspector John Bates, of the Metropolitan Police, described three rooms in Half Moon Court, Holborn, in which nineteen people – eight adults and eleven children – slept, he was asked if he regarded this as over-crowding. 'I think not,' he replied. 'They were small children.' The Inspector told of a visit to No. 10 Prospect Terrace, Gray's Inn Road:

'I spoke to a woman who was living in the parlour on the left-hand side. she looked very ill. She and her husband and four children were occupying this room. One little boy was lying on the floor and the woman told me that they had not seen meat since Xmas time (about 2 weeks ago) and her husband was breaking stones in the stone yard, but on that day he was not able to get work, being very poorly; and I could not see a particle of food in the house. She told me that the landlord refused to take her money because she was a halfpenny short in the rent. She had 4/5½d. wherewith to pay 4/6, and the agent positively refused to take the money and told her she had better put it in a flower-pot until it grew, and she sold her bedstead to raise the money for the rent.'

When the vestry clerk of Clerkenwell, Mr Robert Paget, was asked by Sir Charles Dilke: 'You are not prepared to deny, are you, that there is an immense amount of overcrowding in Clerkenwell?' he replied enigmatically, 'Query what is overcrowding?'

Mr Paget had reservations on most subjects, but he was quite convinced that there was nothing wrong with the Vestry being run by the men who owned these hovels. 'Those who hold property and have something at stake in the Parish are the most suitable men to be elected to administer its local affairs', he said. This may explain why he had held this job for twenty-eight years.

And writing in the late 'eighties, the anonymous author of *My Secret Life*, that comprehensive eleven-volume Baedeker of Victorian sex, evoked a fragrant picture of the West End in his young days:

The angle of the street named as leading out of the Strand was dark of a night and a favourite place for doxies to go to relieve their bladders. The police took no notice of such trifles, provided it was not done in the greater thoroughfare (although I have seen at night women do it openly in the gutter in the Strand): in the particular street, I have seen them pissing almost in rows; yet they mostly went in twos to do that job, for a woman likes a screen, one usually standing up till the other had finished, and then taking her turn. Indeed the pissing in all by-streets of the Strand was continuous, for although the population of London was only half of what it now is, the number of gay ladies seemed double . . .

II

In the famine year, 1847, Alexis Soyer, the accomplished chef of the Reform Club, went to Ireland at the request of the British Government and produced a book called *The Poor Man's Regenerator*. It consists of recipes for feeding very many people at very little cost.

'It will be perceived,' wrote M. Soyer in his foreword, 'that I have omitted all kinds of spice except in those dishes which are intended expressly for them, as I consider they only flatter the appetite and irritate the stomach and make it crave for more food: my object being not to create an appetite but to satisfy it.'

Here are two typical satisfying Soyer *plats du jour*, carefully costed to the last farthing:

Two ounces of dripping	o½
Quarter of a pound of solid meat, at 4d. per lb. (cut into dice one inch square)	1
Quarter pound of onions, sliced thin	
Quarter pound of turnips; the peel will do, or one whole one cut into small dice.	1
Two ounces of leeks; the green tops will do, sliced thin.	
Three ounces of celery	
Three-quarters of a pound of common flour	1
Half a pound of pure barley, or one pound of Scotch	1½
Three ounces of salt	
Quarter of an ounce of brown sugar	¼
Fuel	¾
Two gallons of water	o
	6
Six pounds of bones	3
Ten quarts of water	
Three ounces of salt	
Bay-leaf, etc., ...	
Two onions, cut thin	
Half an ounce of sugar	
Half a pound of vegetables, cut small	1
Half a pound of oatmeal	1
Pound of rice	2½
Two ounces of dripping	o½
	8

The bones can be sold after using for   2

6

In 1850 M. Soyer designed a dish for the Exhibition Banquet given by the Lord Mayor of York to Prince Albert. This dish, apparently intended more to flatter the appetite than to satisfy it, was also carefully costed, as follows:

		£	s.	d.
5 Turtle heads, part of fins, and green fat		£34.	0.	0
24 Capons (the two small *noix* from middle of back only used)		8.	8.	0
18 Turkeys – the same		8.	12.	0
18 Poulards – the same		5.	17.	0
16 Fowls – the same		2.	8.	0
10 Grouse		2.	5.	0
20 Pheasants – *noix* only		3.	0.	0
45 Partridges – the same		3.	7.	0
6 Plovers			9.	0
40 Woodcocks – *noix* only		8.	0.	0
3 Dozen quails, whole..		3.	0.	0
100 Snipes – *noix* only		5.	0.	0
3 Dozen pigeons – *noix* only		0.	14.	0
6 Dozen larks, stuffed		0.	15.	0
Ortolans, from Belgium		5.	0.	0

The garnish, consisting of cocks' combs, truffles, mushrooms, crayfish, olives, American asparagus, croustades, sweetbreads, *quenelles de volaille,* green mangoes, and a new sauce 14. 10. 0

           £105. 5. 0

The total cost of this banquet, in addition to the 'hundred guinea dish', is not known, but when the Corporation of the City of London entertained the newly married Prince and Princess of Wales at the Guildhall in June 1863, the Report of the Royal Reception Committee disclosed that the City's loyal gesture had cost £12,345, made up thus:

	£	s.	d.
Artificers' charges	£3,591.	0.	0.
Toilet articles, perfumery etc.,	208.	0.	0.
Supper, etc.,	1,680.	0.	0.
Decorations after sale	3,591.	0.	0.
Wines, etc.,	584.	0.	0.
Care of Plate	60.	0.	0.
China and Glass	205.	0.	0.
Music	117.	0.	0.
Printing	431.	0.	0.
Lighting and Illuminations	207.	0.	0.
Miscellaneous	1,163.	0.	0.
Gratuities to Officers	508.	0.	0.
	£12,345.	0.	0.

III

'Why is there so much pauperism in this country?' John Bright, the Quaker mill-owner's son, asked his well-fed colleagues in the House of Commons in February 1869. 'This is the great problem in comparison with which many of those piddling questions which sometimes occupy us are as nothing. . . . Is it not upon the face of it a monstrous state of things that the people of this rich England, who lay the whole world under contribution for the flower of its products, and who are a byword among the nations for plethoric wealth, should yet have to confess to the shameful fact that one in thirty of them has not wherewith to support bare existence?' (The population of the United Kingdom was 30,000,000, and there were over one million *registered* paupers.)

'The year which ends today has, in England, been generally prosperous and tranquil,' said *The Times* somewhat in the manner of Mr Derek Hudson, in its *Annual Summary* for 1873. That year, there were 100,000 registered paupers in London. That year, 107 people *officially* died of starvation in the metropolis. 'A hundred human beings slowly tortured out of this world!' commented *Vanity Fair*: 'And after all our statesmen had done for them! Mr Disraeli had given them the franchise and Mr Gladstone the ballot. If this is not enough for dinner, what more would they have?'

If the Victorians did little to abolish poverty, they were not lacking in charity. Alleviating the poor with gifts and good wishes was easier than getting rid of the conditions that produced them; besides, it gave the benefactor a comfortable feeling of virtue. No other age has produced such a luxuriant growth of assorted charities, mostly under the patronage of noblemen and noblewomen. The *Post Office Directory* for 1862 lists over five hundred 'philanthropic and improvement societies', among them the *Aged Pilgrims' Society,* the *Sack Protection Society,* the *Syrian Improvement Society,* and the *Society for the Evangelisation of Foreigners.* Vast sums were spent in converting heathens and heretics to Christianity. The *Society for the Conversion of the Jews* announced at its annual meeting in 1859 that its income the preceding year was £31,305 16s. 4d. and its bag of Jews converted, twenty. *Punch* worked out the price of each convert at £1,565 5s. 9¾d. and commented, 'There are heaps of Christians who are ready to become Jews at a considerably lower figure . . .'

Victorian charity knew no boundaries. In 1875 the Lord Blantyre and the Duke of Portland sat on the *Stafford House Committee for the Relief Among the Turkish Soldiers* ('caused by the severity of the winter and the want of shelter') although, only a few months before, the Turks had murdered 12,000 Christians in Bulgaria, and 11,000,000 more of the faithful were said still to be 'groaning under the yoke'. The Lord and the Duke each contributed a thousand pounds.

According to *Vanity Fair* in 1874, the average income of an English Duke was £70,000: 'The House of Lords represents a collective income of £45,000,000 equal to the revenues of the Church of England.' (The Established Church was not embarrassed by its Founder's badge of poverty, and the superior clergy, at least, had good reason to be satisfied with the ways of God to man. The benefice of the Bishop of London was worth £24,000 a year. Towards the end of his life, Blomfield, in a mood of self-denial, told Lord Palmerston that he would resign his see if he received an annuity of only £6,000. The see of Canterbury was worth £20,000 a year. The Bishops of Oxford and of Durham each jogged along on £10,000 a year. Bishop Sparke of Ely, his son and his son-in-law enjoyed between them £30,000 a year of church endowments.)

In January 1860, while Coventry weavers were eating garbage from the gutter, and sleeping, said *The Spectator*, 'like pigs in the straw', all their bedding having been pawned; while three thousand women in one day gathered at the Thames Police Court seeking relief, and the condition of the poor in many other parts of London was 'appalling', English clergymen were engaged in passionate debate about albs, chasubles and dalmatics, prevenient grace and auricular confession; whether it was permissible to brighten up the service with a stuffed dove, and the supreme evil of Romanism.

'We know what Ritualism means!' cried the Rev. George Chute during one of the violent controversies that followed John Henry Newman's conversion to Rome. 'It means the defilement of your daughters, the seduction of your wives, and all the other evils that abound on the Continent.'

The House of Commons in 1856 rejected a bill which would have regulated the hours of labour in bleaching factories where 'young girls are worked 16, 18 and 20 hours a day, in a temperature varying from 90 to 130 degrees (Fahrenheit), and from some of the apartments in which persons are habitually carried out in a fainting state'. Honourable members pointed out that bills of this kind interfered with manufacture. Were these children relieved, it would be impossible to sell the article they produced at the same rate of profit.

Half a century later, when the Victorian age closed in a glow of Imperialist glory, inner London was still a great sink of sweated workers – a class that ranked lower even than labourers – 'whose plight,' says R. C. K. Ensor, 'public opinion had deplored, without amending, since Tom Hood's day'.

Nor was the condition of other workers much better. 'It is no exaggeration to say that the opening of the twentieth century saw malnutrition more rife in England than it had been since the great dearths of medieval and Tudor times,' says J. C. Drummond in his classic study of five centuries of English diet, *The Englishman's Food*. But apart from a handful of social workers, 'few showed any real concern at the terrible distress in the working-class districts'.

The Government showed a belated and not entirely disinterested concern when Army authorities reported 'the greatest difficulty' in getting enough fit men to fight in South Africa. In some areas, rejections were as high as 60 per cent; throughout the whole country, nearly 40 per cent. Despite the scepticism of the Royal College of Surgeons and the Royal College of Physicians, the Government set up a committee to investigate the deterioration of the national physique.

Its report, published in 1904, is the bleak epitaph of the Victorian age. In some districts, at least a third of the children were undernourished, not only in the sense that their food was bad, but that they were actually hungry, living almost entirely on a semi-starvation ration of bread and jam. Rickets, rotten teeth and stunted growth were the heritage of England's working-class from the richest century in her history. When the century ended, London, the capital of the world's greatest empire, had an infantile death-rate of 279 per 1,000. Seventy years later it was 18 per 1,000.

II

'Tears, Idle Tears'

I

Victorians who showed little or no emotion at the brutal treatment of real children often shed torrents of real tears over the sufferings of a child in a novel, especially if the child were a little girl. 'If anybody can get a pretty little girl to go to heaven prattling about her dolls, and her little brothers and sisters, and quoting texts of Scripture with appropriate gasps, dashes and broken sentences, he may send half the women in London with tears in their eyes, to Mr Mudie's,' said the *Saturday Review* in 1858 (Mr Mudie was the proprietor of one of England's most popular lending libraries):

> This kind of taste has not only been flattered, but prodigiously developed, by Mr Dickens . . . No man can offer to the public so large a stock of death-beds adapted for either sex and for any age from five-and-twenty downwards. There are idiot death-beds, where the patient cries ha! ha!, and points at vacancy – pauper death-beds with unfeeling nurses to match – male and female children's death-beds, where the young ladies or gentlemen sit up in bed, pray to the angels, and see golden water on the walls . . .

The case of Little Nell surely belongs to a textbook of abnormal psychology. When Dickens was writing *The Old Curiosity Shop* in monthly parts, her impending death was a matter of enormous concern to himself, his friends and a great number of strangers, many of whom wrote to him pleading to save her life. His friend and biographer John Forster – who himself had 'a good cry' over the last chapters of Mrs Gaskell's *Ruth* – describes Dickens's unspeakable anguish as Nell approached her end. 'I am breaking my heart over the story and cannot bear to finish it,' Dickens wrote a week before he disposed of her. And when the dreadful deed was done: 'I am the wretchedest of the wretched . . . Nobody will miss her like I shall.' A week later he wrote: 'I am . . . nearly dead with work and grief for the loss of the child.' And: 'All the night I have been pursued by the child.'

There may be something in the theory that Dickens's grotesque grief derived from his identification of Nell with his dead sister-in-law, Mary Hogarth, with whom he had been in love. But what of the sardonic Carlyle, who 'wept like a child' over Nell's death; or Daniel O'Connell, who groaned, 'He should not have killed her,' and threw his book out of the window; or Walter Savage Landor, who, when he threw his cook out of the window was worried only about the violets below, but was overcome by the death of Nell, and when he was able to speak, compared her with Juliet and Desdemona? And what of Lord Jeffrey, the savage critic of the *Edinburgh Review*? He was found by a woman neighbour with his head on his library table; when he looked up with tear-filled eyes she begged to be excused; she had not known he had got bad news – was someone dead? 'Yes, indeed,' replied Jeffrey, 'I am a great goose to have given way so, but I couldn't help it. You'll be sorry to hear that Little Nelly, Boz's Little Nelly, is dead.' Another great goose was the actor William Charles Macready, who had begged Dickens to spare the life of Nell. *The Old Curiosity Shop* was then appearing in *Master Humphrey's Clock*.' I saw one print in it of the dear child that gave a dead chill through my blood,' Macready wrote in his diary. 'I dread to read it, but must get it over. Later I have read the two numbers; I never read printed words that gave me so much pain. I could not weep for some time . . .'

In this almost universal orgy of grief, it is refreshing to read that Swinburne thought Little Nell was as monstrous as a baby with two heads.

When Dickens was writing *A Christmas Carol* he 'wept over it and laughed and wept again'. He had 'a real good cry' over *The Chimes*, and Gilbert A'Beckett, too, cried 'much and painfully' over it. Then came *Dombey and Son*, and a cloudburst of tears that recalled the deluge at the death of Little Nell. Dickens could not sleep after he had written of Paul Dombey's death; he walked the streets of Paris distractedly all night. Lord Jeffrey was again convulsed: 'I have so cried and sobbed over it last night and again this morning,' he wrote to Dickens, 'and felt my heart purified by these tears, and blessed you and loved you for making me shed them.' Of what was his heart purified? Of the stain of indifference to the thousands of children, less privileged than Paul Dombey, who suffered in England's slums and workhouses and gaols? Even Macaulay, who later denounced the 'sullen socialism' of *Hard Times*, cried 'as if my heart would break' over Paul; and Milnes, the cynical student of de Sade, and Thackeray, the worldly satirist, were both moved to tears by Paul's death. Macaulay, even more curiously, cried over Tennyson's *Guinevere*, and Dickens over Wilkie Collins's *Ann Rodway*. Thackeray, like Dickens, could cry over his own puppets. James Russell Lowell sat in Thackeray's library while Thackeray, looking haggard and ill, read the narrative of Colonel Newcome's death; tears flowed down his face and the last words were lost in a heavy sob.

'Nothing in the field of fiction is to be found in English literature surpassing the death of Jo,' wrote Dean Ramsay, but he did not comment on this paragraph which appeared in Dickens's *Household Narrative of Current Events* at the time when *Bleak House* was being written:

Two little children, whose heads scarcely reached the top of the dock, were charged at Bow Street on the 7th with stealing a loaf out of a Baker's shop. They said, in defence, that they were starving, and their appearance showed that they spoke the truth. They were sentenced to be whipped in the House of Correction.

A few years later a correspondent, 'Jacob Omnium' (the essayist Matthew Higgins), wrote to *The Times* about the brutality of flogging in reformatories and juvenile prisons:

40 years ago, flogging was much more in vogue than it is now. The usual dose, even in those flogging days, was from 8 to 10 cuts. In grave cases, 14 to 16 cuts, and a fresh birch, but such terrible executions were happily rare.

I do not think that flogging is so much approved now as a means of imparting knowledge to the young as it used to be. In our lower and middle class schools it has almost entirely disappeared, although still adhered to in our upper class schools as a time-honoured institution. The children of the rich never received more than 12 or 16 cuts in Dr. Keate's palmiest days. Here is what we administered in 1857-8-9 to the children of the poor:

67 criminals of 12	
41	of 11
34	of 10
12	of 9
3	of 8
1	of 7

were flogged with birch or cat.
A boy of 11 got 48 lashes with the cat for shouting in his cell.
A boy of 10 got 48 lashes for not picking cotton properly.
A boy of 14 got 60 lashes for idleness at the crank.

It is not without significance that while the *Royal Society for the Prevention of Cruelty to Animals* was founded in 1824, *The National Society for the Prevention of Cruelty to Children* was not founded till 1884.

II

Little Nell is a symbol not only of the strange Victorian cult of tears, but of a more sombre, and perhaps related, quirk of the Victorian psyche – the passion of the mature man for the young girl. It may not be extravagant to suggest that all the men who wept over Little Nell were, like Dickens himself, in love with her. Ruskin was nearly forty when he fell in love with the twelve-year-old Rose La Touche, though he did not propose to her till she was eighteen. Edward White Benson, the future Archbishop of Canterbury, decided to marry Mary Sidgwick, a little fair girl of eleven, when he was twenty-three. A year later, he took Mary on his knee and asked her if she thought it would ever come to pass that they should be married. 'Instantly, without a word, a rush of tears fell down her cheeks,' he recorded in his diary. 'I told her that she was often in my thoughts, and that I believed I should never love anyone so much as I should love her if she grew up as it seemed likely.' Mary 'said nothing childish or silly', but affected Mr Benson very much by 'quietly laying the ends of my handkerchief together and tying them in a knot, and quietly putting them in my hand'. She then quoted some passages from *The Princess*. They were married when she was seventeen.

The Rev. Charles Dodgson (Lewis Carroll) too liked to take little girls on his knee, and kiss them, but when a girl grew close to nubility, he abandoned her and found another child friend. Isa Bowman recalls his kissing her passionately when she was about ten or eleven.

Many of Carroll's letters discuss kissing little girls, and he liked to draw or photograph them in the nude. He had no interest in male or grown-up female models. 'I confess I do *not* admire naked boys in pictures,' he wrote. 'They always seem to *need* clothes, whereas one hardly sees why the lovely forms of girls should *ever* be covered up.' Twelve was his ideal age for a girl. 'Girls are so thin from seven to ten,' he said. Most of his friendships with girls ended when they reached the age of fourteen or fifteen. His diary for 1889 records that he kissed a girl who he thought was only fourteen, but turned out to be seventeen. He wrote a 'mock apology' to her mother who replied sternly: 'We shall take care it does not recur.' Mrs A. L. Mayhew, wife of the chaplain of Wadham, offended him by refusing to let him photograph her eleven-year-old daughter in the nude. To another mother, in 1895, he wrote:

> The being intrusted with the care of Ethel for a day is such a great advance on mere acquaintanceship that I ventured to ask if I may regard myself as on 'kissing' terms with her, as I am with many a girl-friend a great deal older than *she* is. Considering that – she being 17 and I 63 – I am quite old enough to be her *grandfather*, I hope you won't think it a very out-of-the-way suggestion.

Discussing Carroll's 'romantic interest in little girls', Derek Hudson says guardedly, 'it is plain that, if they were something less than sweethearts to him, they were considerably more than daughters.' Hugh Kingsmill argues that the Victorians' sense of guilt produced their cult of innocence, with as objects of worship those who were immune from sexual tempta-tion: the very old and the very young, and, by an important convention, all gentlewomen, mothers, wives, sisters and daughters unless otherwise specified. The clash between an awakening imagination and the sense of guilt is naturally most frequent in adolescence: hence the adolescent strain in the Victorian writers of genius, and their attraction towards that period of life.

'Nonsense poetry like that of Lear and Lewis Carroll could not have been written with such beautiful perfection by a nation that preserved a complete psychological balance,' says Dr H. G. J. Renier, and Mr E. L. Woodward suggests that 'a good deal of the Victorian "nonsense" verse is a substitute for the bawdy of earlier periods'.

III

At Wadham Lewis Carroll had known Robert Francis Kilvert, later the vicar of Bredwardine, on the Wye. Kilvert, like Carroll, had a great interest in little girls, and his diary, a sensitive picture of English country life in the seventies, is embroidered with lyrical descriptions of young girls' 'round plump limbs', 'rosy dimpled bottoms', 'budding breasts', 'thighs white and soft and rosy and warm', 'blooming cheeks', 'sweet red lips' and 'long loving kisses'. The kisses of this nineteenth-century Johannes Secundus are recorded with an ecstatic candour. When little Janet Vaughan looked up from her simple division sums to be kissed by him, Kilvert wrote in his diary: 'Shall I confess that I travelled 10 miles today over the hills for a kiss.' Unlike Carroll, Kilvert was attracted even by very young girls. He records a long session of 'sweet kisses and caresses' with beautiful Carrie Britton, who was seven:

I was lost to everything but love and the embraces and the sweet kisses and caresses of the child. At last . . . with one long loving clasp and kiss I reluctantly rose to go. It was hard to leave the child . . . I was exhausted with emotion.

All this recalls Quilp's lickerish response to Little Nell's kisses:

'Ah!' said the dwarf, smacking his lips, 'what a nice kiss that was – just upon the rosy part. What a capital kiss . . . such a chubby, rosy, cosy, little Nell!'

But Kilvert's emotion for kissing little girls was curiously mixed with flagellation fantasies about them. At a period of English life when the birch was almost as important a spiritual guide as the bible, he had many opportunities for indulging these. There is an inescapable gusto about the way he describes the home life of the three Corfield girls, Annie, Phoebe and Tizzie:

> How unkindly their father uses them. The neighbours hear the sound of the whip on their naked flesh . . . It seems that when he comes home late he makes the girls get out of bed and strip themselves naked and then he flogs them severely or else he pulls the bedclothes off them and whips them all three as they lie in bed together writhing and screaming under the castigation.

This, you would think, tells the story. But Kilvert is obviously enjoying it, and continues:

> It is said that sometimes Corfield strips the poor girls naked holds them face downwards across his knees on a bed or chair and whips their bare bottoms so cruelly that the blood runs down their legs. The neighbours fear that there is little doubt that the girls are flogged on their naked bodies till the blood comes . . .

And so on for many more lines of the same sort of thing. Even more revealing is Kilvert's account of the incorrigible Fanny Strange, which requires three entries in his diary.

Thursday 6, August.
I received this evening a wild strange unhappy note from Susan Strange begging me to come and see her as soon as possible. She . . . was troubled about her daughter Fanny who grieves her sadly by frequently lying and stealing. 'I do flog her,' she said. 'And the other morning she was a naughty girl and her brother Joseph brought her in to me in her shimmy while I was in bed. I held her hands while Joseph and Charlie whipped her on her naked bottom as hard as ever they were able to flog her.' I was rather astonished at this system of correction which set two brothers to whip their sister's naked bottom while their mother held her hands, but the poor mother was sick and weak, the girl deserved instant and severe chastisement and merited her flogging richly.

Friday, 7 August.
I went to see Mrs Strange again this afternoon . . . She told me that her child Fanny was still incorrigible though she had been severely 'whipped six times or more this week and on some days she had been flogged twice severely on her naked bottom'.

Saturday, 8 August.
. . . I got a message . . . that little Fanny Strange had suddenly been taken ill and wanted to see me. I went immediately. The little child was in bed upstairs. I sat down by the bed and took her little hot hand. She seemed

very feverish but was quite sensible and appeared to be much softened and humbled. If so the severe chastisement she had undergone may have had a happy effect and have broken her self-will and cured her of her faults. She has during the last few weeks been repeatedly stripped and has had her bottom flogged naked with great severity . . . The severest whippings her mother could inflict on her bare flesh seemed to have no effect on her. She was whipped every day, and often twice or three times in a day and then when her father came home at night he got a stout switch, stripped the girl naked, laid her on her face across his knees and whipped her bare bottom and thighs again till they were covered with weals and the blood came.

Did the good shepherd, when he learnt of these educational methods, protest to Mr and Mrs Strange in the compassionate words of his Master? (Luke 18: 16). On the contrary, he expressed an unshepherdly desire to participate: 'I asked her mother if it would shame the girl and have a good effect if I were to whip her myself or if she were to flog her in my presence. "No," she said, "she is so hardened that she wouldn't care if I made her strip herself bare and then flogged her on her naked bottom before you. You can whip her as much as you please."'

And what would the Viennese bloodhounds have made of this story of another little girl's misadventure?

She was a perfect little beauty with a plump rosy face, dark hair, and lovely soft dark eyes . . . I lifted her into the swing and away she went. But about the sixth flight the girl suddenly slipped . . . Unfortunately her clothes had got hitched upon the seat of the swing and were all pulled up round her waist and it instantly became apparent that she wore no drawers. A titter and then a shout of laughter ran through the crowd as the girl's plump person was seen naked hanging from the swing . . . her flesh was plump and smooth and *in excellent whipping condition*.

The italics are mine.

The Rev. Francis Kilvert's interest in these operations was shared by a surprising number of his contemporaries; so many, indeed, that nineteenth-century England became known, in Iwan Bloch's phrase, as 'the classic land of sexual flagellation'. 'Monckton Milnes', says Mr Pope-Hennessy, 'shared with Thackeray, with Burton, with Swinburne the specially English interest in flagellation. . . . His interest in boys' reformatories went hand in hand with an interest in flogging and a collector's attitude to books on school punishments.' George Augustus Sala had a similar quirk. 'All his life,' says his biographer, Mr Ralph Straus, 'the question of corporal punishment was to remain vividly before him . . . As so often happens, his very horror of flagellation proved to be for him its greatest attraction, and, as his private correspondence shows, he could never banish an eager interest in its practice.' Sala is reputed to have been the part author of *Mysteries of Verbena House*, a novel which 'Pisanus Fraxi' (H. S. Ashbee) calls the 'truest picture of English flagellomania' ever written.

'There is nothing secretive about Monckton Milnes' attitude to these matters,' says his biographer. That his idiosyncrasies were generally known is clear from a letter Sir William Hardman, the Falstaffian editor of the *Morning Post*, wrote to his friend, Edward Holroyd in 1866, when Governor Eyre's brutal suppression of the Jamaican rebellion was being debated in London: 'An indignant correspondent of the *Daily News* complains of the mode of flogging women in Jamaica,' wrote Hardman. '"Men", he says, "are flogged on their backs and shoulders . . . women on their naked posteriors".' Hardman's comment was: 'I daresay the women deserved it . . . Anyhow, the whipping of women would have gratified the senses of Lord Houghton (Monckton Milnes) and would probably have culminated in his asking to be similarly castigated himself.'

Whether Monckton Milnes had more than a theoretical interest in flagellation is uncertain, but at least two of his close friends enjoyed its practice, actively or passively. The eccentric, indefatigable collector of pornography, Frederic Hankey, told Saint-Victor that Paris was less fun than London because in London he could go to Mrs Jenkin's house and whip the girls: 'You take class with them,' he explained. 'Then you whip them – the little ones, oh! not very hard, but the big ones, very hard indeed.'

Swinburne's life-long obsession with the birch gained him a European reputation as the archetype of *le vice anglais*. His floggings at Eton under the Rev. James Leigh Joynes, whom Mr Pope-Hennessy calls 'a practised and sadistic tutor', seem to have developed this appetite. Mr Ralph Nevill affectionately remembers Joynes 'laying with a will into a boy', who received thirty-two strokes with two birches – 'the first one after a time became useless owing to the force with which it was used.' Mr Joynes, as Swinburne confided to Monckton Milnes, was such an enthusiast that he had flogged Swinburne on the sea-shore, as he emerged naked from a swim, and in a scented fir-wood, an experience described by his pupil as 'real delicate torment'. On another occasion, as an esoteric treat, he allowed Swinburne to saturate his face with eau-de-Cologne before being flogged. In later life Swinburne recalled these incidents with a pleasurable vividness. 'I should like to see two things at Eton,' he wrote in 1867, 'the river and the block.' And he recreated his experiences on the block with tiresome pertinacity in his correspondence, in his two novels, *Love's Cross Currents* and *Lesbia Brandon*, and in reams of puerile verse such as the *Whippingham Papers* and *The Flogging Block*.

The man who wrote:

> *When the hounds of spring are on winter's traces*
> *The mother of months in meadow or plain*
> *Fills the shadows and windy places*
> *With lisp of leaves and ripple of rain.*

also wrote:

> *Every fresh cut well laid on*
> *The bare breech of Algernon*
> *Makes the swelled flesh rise in ridges*
> *Thick as summer swarms of midges.*

Swinburne, as the flamboyant eroticism of his poetry suggests, and despite his schoolboyish boast that he was Adah Menken's lover, was apparently incapable of normal sexual experience, but seems to have enjoyed being flogged by women. 'My life has been enlivened of late by a fair friend who keeps a *maison de supplices à la Rodin,*' he wrote in the 'sixties. The Rodin, of course, was the gentleman in de Sade's *Justine,* and the *maison,* according to M. Lafourcade, was in the Euston road. 'One of the great charms of birching,' Swinburne explained, 'lies in the sentiment that the floggee is the powerless victim of the furious rage of a beautiful woman.' When no beautiful woman was on hand, the unlovely and unscrupulous Charles Augustus Howell was a willing substitute. Howell, who had been Ruskin's secretary, and was the licensed harpy of Swinburne, Whistler, and the pre-Raphaelites, was also, in the words of Swinburne's most intransigent champion, Randolph Hughes, 'a connoisseur in the art of Flagellation, equally urbane as donor or recipient'.

Of the many flagellation-hostesses of mid-Victorian London, the most celebrated was Sarah Potter, known as Mother Stewart, who maintained two 'educational' establishments, one in Wardour street, Soho, the other, and the more select, in the King's road, Chelsea, near Cremorne Gardens. Some details of the curriculum of the Soho academy emerged in 1863, when Mrs Potter, 'a married woman, respectably connected', was charged with assaulting Agnes Thompson, a good-looking girl of fourteen. Officers brought into court, said *The Times,* 'a number of birch-rods, two bunches of dried furze, and other articles', and Miss Thompson related a strange story:

> About twelve months before, she told the court, she was walking in the street when she was spoken to by a gentleman who induced her to accompany him to a house in George street, where he 'effected her ruin'. About a week later, she met a woman who took her to a house in Wardour street. She was there about seven months and led an immoral

life. She was not allowed to leave. She was beaten by a man with a birch-rod on her naked body. The servant was sent up with the birch-rod, the man locked the door and beat her. She cried out, and when Mrs. Potter came, said to her: 'You did not tell me when you sent me to the room what was going to be done.' The prisoner said to her: 'Oh, never mind. He did not hurt you.' She was also beaten by a person who goes by the name of Sealskin and by another known as The Count. Other girls were treated in the same way. She was in the room once when the servant was beaten by a man. She had been strapped to some steps while being beaten, she could not move hand or foot, and could not cry out as a towel was forced into her mouth. (The steps and four straps were produced.) She had seen blood flow from wounds inflicted on the servant. Last month she was sent away and went to a woman in the same street who got her a doctor. The doctor sent her to the Society for the Protection of Women and Children, which prosecuted.

Catherine Stewart, 17, told a similar story. She was strapped to a folding ladder without any clothes on. After she was flogged, the gentleman gave prisoner money and prisoner gave her a sovereign. The room in which she was flogged was called 'the schoolroom'. On the second occasion she was flogged for about 10 minutes very severely and received half a sovereign. She left next day.

Alice Stewart said she met prisoner in Wardour street and was told to go to 'the schoolroom'. She found there a short, fat gentleman. She was fastened to the ladder and flogged. The lashes were very severe and she screamed 'Police', and said she could bear it no longer. The flogging brought blood from her person.

The prosecutor asked for the case to be dealt with summarily, 'for the ends of public morality, to prevent a repetition of the disgusting disclosures'. The magistrate regretted that 'the wretches who had misused the wealth bestowed upon them for better purposes than to stimulate their passions should have escaped the just punishment of their revolting conduct', and sentenced Mother Stewart to six months in the House of Correction.

Sealskin, The Count, and the short fat gentleman may have followed with attention a series of letters that appeared in the *Englishwoman's Domestic Magazine* in 1868 on the ritual and rationale of flogging girls in the home. After it had continued for about six months, the *Saturday Review*, in an article headed 'Birch in the Boudoir', commented:

That in the year 1869, there should be living in England, and in London, a considerable number of women, many apparently in good society, and some of them titled, who are in the regular habit of stripping and flogging with birches, apple-twigs, or leather straps, their daughters of thirteen years old and upward, must appear to foreigners simply incredible, and to most Englishmen very queer. Yet that such is the case is amply proved ... They seem to glory in the privilege of thrashing their girls. They give faithful representations, carefully drawn from life, of their own pet mode of conducting the operation. The preliminaries, the place of execution ... the instrument of torture, the behaviour of the victim, during and after the infliction of the flogging, in short the most minute details of the entire process, are described with that graphic force which some women exhibit when writing on a subject which powerfully interests and excites them. The writers do not even take the line of apologising for the inhumanity or of endeavouring to palliate the shame, which must be involved in the process of stripping and flogging a girl of fifteen or sixteen years old. On the contrary, some of them, who seem to have a sort of mission for propagating the doctrine of flogging girls, are most keen in recommending means whereby the pain may be made as severe and the shame as overwhelming to the sufferer as possible ... 'Even at the age of 18,' writes one enthusiastic mother, 'I still administer corporal chastisement.'

'Is it possible,' the *Saturday Review* asked, 'that before long the only creatures in England, besides cattle, that are flogged, will be English criminals and English girls?'

IV

The Victorian pedagogue – and often his disciple, the Victorian parent – was wrapped in a nauseous aura of blended piety, benevolence and sadism. The traditional phrase, the slogan of the pious flagellant, 'This hurts me more than it hurts you,' was an unconscious inversion of his true feelings: 'This pleases me more than it hurts you,' and he saw nothing incongruous in turning from a savage assault on a small boy to an unctuous invocation of Christian compassion. A former pupil of the Rev. S. Baring-Gould, the prolific hymnologist, novelist, and father, recalled a typical incident of his schooldays. 'I was sent to Mr Baring-Gould. He gave me thirty-two cuts and went back to writing *Onward Christian Soldiers*.' A verse of this popular hymn reads:

> *We are not divided,*
> *All one body we,*
> *One in hope and doctrine,*
> *One in charity.*

It is not surprising that Mr Baring-Gould's biographer, William Purcell, notes 'the elements of brutality' in much of his writings and finds in his best novel, *Mehalah*, a marked strain of brutality 'mingled with what can fairly be called sadistic pleasure'.

Some of these men of God saw evidence of divine planning in the fact that children had floggable bottoms. The Rev. Anthony F. Thompson, headmaster of St John's Foundation School, London, who believed that birching 'was an improver of physical health rather than the contrary', wrote appreciatively of 'that part of the body apparently allotted by nature to such exercitation'. The Rev. Francis Kilvert, in a philosophical moment, had a similar thought: 'Were bottoms so formed,' he asked his diary, 'that they might be whipped?' Many years before, Mr B. Batty, author of a sixteenth-century devotional work, *The Christian Man's Closet*, had praised God's wisdom and foresight in endowing children with bottoms on which they could be beaten repeatedly without permanent damage. (Anthony Trollope perceived a similar proof of benevolent Design in the fact that hounds chased foxes 'in compliance with an instinct given by God'.)

'I cannot escape the conclusion', says Mr G. M. Young, writing in *Victorian England*, 'that the current religion did sometimes act as a provocative to sadism.' The inescapable corollary is that the clerical domination of English education played a not insignificant part in the English cult of flagellation. 'It may safely be accepted as an axiom,' said *Vanity Fair* in 1876, 'that a good schoolmaster is never a good clergyman and vice versa, for in truth the birch is not wholly compatible with brotherly love.' But it is wholly compatible with a pathological desire to inflict pain, and the complementary desire to have pain inflicted. A century before the idiosyncratic Marquis endowed sadism with a name and a canon, Samuel Butler wrote of 'pedants' who

> . . . *out of school-boys' breeches*
> *Do claw and curry their own itches.*

Marryat says of Root the pedagogue in *Rattlin' the Reefer*, who sets aside an hour each day for birching his pupils, 'I believe, and I make the assertion in all honesty, that he received a sensual enjoyment by the act of inflicting punishment'; and Dickens acutely recognized that Mr Creakle's delight in cutting a boy with his cane – 'a chubby boy especially' – was 'like the satisfaction of a craving appetite'.

Later writers have noted more explicitly the perverted sexual basis of the English passion for flogging. Henry Salt, after pointing out that what Dean Inge calls 'the wholesome birch' has not very wholesome associations with the brothel, says it was 'in full enjoyment' in English schools because 'it gave satisfaction to those who wielded it'. Sir Charles Oman, describing an orgy of flagellation that Winchester experienced in 1872, attributes it to 'the same pleasure in inflicting pain which inspired the too-celebrated Marquis de Sade'. Among the most obscene passages in English literature is Roger Fry's account, quoted in Virginia Woolf's biography of Fry, of a birching at the Rev. Sneyd-Kynnersley's select school, which Winston Churchill also attended, in the late 'seventies. Mr Sneyd-Kynnersley, a 'bigoted and ignorant High Church Tory', used to tell parents that there were no punishments at his school, by which he meant that the only punishment was a ferocious birching carried out by himself. 'He had an intense sadistic pleasure in these floggings,' wrote Fry.

Dr Wingfield-Stratford, writing of Eton in the nineties, says its 'cultivated lust for flagellation' had 'something of the sacredness attaching to a religious ritual'. A popular high priest of these rites was the Lower Master, Austen Leigh, known 'from his skill, not to speak of delight, in drawing blood from the lower boys whom he was privileged to birch', as the Flea. 'This great Eton character enjoyed – and I think "enjoyed" is the literally correct word – the reputation of a jolly old sadist, naked and unashamed.'

A member of the 'other classes', Professor John Nichol, felt it necessary to apologize to his friend Swinburne for his ignorance of birching. In a letter about *Lesbia Brandon* he wrote: 'Not having been a public-school boy, I was never properly flogged, only cuffed and caned.' But to the *cognoscenti*, even the word 'flogged' was in poor taste. 'If a fellow says flogged, it may be a whip, don't you see, or a strap,' says the eleven-year-old Reginald Harewood, in *Love's Cross Currents*. 'That's caddish.' Young gentlemen, unlike young cads, were always 'swished'.

When Dr E. C. Weldon, Bishop of Calcutta, and a former head of Harrow, wrote his *Recollections* in 1915, he noted the 'curious paradox' that the upper classes submitted to such chastisement as the lower resented and resisted. 'It is far easier to flog a peer's son than a pauper's,' he said. More recently the late Sir Shane Leslie has brooded over the horrid possibility of paupers imposing their rude prejudices on Eton. 'The swishing over the time-honoured block should never be abolished,' he writes in *Film of Memory*. 'No doubt it will run danger of abolition should Eton ever come under Socialist conditions. When the sons of working-men are allotted places at Eton, no doubt hereditary and aristocratic punishments will be reduced or done away with.'

Foreigners who had not been privileged to receive what was known as the 'Eton confirmation' over the block, sometimes expressed ill-bred surprise at the upper-class Englishmen's spirited defence of birching. 'The practice has long been extinct in foreign schools,' said the *Saturday Review* in 1862, 'and as ... Englishmen realise the contempt with which foreigners regard it as a relic of barbarism, the cry for its suppression in English education will become louder.' After watching a routine flogging at Harrow, Taine wrote: 'There is hardly a headmaster in France who would accept, at such a price, a salary of £6,000 a year'; and the French commissioners who reported on English schools in 1869 expressed surprise that their headmasters with their extensive learning, dignified social position and huge salaries should 'condescend to use the birch'. (Matthew Higgins estimated that the headmaster of Eton received £7,500 a year, of which about £1,500 came from 'leaving money' – a tip of from £10 to £50 deposited on a plate in the head's room by departing pupils.)

'The second quarter of the nineteenth century', says Dr Wingfield-Stratford, 'was an age of reforming headmasters and much of anarchic brutality was purged away.' But the birch remained. The greatest of these reformers was Dr Arnold, who birched, not with the anarchic brutality of a Keate, but with the majestic brutality of a Jehovah. When there was a press controversy about brutal beatings at Rugby, Dr Arnold said with some hauteur: 'I do not choose to discuss the thickness of a praeposter's sticks, or the greater or less blackness of a boy's bruises.' His most distinguished follower was the Rev. Edward Thring, of Uppingham, to whom the *Dictionary of National Biography* devotes nearly two pages. Like many of his colleagues, he was an ignorant and arrogant tyrant, who, too, clung tenaciously to his birch. In his diary he describes a public flogging as 'one more of the great days of the school'. He once flogged two brothers, one aged nineteen, the other eighteen, because they missed a railway connection and returned from their Christmas holidays a few hours late. When their father protested, Mr Thring, who said he always 'tried to walk with Christ', rebuked him for 'teaching his boys to criticize authority and speak evil of Governments', and he was upheld by the school Governors and the Bishop of London. Similarly, the Governors of Shrewsbury rejected the protest of a parent whose son, for having ale in his study, had received eighty-eight strokes, with two birches, from the Rev. Mr Moss, and the Bishop of Manchester pronounced that the flogging was 'not excessive'.

In 1856 Mr Morgan Thomas sent his boys to Eton with the express injunction that they should refuse to submit to flogging. When one was caught smoking, and followed out his father's instruction, he was asked to leave the school. There followed a long correspondence between Mr Thomas and the Eton authorities, in the course of which Mr Thomas described the practice of flogging as, among other things, degrading, revolting, beastly, disgraceful, dirty and inefficient. When Eton responded coldly to this attack on one of its proudest traditions, Mr Thomas sent the entire correspondence to *The Times*. To his surprise *The Times* published a warm defence of Eton and its four foot six inch birch, and an equally warm condemnation of Mr Thomas, and his breach of manners. He was accused of conspiring with his sons against the discipline of the school. 'As to the alleged indecency and degradation of such exhibitions, we are greatly mistaken if 99 out of 100 Etonians would not pronounce it to be downright nonsense.' To this Mr Thomas replied with spirit: '*The Times*', he said, 'most justly hurls its indignation against the "revolting" lashings and tortures of Neapolitan dungeons but reserves its sympathies for the birchings of Eton.' This drew a second leader, longer and more lethal, from Printing House Square. 'A very large proportion of the British aristocracy has passed through the ordeal of the birch, and though they do not claim a monopoly of honourable sentiment, yet they may at least be compared advantageously with other classes, and even with other aristocracies.' These aristocrats, *The Times* explained proudly, would much rather be birched than behave in the caddish way Mr Thomas had behaved.

Occasionally, too, a public school headmaster revolted against what Henry Salt, a one-time Eton master, called the 'rank old practice' of birching. When Dr Lyttelton was head of Eton he substituted the cane for the birch, but this uncouth violation of custom was soon corrected by his successor. An earlier Eton headmaster, Dr Warre, was in Dr Wingfield-Stratford's words, 'so utterly sickened and revolted' by the 'whole beastly ritual of the block', that he averted his eyes and 'used the birch rather as a symbol of disgrace than as an instrument of torture'. This deviation, too, was displeasing to the enthusiasts, among them Sir Shane Leslie, who complained that unlike Dr Hornby, his predecessor, Warre 'only scraped and scratched a boy'. Most of the learned, dignified, and highly paid headmasters, however, continued to wield the blue-blood-stained birch with enthusiasm.

V

In the index of *The Times* for 1877, under the heading of 'Inquests', appears this idiosyncratic entry:

> *On William Arthur Gibbs, Who committed suicide from the*
> *Irritation of a Monitor in Christ's Hospital, 7 July*

Gibbs was a twelve-year-old schoolboy who had come from the Hertford preparatory school for Christ's Hospital after the Easter holiday. He ran away from school because he was bullied, was brought back, and flogged. The bullying continued and he again ran away. Once more he was taken back and locked in the school infirmary to await his second flogging. Next morning he was found hanging by a cord from the ventilator, dead. Evidence was given at the inquest that he had been systematically terrorized by a monitor named Copland, though the headmaster, the Rev. Charles Lee, said he had not heard of it. After going back home, Gibbs had said to his father: 'Pa, sooner than I would go back under that Copland, I would hang myself.' He also spoke of the shame of the birching. The jury found that the boy, who was shown to have been lively and amiable, if stubborn, had committed suicide in a state of 'temporary insanity'. It was a comfortable finding, but a few days later a member of the House of Commons asked the Home Secretary to inquire into young Gibbs's death. *The Times* endorsed the suggestion and pointed out that the coroner's verdict was 'so little warranted by the apparent facts' that the 'nature and severity' of punishments at Christ's Hospital should be fully investigated. 'Was it the possibility of a second flogging,' asked *The Times*, 'which could have driven Gibbs to his death?' Modern life, it said, had become in every way so much more humane and modern school life had so largely shared in the general improvement, that instances of inhumanity which would have attracted no notice once would now justly be considered shocking.

The extent to which Christ's Hospital had shared in this increasing humanity was defined by a letter which an old Bluecoat boy wrote to *The Times*. He was the Rev. Andrew Drew, of St Anthony's Nunhead, and, as far as I can find, the only professional follower of Christ who publicly disapproved of the Christian methods of Christ's Hospital:

> The seven years I spent in the school were years of misery and suffering. The food was utterly insufficient, the treatment was such as to make every boy detest the school, the punishments were simply brutal in their severity and often meted out with scant justice. Gibbs knew what he would get if he were alive in the morning. Only an old Bluecoat boy knows what a Christ's Hospital flogging is.

As an illustration, Mr Drew told the story of a 'small and delicate lad called Blount', who slept in the next bed to him. A big boy had compelled Blount to steal some lumps of sugar from the monitor's sugar-basin. The big boy ate all the sugar himself but when the facts became known, Blount only was flogged.

> That night, [wrote Mr Drew] poor little Blount could not sleep and he begged me to help him. I accordingly took his shirt off and found his back, from the shoulders down to the waist, one mass of lacerated flesh, the blood sticking to his shirt so as to cause agony in getting it off. I then, with my finger, pulled out of his back at least a dozen pieces of birch-rod which had penetrated deep into the flesh . . . I have since seen the back of a sailor after three dozen with a naval 'cat' and I solemnly declare that the injury done to the sailor's back did not compare with that done to the Bluecoat boy.

Mr Drew explained the *modus operandi* of punishment at Christ's Hospital:

> Two men were required . . . One takes hold of the boy, holds him on his back by the wrists, and keeps him suspended. The other strips off his coat and armed with a large and heavy rod, gives 15 cuts to the boys bare back, and these with might and main.

This was a 'mild flogging'. For more serious offences, such as running away, the boy received 15 cuts on the back and 15 more 'in another place with a fresh rod'.

Mr Drew's letter evoked a spate of replies, selections from which filled three columns in one issue of *The Times*. Many of the correspondents were old Bluecoats who resented the attacks made on their school in the name of 'mawkish sentimentality'. ('Mawkish' and 'sentimental' remain the stock epithets hurled at anyone in England who protests against sanctified brutality.) 'Because Blount was soundly flogged for thieving, and very properly, so I think,' wrote the Rev. James Cohen, Vicar of Heston, 'it does not follow that "poor little Gibbs was done to death" etc.'

But other Bluecoats amplified Mr Drew's report. 'I can quite understand a lad committing suicide to avoid the repetition of the torture,' wrote one. Another described the pedagogy at Hertford, where boys were received from seven years of age to eleven:

I once witnessed the headmaster make a most savage attack on a boy simply because he did not know anything about aspirating the letter H. His name was Hallam. Every time he was told to repeat his name, which he did as Allam, there was a fresh onslaught on every part of his body, until executioner and victim sank exhausted, the former into his chair, the latter onto the floor, whence the beadle took him in a sheet to the infirmary.

The same writer described the headmaster at the London school beating boys 'until he foamed at the mouth'.

Loyal Bluecoats rallied again to the defence of their old school with a meeting at Keenan's Hotel, Cheapside. The Rev. Thomas Harris took the chair and declared there had been 'a good deal of sickly sentimentality with respect to the punishment of boys'. One of the sentimentalists, Mr Tidy, speaking from experience, said the treatment of boys was 'most cruel'. He himself had been taken up by one porter and flogged by another while the Warden exhorted the operator to 'lay on harder'. As a result, Mr Tidy had been unable to sit down for two or three weeks, and carried the marks on his body for ten years.

A House of Commons committee which sat for nine days heard masters, pupils and old boys explain the varieties of corporal punishment, some officially recognized, others hallowed by long usage, employed at the 'religious, royal and ancient Foundation' of Christ's Hospital. The cane, the prime mover of the establishment, was used in many ways, from simple 'caking', or caning on the hands (across or along the palm, according to whim) to more ritualistic 'tetching', in which a boy was turned over a form while two other boys pulled his breeches tight. In less formal moods, masters would simply cane a boy on the head, back or legs – an old

Bluecoat had seen a boy receive a cut in the eye with a cane but he thought this was 'purely accidental' – or punch him on the ear. By tradition, only 'cakings' had to be entered in the punishment book.

Caning was usually invoked as a stimulus to learning. 'He certainly used the cane,' said an old boy apologetically of one master, 'but we were commencing Greek at the time and I suppose there was a good deal of coarse work.' Several boy witnesses explained that Gibbs was one of eleven boys in a class who were caned every day regularly, to induce them to improve their position in class. Another old boy mentioned a master with a class of fifty boys: endowed, apparently, with inexhaustible energy, 'in the course of the morning, he had caned the whole class five or six times'.

The committee was told that for serious offences, such as running away, younger culprits were birched on their bare buttocks, older ones, on the bare back. One beadle acted as school executioner, and another beadle, or a big boy, as the 'horse' on whose back the victim was hoisted. This process was known delicately as 'brushing' and the executioner as the 'brush beadle'. School officials said birching was limited to twelve strokes. It was explained that two birches were sometimes used on the one boy, because a birch becomes less efficient with use.

Boys were subject to two jurisdictions; in school hours, punishments were imposed by the masters, in play hours and in the sleeping wards, by the warden, a retired major. The headmaster had no overall authority.

The commission also heard evidence about the school diet. Charles Lamb has given a famous description of the food at Christ's Hospital when he was a pupil there in the 1780s;

> Our Monday's milk porritch, blue and tastless, and the pease soup of Saturday, coarse and choking . . . Wednesday's mess of millet . . . scanty mutton scrags on Friday – and rather more savoury, but grudging portions of the same flesh, rotten-roasted or rare, on the Tuesdays.

A century later, the diet had been improved by the addition of potatoes, to counteract scurvy, and occasional greens. But it was still grossly inadequate for hungry boys. Breakfast consisted of seven and half ounces of bread, half a pint of milk (with or without hot or cold water) three-quarters of an ounce of dripping; dinner, three ounces bread, four ounces meat, eight ounces potatoes; with lettuces and greens (and only four ounces potatoes) three days a week.

A former pupil said in his day the meat was often 'prismatic in colour from being kept so long in hot weather'. He believed that the steward responsible for catering had lost his sense of taste through excessive snuff-taking.

The report of the committee was adroitly evasive. Much of it was devoted to trying to prove that Gibbs had been a difficult pupil, whose word was not to be relied on, despite the fact that he came from preparatory school with a good report on his diligence and progress. It was admitted that he had been often caned and assaulted by masters and monitors at Christ's Hospital, but the committee was not prepared to advise the discontinuance of corporal punishment 'at present'. However, 'the evidence made it clear that a closer supervision of caning should be exercised'. As for flogging, 'it cannot be said to be severe – the ordinary number of stripes is six or eight, and in no case does the number exceed ten or twelve, and only a single rod is used'. The committee found there had been an exceptionally large number of floggings in 1876.

The last word in this melancholy symposium came from Gibbs's father, a small London tradesman, who wrote a dignified letter to *The Times* in defence of his son's character. Young Gibbs, he said, was a kind-hearted, amiable boy. 'Only recently did he have some eggs boiled to take with a case of pepper and mustard (things not found by the school) to give monitor Copland, as he said, to induce Copland to treat him better.'

English public schools are proud of their traditions. (Traditions, of course, are always 'time-honoured', never 'time-dishonoured'.) It must have been a proud day for Christ's Hospital, when forty-six years later, another of its pupils committed suicide after being kicked for playing football with insufficient enthusiasm. The head of the school, interviewed by a London newspaper, said there was no harm 'in a mild kick occasionally'. George Bernard Shaw's comment was: 'I do not blame the boys who did the kicking. They are evidently just as much the victims of the system as the boy they kicked.'

III

The Gallows-watchers

I

'Sir,' said Dr Johnson, 'executions are intended to draw spectators. If they do not draw spectators, they don't answer the purpose.' Eminent Victorians shared the eighteenth-century belief that it did people good to see a man or woman strangled, and they had, for many years, a powerful spokesman in *The Times*. It is curious to find Mr E. E. Kellett writing in the Oxford University Press's authoritative *Early Victorian England*, that *The Times* 'strongly advocated the abolition of public executions'. In fact, almost until the last murderer's body twitched before a happy crowd, *The Times* repeatedly and vehemently defended public hangings against 'sentimentalists' like Thackeray, Dickens and Douglas Jerrold. It came to the 'necessary conclusion' that 'if executions are performed publicly for the sake of teaching public lessons . . . the more spectators there are the better'.

Whether the many thousands who flocked to public executions during the first three decades of Victoria's reign were aware of their educational value is doubtful. It seems more likely that they went along just for fun. Public flogging had been abolished in 1817 – a woman was flogged at the cart's tail through the City of London as late as 1811 – and bull-baiting in 1838; but fortunately for sadists, vulgar, genteel, or noble, the more exciting entertainment of a public hanging survived until 1868. And hangings, unlike other blood sports, were essentially democratic. Deer-stalking and fox-hunting, though legal, were the privilege of a few. Cockfighting, though still popular, was illegal. Public executions were legal, free and frequent, enjoyed by noblemen and pickpockets, ladies and whores, gentlemen and artisans, rich and poor, young and old, alike.

Contemporary reports often stress their carnival-like atmosphere. The Venerable Archdeacon Bickersteth, describing the first execution he witnessed (at Shrewsbury in 1841) told a Select Committee of the House of Lords in 1856:

> The town was converted for the day into a fair. The country people flocked in their holiday dresses, and the whole town was a scene of drunkenness and debauchery of every kind . . . A very large number of children were present: children and females constituted the larger proportion of the attendance.

'They came just as they would to a bull-baiting or a cockfight,' wrote another citizen of Shrewsbury. Mr C. G. Hodgson, Superintendent of City of London Police, agreed: 'They go as they would to a theatre, or the exhibition of a bull-fight,' he said.

A writer in *Household Words* ironically described the hanging of Mrs French, at Lewes in 1852, under the heading of 'Open Air Entertainment'. In front of the gaol were about ten thousand people, screaming, fighting, roaring with gypsy jollity: 'married couples with their families, loving couples, old men and young!''

It was a rare sight! Stout yeomen on horseback, with flowers in their coats, and in their horses' headstalls; lounging dragoons from the cavalry barracks . . . women in crowds, gaily dressed, very merry, holding up their little children to see the show; white-haired old agriculturists in snowy smock frocks, and leaning on sticks; picturesque old dames in scarlet cloaks . . . tribes of brown-faced urchins, farm-labourers, bird-catchers and bird-scarers; crowds of navvies, rough customers . . . very chalky indeed, striped night-capped, gigantic shoed, and carrying little kegs of beer slung by their sides. Also, gangs of true genuine British scamps . . .

Hawkers peddled cakes and fruit and roughly illustrated broadsheets: *'The last dying speech and confessions of Sarah Ann French, executed at Lewes for the murder of her husband at Chiddingley.'* Most of the better shops were closed, but public houses and beer-shops were crowded:

Eager conversations were carried on in these hostelries . . . Old stagers related their impressions and reminiscences of former murders and hangings. Of Holloway; of Corder, Maria Marten and the Red Barn; of men hanged for setting fire to hayricks, for smuggling, and for burglary; of criminals who had gone to the gallows singing psalms, or who had been hanged in chains, or brought to life again by the touch of the surgeon's anatomising knife.

After the execution, as hangman Calcraft 'gazed on his work complacently', the 'elements of the crowd, swaying more than ever, made a great rush to the beer-houses, or refreshed themselves from their own private stores – yelling, screaming, and laughing heartily'.

Mr Hilary Nicholas Nissen, a sheriff of the City of London, told a Royal Commission in 1865: 'The executioner comes to the scaffold, dressed in his ordinary way, a dirty wide-awake hat and a shooting jacket, and he takes out a pocket-knife and cuts the cords by which the body is suspended . . . the whole thing appears to me to be regarded as a matter of entertainment by the crowd.'

As entertainment, a good hanging ranked with a royal procession or a state funeral, and rooms with a view of the gallows commanded comparably high prices. In 1849, when the Mannings were hanged at Horse-monger Gaol, windows were rented at from one to three guineas each. Three years later, when the funeral of the Duke of Wellington passed along the Strand and Fleet street, a second-floor could be hired for £10, and third floor for £7 10s., each containing two windows. In 1863, when Princess Alexandra drove through London on the eve of her wedding to Edward, Prince of Wales, rooms along the route were available for very little more.

One of the *Ingoldsby Legends* tells how Lord Tomnoddy, Lieutenant Tregooze and Sir Carnaby Jenks of the Blues, take the first floor of the Magpie and Stump, opposite the Old Bailey, the night before an execution, but they drink so much gin-toddy and punch, and eat so many fowls and rabbits and lobsters and kidneys, and smoke so many cigars, that all fall asleep:

> *'Why, Captain! My Lord! – Here's the devil to pay!*
> *The fellow's been cut down and taken away!*
> *What's to be done? We've missed all the fun!*
> *Why, they'll laugh at and quiz us all over the town,*
> *We are all of us done so uncommonly brown!'*

The Earl of Malmesbury, one of the twenty-five peers who voted against the *Capital Punishments Within Prisons Bill* of 1866, answering the objection that people indulged in obscene language at executions, said: 'The same thing occurred on great public spectacles such as the funeral of the late Lord Palmerston, or at Her Majesty's coronation. . . These people were obscene, not because of what was taking place, but because it was their habit to be obscene.' Malmesbury spoke with authority; he was an enthusiastic patron of executions.

The House of Lords Committee of 1856, with the Bishop of Oxford in the chair, unanimously recommended that executions be carried out in private. The argument that public hanging was a deterrent to crime had long been demolished – with the cognate argument that an executed criminal rotting publicly on a gibbet was a deterrent. A prison chaplain, the Rev. W. Roberts, told the 1856 Committee that of 167 persons awaiting execution in Bristol prison, 164 had witnessed at least one execution. But despite the recommendation of the Lords, these popular carnivals of blood-lust went on for another twelve years. It was not till 1868, two years after a Royal Commission had repeated the recommendation, that public hanging was abolished in England. Most of the Australian colonies had abolished it in 1853.

'Posterity will probably wonder how the age which would have scouted the idea of any wholesome effect being wrought by public floggings, could have remained so long under the belief that any manner of good could be done by the system of public executions,' wrote Justin McCarthy in 1881. A later posterity will probably wonder how the present age could have remained so long under the belief that any manner of good could be done by its system of private executions.

II

An enterprising showman of the 'forties catered for the Londoners' appetite for executions by pretending to hang himself in public for a small fee. He ended his career by hanging himself too realistically on a temporary gallows erected on Waterloo Bridge.

'Hanging is as much a part of the British tradition as counting in shillings and pence,' says Arthur Koestler. 'Generations of children have squeaked in delight at the appearance of the puppet hangmen in the Punch and Judy shows.' And he comments acutely that to Englishmen 'hanging has a kind of macabre cosiness, like a slightly off-colour joke, which only foreigners, abolitionists and other humourless creatures are unable to share'.

The peculiar British interest in hanging naturally made a public hero of the hangman. William Calcraft, the master-hangman of the nineteenth century, had a place in the affections of the Victorian public similar to that enjoyed today by a man who can run 1,760 yards at an average speed of 15 m.p.h., or by a woman who measures sixteen inches more round the breasts than round the waist. Monckton Milnes strenuously opposed hanging – but he collected hangman Calcraft's autographs.

Calcraft, one of four English executioners honoured by inclusion in the *Dictionary of National Biography*, was successively a lady's shoemaker, a watchman at Reid's brewery, and a butler to a gentleman at Greenwich, before he found his vocation. The discovery was accidental, perhaps providential. In a period of unemployment when he was hawking pies round the scaffold at Newgate, he met the hangman, John Foxton, and through him was given the relatively unskilled job of flogging juvenile offenders at ten shillings a week. The meeting took place in 1828 at the hanging of Joseph Hunton, a Quaker convicted of forgery. (Before £1 and £2 Bank of England notes were withdrawn, forging small notes was a popular pastime. In 1820, 154 men were charged at the Old Bailey with this crime.) Hunton was executed at Newgate with three young burglars, Messrs Abbott, James and Mahoney, but, as a gentleman and a Quaker, he was the star turn. The audience extended on one side of the scaffold in a solid mass from the barrier at the end of Fleet Lane to the end of the Old Bailey in Ludgate Hill, and on the other, as far as Cook Lane at the end of Giltspur Street. While other entrepreneurs cried their hot potatoes and coffee, Calcraft, a short, active man with dark restless eyes, threaded his

'Calcraft's first interview with the executioner.'

way through the crowd dispensing his pies. The execution over, Calcraft lingered by the scaffold. 'I saw their executioner come out from underneath the gallows,' he recalled years later in his autobiography:

He appeared to be weak and faint. Poor chap! he wasn't up to his business, and was evidently a good deal flurried, or maybe he was a bit frightened, for it was a mob on that morning and no mistake. I stood within a few yards of him, and . . . and got a pint of porter which I handed to him as he stood underneath the steps of the gallows. He drained off the largest portion, and handed me the remainder, which I refused.

'Ah, that's it – is it?' said he, 'too proud, I suppose, to drink with a hangman.'

'I ain't proud at all,' I answered, 'but maybe you'd like the remainder yourself in a few minutes. I can get what I want – as much as I like over the way – but just to show you that you are mistaken I will drink with you, and so here's better luck to both of us.'

'I suppose you can do with a little?'

'With what?'

'A little better luck!'

'You never spoke a truer word, my friend. Things have gone precious hard with me of late. Had not this been the case you would not see me selling pies on a morning like this.'

'Umph! and you are not altogether a bad sort, I should say,' ventured Foxton.

'I ain't afraid of work, and don't much care what sort it is. Now I'll tell you what I'll do, if you've no objection.'

'What may that be?'

'Well, I'll take to your line of business when you give it up.'

'What! turn hangman,' asked he, in a tone of surprise.

'That's it.'

Next year, he helped Foxton in an emergency by hanging two men at Lincoln, and with such *expertise* that on Foxton's death in 1829 Calcraft inherited the post of public executioner to the City of London. His retainer was a guinea a week, with a guinea refresher for each hanging, and the right to accept country engagements at £10 per neck. These earnings were augmented by a fee of half a crown for floggings, with an out-of-pocket allowance for 'cats' and birch-rods.

For over forty-five years Calcraft enjoyed his great national esteem. In 1855 he published *The Hangman's letter to the Queen* in reply to an attack on his life, character and profession made in a pamphlet titled *Groans from the Gallows*. In it he proposed that the gallows be replaced by a machine of his own invention. Unfortunately, no copy of the letter seems to have survived, and the details of the new device remain unknown. He was seventy-four when he carried out his last execution in 1874, though after 1868, of course, he was denied the artistic satisfaction of performing in public. But his memory was kept evergreen by broadsides, comic songs and spurious biographies, in which London streetsellers did a brisk trade. In one of these 'biographies', *Voice from the Gaol! or the Horrors of the Condemned Cell!* he is described, twenty-five years before his retirement, as a man whose

> nervous system is fast breaking down every day rendering him less able to endure the excruciating and agonising torments he is hourly suffering . . . every fresh victim he is required to strangle being so much additional fuel thrown upon that mental flame which is scorching him!

An authentic, if ghosted, autobiography, *The Life and Recollections of William Calcraft, the Hangman,* was published in London in 1870.

When Henry Mayhew was making his historic survey of *London Labour and the London Poor* in 1851, Calcraft was as popular a subject for broadsheets and ballads as Pope Pius IX, whose recent bull setting up a hierarchy in England, with Cardinal Wiseman as archbishop, was not popular. A Cockney 'running patterer' – the Victorian descendant of the jester or troubadour – told Mayhew that he named items of his clothing 'after them I earn money by to buy them with'. The Pope and Cardinal Wiseman had shod him; 'My shoes I call Pope Pius; my trousers and braces, Calcraft.'

About this time, Calcraft was charged with having refused to support his seventy-three-year-old mother, an occupant of Hatfield Peveril workhouse, 'he being of sufficient ability to do so,' and the patterer 'worked him' down in Essex and sold the 'limping old body' a copy of the penny broadsheet composed for the occasion. Calcraft himself bought two copies outside his house in Devizes Street, Hoxton.

His appearance at Worship Street to answer the charge excited 'a considerable degree of interest', *The Times* reported. The court was inconveniently crowded, 'a number of well dressed women' being present. 'Well, I should be happy to support her if it was in my power,' Calcraft told the magistrate, 'I admit that I receive a guinea a week from the city, but that is all we have to live on, and when you deduct out of that 4/6 a week for rent, and the cost of a Sunday's dinner, you will find there is not much left.' His mother, he said, was in better circumstances than he; she had a large quantity of good furniture and a number of silver spoons. But Calcraft was told he was clearly liable for her support by an act of Queen Elizabeth, and an order was made upon him to contribute three shillings a week to the workhouse.

Swinburne introduced Calcraft into his unpublished French verse drama

La Sœur de la Reine, an irreverent burlesque on the early life of Queen Victoria. In the last act, the Queen sends for Calcraft, and commands him to do away with Princess Katy, an illegitimate daughter of Victoria and Lord John Russell, who, though she has taken to the streets, may one day claim the throne. Calcraft stubbornly refuses, and Victoria tries to tempt him with a knighthood: '*Levez-vous, Sir Calcraft, Pair d'Angleterre!*' But the honest fellow is unmoved. '*Pardon, Madame,*' he says, '*Je ne suis que le bourreau de Londres.*'

There is a whimsical reference to him in *The Bab Ballads* where Anne Prothero says:

> *In busy times he laboured at his gentle craft all day –*
> *'No doubt you mean his Cal-craft,' you amusingly will say –*
> *But, no – he didn't operate with common bits of string,*
> *He was a Public Hangman, which is quite another thing.*

William Calcraft, public hangman from 1829 to 1874.

Calcraft retired on a pension of twenty-five shillings a week. As a tech-
nician he was sometimes criticized. A witness told the Royal Commission
on Capital Punishment in 1866 that his methods were very rough, 'much
the same as if he had been hanging a dog'. This was unfair, because he was
fond of dogs. 'He was of kindly disposition,' says his biographer, 'very
fond of his children and grandchildren, and took a great interest in his
pigeons and other pet animals. They included rabbits and a pony which
used to follow him round affectionately.'

III

Vintage years for public executions were 1840, 1849, and 1864. The execution of Courvoisier in 1840 for the murder of Lord William Russell was a
brilliant social and literary occasion. Thackeray wrote about it in a famous
magazine article, and Dickens was there, too. Gallows-watchers in 1849
had two memorable experiences: the execution of the godly James Rush
outside Norwich castle, and the joint execution at Newgate of Mr and Mrs
Manning – an event, with its sentimental domestic overtones, of peculiar
interest to mid-Victorians. Dickens described it in a passionate letter to
The Times. But 1864 was the year of wonders for the *amateur* of the scaffold,
offering a series of unexampled spectacles, from the multiple execution of
five Malay pirates in February, to the execution of Franz Muller, England's
first train murderer, in November.

IV

With an English peer the victim and a Swiss valet the villain, the Courvoisier case made a potent appeal to two national characteristics – snobbery
and xenophobia. (It is surely not without significance that foreigners were
involved in four out of the five more popular executions of the century.)
One morning in 1840 Lord William Russell's housemaid found her master
dead in bed with his throat cut. Lord William, a veteran of Waterloo and a
scion of the House of Bedford, was a seventy-three-year-old widower who
lived alone in Norfolk Street, Park Lane. His staff consisted of a cook, a
housemaid, and a confidential valet, François Benjamin Courvoisier, who
was charged with the murder. On the second day of the trial, after pleading
not guilty, he confessed to his lawyers that he had cut his master's throat
with a carving knife because Lord William, in a peevish mood, had given
him notice. Courvoisier's leading counsel, Mr Charles Phillips, communicated the confession to the trial judge, Baron Martin, who told Phillips
that he must continue to defend his client to his utmost ability. Whether
this justified Phillips imploring the jury, in an impassioned address, 'not to
send an innocent man to the gallows' is still a matter for debate. So is the

theory that Courvoisier, to avoid bloodstains on his clothes, stripped himself naked before attacking his master, thus anticipating the *modus operandi* of Mr William Wallace, the Liverpool wife murderer, by ninety-one years.

A statement in *The Times* that Courvoisier got the idea of murdering Lord William Russell from Harrison Ainsworth's *Jack Shepherd* was indignantly denied by Mr Ainsworth in a letter to which William Evans, the Sheriff of London and Middlesex, replied sharply: 'I think it my duty to state distinctly that Courvoisier did assert to me that the idea of murdering his master was first suggested to him by a perusal of the book called *Jack Shepherd* and that the said book was lent to him by a valet of the Duke of Bedford.'

Foreign servants in London raised a fund for Courvoisier's defence, and England's 'nobility and gentry' clamoured for tickets of admission to the trial. These included the Duke of Sussex, the Earl of Mansfield, the Earl of Cavan, Lord and Lady Arthur Lennox, Lady Granville Somerset, and many other 'ladies of rank'. Some of the nobility were further privileged by being admitted to the gallery of the prison chapel at Newgate on the Sunday before the hanging, to hear the execution sermon preached. Among these fortunate card-holders were Adolphus Fitz Clarence, Lord Coventry, Lord Bruce, Lord Alfred Paget, and some unnamed ladies.

Lord Alfred Paget was also among the six hundred noblemen and gentlemen admitted to the prison early on the morning of the execution. In this distinguished party was the actor Charles Kean, following the example of his father, Edmund Kean, who had attended the hanging of Thistlewood, one of the Cato Street conspirators, with a view, he explained, to his 'professional studies'. The Earl of Malmesbury, who followed Courvoisier's execution procession from the condemned cell to the scaffold, was 'not a little shocked' to see 'punch, or some beverage of the sort', handed around as if it were a 'pleasant festivity'. 'It seems to be the custom,' he noted in his diary, 'and the sooner it is abolished the better.' However, he did not think public executions should be abolished.

Occupants of houses with a view of the gallows hired out rooms, windows, and even perches on roofs, for high fees. The attic storey of Lamb's Coffee House was let for £5, and windows for £2 each. Sir William Watkin Wynn and his friends took a room for the night at The George public house, to the south of the drop, and the indefatigable Lord Alfred Paget entertained a party, including ladies of rank and fashion, in a room next door. Hundreds of less fortunate citizens took up a position near the gallows early on Sunday morning 'cheerfully exposing themselves to the inconvenience of standing in the open during the whole of the night,' said *The Times*, 'in order that their curiosity might be fully gratified in the morning.' During the preliminary celebrations a well-dressed woman fell out of a first-floor window on to the crowd but neither she nor anyone else was much hurt, and the under-sheriffs expressed satisfaction 'at the un-heard of circumstance' that, despite the huge attendance, estimated at fifty thousand people, no serious accident occurred.

'The greatest poet in the House of Commons came here yesterday morning at half-past three,' Thackeray wrote to Mrs Proctor, 'and we drove together in his famous fly . . . to see Courvoisier killed. It was a horrible sight, indeed.' The poet was Monckton Milnes, the future Lord Houghton. For weeks, the memory of the 'horrible sight' weighed on Thackeray's mind 'like cold plum pudding on the stomach'. To exorcise it, he wrote the article 'Going to See a Man Hanged', published in *Fraser's Magazine* in August.

Monckton Milnes spent the night before the hanging at his club, in jovial company. For hours Thackeray tried to sleep but could not. He had been asleep only half an hour when Milnes arrived for breakfast. The party washed down a tough fowl with sherry and soda-water and set out at 4 a.m. for Snow Hill. Twenty minutes later they were looking at the gallows, jutting out 'black and ready', from a little door in Newgate Prison.

People in the street were talking in groups, the newcomers questioning the *habitués*. Did the victim hang with his face towards the clock or towards Ludgate Hill? Was the rope round his neck when he came on the scaffold? Had Lord Waterford taken a window?

The best standing positions, close to the scaffold, were chiefly occupied by 'stunted, ill-grown lads, in rugged fustian, youths of 16 or 17' with girls of the same age. One girl particularly interested Thackeray. Cruickshank and Dickens, he thought, might have used her for a study of Nancy:

> The girl was a young thief's mistress evidently; if attacked, ready to reply without a particle of modesty; could give as good ribaldry as she got; made no secret as to her profession and means of livelihood. But with all this, there was something good about the girl; a sort of devil-may-care candour and simplicity that one could not fail to see. She had a friend with her of the same age and class, of whom she seemed to be very fond, and who looked up to her for protection. Both of these women had beautiful eyes. Devil-may-care's were extraordinarily bright and blue, and admirably fair complexion, and a large red mouth full of white teeth. *Au reste*, ugly, stunted, thick-limbed, and by no means a beauty. Her friend could not be more than fifteen.

Thackeray compared these girls with their fictional counterparts in 'late fashionable novels'. 'Bah! what figments these novelists tell us,' he con-cluded. 'Boz, who knows life well, knows that his Miss Nancy is the most unreal fantastical personage possible . . . He dare not tell the truth concerning such young ladies.' As a novelist Thackeray was not more realistic about 'such young ladies' than Dickens. Nor, apparently, did he know that Dickens, with his friends Maclise and Burnett, was watching the execution from a first-floor window opposite the gallows. 'Why, there stands Thackeray!' cried Dickens, recognizing the tall figure towering above the crowd.

In other windows Thackeray noted 'young dandies with moustaches and cigars', quiet fat family parties of simple tradesmen and their wives, who sat calmly sipping tea, and less quiet parties of 'Mohocks', bloods in the boisterous tradition of the eighteenth century, who amused themselves by squirting soda-water on the crowd. One roof-top gallery was occupied by a party of 'tipsy dissolute young men, of the Dick Swiveller cast', who with their women were winding up a pleasant Sunday evening spent 'in some of those delectable night-houses', near Covent Garden.

The debauch was not over yet, and the women of the party were giggling, drinking and romping, as is the wont of these delicate creatures; sprawling here and there, and falling upon the knees of one or other of the males. Their scarves were off their shoulders, and you saw the sun shining down upon the bare white flesh, and the shoulder-points glittering like burning glasses.

More respectable members of the audience were indignant 'at some of the proceedings of this debauched crew', and 'at last raised up such a yell as frightened them into shame'. But for the most part, the crowd was 'extraordinarily gentle and good-humoured'. The mood was festive, 'jokes bandying about here and there, and jolly laughs breaking out'. With these diversions, and the contemplation of workmen knocking and hammering at the scaffold, the hours of waiting passed pleasantly, till the bell of St Sepulchre's clock began to toll the chimes of eight.

As the clock began to strike, an immense sway and movement swept over the whole of that vast dense crowd. They were all uncovered directly, and a great murmur arose, more awful, bizarre, and indescribable than any sound I had ever heard before. Women and children began to shriek horribly.

Thackeray shut his eyes a moment before the drop fell, but he could not escape from his memories of the 'butchery'. He felt 'ashamed and degraded at the brutal curiosity' which had taken him to 'that brutal sight' and he prayed 'to Almighty God to cause this disgraceful sin to pass from among us, and to cleanse our land of blood'. It was more than a quarter of a century before his prayer was answered.

V

As well as broadsheet ballads, plaster casts of Courvoisier's head taken after execution were soon on sale in London. Phrenologists discussed them learnedly. Dr John Elliotson, after examining a cast and finding that Courvoisier was 'phrenologically speaking, unhappily organized' – the higher intellectual faculties, Compassion, Causality, and Wit, were small, and the Organ of the Disposition to do Violence, *very large* – made a surprising plea for the abolition of capital punishment; a plea that has not lost its validity today;

> I trust that the punishment of death will not long continue to disgrace our country. It was devised in the barbarous stages of society, and now that we are advancing in civilisation, should cease. I will not adduce arguments against it as contrary to the spirit of Christianity, because they ought to be calculated for Jews, Mahometans, Deists, and all the human race. Neither will I argue against it on the ground that we have no right to destroy human life, because we unquestionably have this right in some instances, as when our own life or that of others is threatened by an assassin; and because the man who has taken the life of another can hardly complain of his own being insufficient, unnecessary, and injurious – of its not tending to the greatest happiness of the greatest number.
>
> That it is unnecessary is proved by the crimes to which it has been adjudged not being more frequent at present in those countries which have abolished it, or lessened its infliction, than when it was adopted unsparingly. The permanent confinement of a criminal gives as great security to society as his destruction; and the fear of permanent imprisonment for crime deters much more than the fear of death. The consideration of the hardship of society being at the charge of supporting a criminal is of no weight, because he can be made to labour for his own support, and for the accumulation of a fund to maintain him when he can work no longer.
>
> That it is injurious is evident, because it hardens the hearts of the wicked, and of society at large. The ill-disposed, regarding it as mild compared with permanent imprisonment, are not deterred by it from crime; and, looking upon death with the less horror, hesitate the less at murder. Society becomes less inclined to attempt the reformation of criminals, and, becoming habituated to violent death, must become less disposed to benevolence, and less averse from malevolence; to say nothing of the horror of society hiring an individual as an executioner of his fellow-men, and thus destroying the best feelings of his nature.

Not only in his opposition to capital punishment was Dr Elliotson a non-conformist. 'His desire to be original led Elliotson into many eccentricities,' says the *Dictionary of National Biography*. He frequently administered large quantities of drugs which his colleagues regarded as poisonous; he discarded the orthodox knee-breeches and silk stockings of his profession for layman's trousers; he was one of the first doctors in England to wear a beard and use a stethoscope. He founded the Phrenological Society, and a mesmeric hospital where many eminent Victorians were treated. Thackeray dedicated *Pendennis* to him in gratitude for his services, and Dickens a volume of short stories which Dickens had edited for a friend. His name, says Forster, 'was for nearly thirty years a synonym with us all for unwearied, self-sacrificing, beneficent service to every one in need'.

VI

Patrick O'Connor was a Customs House gauger who had made about £10,000 by lending money at high interest to small tradesmen. Most of it was invested in railway shares. O'Connor had a lecherous as well as a usurious eye; he had been the lover of Marie le Roux, a buxom, dark Swiss girl, before her marriage to Manning, when she was lady's maid to Lady Blantyre, daughter of the Duchess of Sutherland. Frederick Manning was a former guard on the Great Western Railway, who, dismissed for suspected complicity in big train robberies, had unsuccessfully conducted an inn at Taunton. He hoped to get a Government position through his wife's influence with the nobility. After their marriage, O'Connor, with Manning's urbane approval, maintained his intimacy with Mrs Manning, and often walked from his house in the Mile End Road to enjoy the hospitality of her kitchen and her bedroom at 3 Miniver Place, Bermondsey.

Mrs Manning was an exceptional hostess. In addition to her generous personal hospitality, she arranged to present O'Connor to an 'eligible' young lady called Massey. (*The Times* delicately described Miss Massey as a 'fair young stranger' and O'Connor as a 'male' flirt.) But, while she was receiving O'Connor with a flattering show of affection and ardour, she was planning to kill and rob him.

According to Manning's final confession, his wife told him a month before the murder that she was determined to kill O'Connor for his money. When he tried to dissuade her, she bought a dozen bottles of brandy and plied him with it till he was 'not in his right mind'. Mrs Manning also bought a small pair of pistols and instructed her husband to dig a grave for O'Connor by the kitchen stove, on the pretence that the drains needed attention. Victorian drains always needed attention. On the night of the murder, when O'Connor came for dinner, Mrs Manning induced him to go downstairs to the kitchen to wash his hands because Miss Massey was expected. 'You know she is a very particular lady,' Mrs Manning reminded him. The appeal to gallantry was irresistible. O'Connor descended the stairs to the kitchen tap and was shot in the back of his head by his hostess. Mr Manning was perturbed, but Mrs Manning called him a 'damned coward' and threatened to serve him the same way if he did not help to dispose of the body. Thus challenged, Mr Manning followed her downstairs where he found O'Connor kneeling beside his grave, moaning. 'I never liked him very much,' Mr Manning said, simply. 'I battered in his skull with a ripping chisel.' Then he helped his wife to push the body into the hearthstone grave and cover it with quicklime.

Mrs Manning changed her dress, took a cab to O'Connor's lodgings and rifled them thoroughly. A few days later, she cooked her husband a hearty goose dinner over the kitchen fire near which O'Connor's body was buried. After dinner, she and her husband stripped the house, abandoned it, and separated.

Mrs Manning took lodgings in Edinburgh where she was arrested when she rashly tried to sell some of the stolen railway shares. In one of her boxes, with more of the loot, police found the *Psalms of David* in French, and a pious work in English, *Familiar Devotions for Every Day in the Year*. Manning was arrested in Jersey about a week later. In the pursuit of Mrs Manning the electric telegraph, recently installed between London and Edinburgh, demonstrated its potentialities. As the *Annual Register* said: 'By the magic of modern science, which in this case is made the handmaid of retributive justice,' a police message had been transmitted from London to Edinburgh 'with a speed that equals the velocity of the thunderbolt'.

The joint trial of the Mannings was an even more resplendent social event than the trial of Courvoisier. The court was filled with 'notabilities' – noblemen and 'ladies of fashion'. Among the less-fashionable ladies who managed to gain admission was Madame Tussaud, proprietress of the waxworks in Baker Street, whose visit, as *Punch* said, was 'purely one of business'. The audience was not disappointed. Mrs Manning made no attempt to conceal her contempt for both the English law and her English husband. 'I think that I am not treated like a Christian, but like a wild beast of the forest,' she said, in a long and spirited debate with Mr Justice Cresswell after he had put on the black cap and was about to pronounce the sentence of death. And pointing scornfully to her husband she said: 'If I had wished to commit murder, how much more likely it is that I should have murdered that man.'

When the judge tried to resume his speech, Mrs Manning cried 'No! No! I won't stand it. You ought to be ashamed of yourselves. There is neither law nor justice here!' She turned to leave the dock, but was prevented by the governor of Newgate. She then picked up a handful of rue which was strewn upon the bench in front of the dock – a custom going back to the days when gaol fever was common – and threw it contemptuously into the body of the court, exclaiming 'Base, shameful, England!'

The behaviour of husband and wife before their execution conformed to the richest traditions of Victorian melodrama. For a time, each continued to accuse the other of being solely responsible for the murder. Mrs Manning remained an obdurate prisoner, frequently shouting 'Damn seize you all!' and denouncing her husband with great vehemence.

After emitting his first confession, in which he swore that he had 'never injured a hair of O'Connor's head', Manning fastidiously asked the prison governor, Mr Keene, to save his own head from the indignity of being copied for display by Madame Tussaud. Mr Keene promised to do his best, and, at Manning's request, knelt in the condemned cell with two turnkeys, Manning, and a solicitor, while all 'engaged in prayer'. Such tableaux were not uncommon in Victorian prisons.

From their separate cells Mr and Mrs Manning exchanged long letters, dripping with piety and reciprocal accusations. 'I address you as a fellow sinner and fellow sufferer, and not as my wife, since the contract must be considered as cancelled extending as it does until death and not beyond it, and both of us standing as we do on the brink of eternity,' Manning began one. 'Believe me, I upbraid you not, but trust you will be assured that I forgive every one, as I pray and hope to be forgiven by God.' When he expressed a fervent wish to see his wife, Mrs Manning replied coldly with a request that Mr Manning state the facts – that she was not in the house when O'Connor met his death. She would then be happy to see him. 'The Lord God will forgive you and comfort you,' she wrote. 'I upbraid you not . . . My life and hope is in your hands. You can, if you will, save me.' Mr Manning made no attempt to do this and finally made a full confession of their joint complicity. Mrs Manning doggedly and contemptuously refused to confess. Their personal differences, however, were resolved on the morning of the execution, when they met in the chapel, kissed, and expressed a mutual hope to meet in Heaven. For the benefit of the audience, the act of reconciliation was repeated with a handshake on the gallows.

'She died with perfect composure, thinking apparently of nothing but exhibiting her beautiful figure to the best advantage,' the Earl of Malmesbury noted in his diary. 'Her dress was very handsome, being of black satin, with a lace *canezou*, and a black veil over her head. The attendants wished her to put on a cloak, but the proposal annoyed her so that they did not press it.' Mrs Manning's choice of black satin was unfortunate for the trade.

'This preference', says Major Griffiths in his *Chronicles of Newgate*, 'brought the costly stuff into disrepute, and its unpopularity lasted for nearly 30 years.' *The Times* compared her with Jezebel, 'the daring foreigner', who, too, was 'painted and attired even unto death'. She was also compared to Lady Macbeth and Clytemnestra. In the streets a common remark was: 'Thank God she is not an Englishwoman.'

'For days past . . . Horsemonger lane and its immediate neighbourhood had presented the appearance of a great fair,' said *The Times*, describing the scene on the morning of the execution. 'Even on Sunday the throng of people pouring in the direction of the gaol never ceased. The surrounding beer-shops were crowded. Windows commanding a view of the scaffold rose to a Californian price. Platforms were run up in every direction, with more attention to profit than to security or law.' On the outskirts of the crowd were men and women from 'fashionable clubs at the West End' and 'luxurious homes', who had paid 2 or 3 guineas for a seat 'to gratify their morbid curiosity'. Many of them watched the proceedings through field-glasses.

Admission to some of the houses was by printed ticket:

> *Admit the Bearer*
> *To one Front Seat.*
> *At M——　——'s*
> *No —— Winter Terrace.*
> *Paid £1. 0. 0d.*

In the orgiastic excitement of the climax Mrs Hannah Manning, a 'masculine looking woman', indignant at being jostled, knocked down a neighbour from the same court, Mrs Ann Collins, crying out that she carried a knife and would have Mrs Collins's 'heart's blood', and would gladly 'swing for her on the same drop as Marie Manning, my namesake.' She was arrested and bound over to keep the peace. Another member of the audience, Catherine Read, aged thirty, was crushed to death against a barrier. But the authorities were pleased by the comparative decorum of the crowd, and, particularly, by the inactivity of the pick-pockets, who, discouraged by the presence of five hundred constables, were not very busy.

On the day before the execution Dickens wrote to Leech: 'We have taken the whole of the roof (and the back kitchen) [of a house opposite the gallows] for the extremely moderate sum of Ten Guineas, or two guineas each.' Dickens had seen at least two executions – the description of Fagin's hanging, written in 1837, was based on first-hand observation – and, for a while, he could not make up his mind whether or not to see the Mannings hanged. A week before, he had written to Leech;

The doleful weather, the beastly nature of the scene, the having no excuse for going (after seeing Courvoisier) and the constantly recurring desire to avoid another such horrible and odious impression, decide me to cry off.

But a party was made up that included Leech and John Forster, and Dickens suggested they meet for supper at the Piazza Coffee House, Covent Garden, 'at 11 exactly'.

Dickens was profoundly moved by the hideous behaviour of the crowd. It was so 'indescribably frightful' that for some time afterwards he felt as if he were 'living in a city of devils'. Three years before, he had written three letters to the *Daily News* condemning public executions as barbarous and useless, and advocating the 'total abolition of the Punishment of Death'. He now wrote to *The Times*, at white heat, 'most earnestly' beseeching the Home Secretary, Sir George Grey, to originate legislation at least to abolish public hangings. 'I have seen, habitually, some of the worst sources of general contamination and corruption in this country, and I think there are not many phases of London life that could surprise me now,' he said. But he was 'solemnly convinced' that 'nothing that ingenuity could devise' could work such ruin in the same compass of time as one public execution:

I believe that a sight so inconceivably awful as the wickedness and levity of the immediate crowd . . . could be imagined by no man, and could be presented in no heathen land under the sun. The horrors of the Gibbet and of the crime . . . faded in my mind before the atrocious bearing, looks and language, of the assembled spectators. When I came upon the scene at midnight, the shrillness of the cries and howls that were raised from time to time, denoting that they came from a concourse of boys and girls already assembled in the best places, made my blood run cold. As the night went on, screeching and laughing, and yelling in strong chorus of parodies of Negro melodies, with substitutions of 'Mrs. Manning' for 'Susannah' and the like, were added to these. When the day dawned, thieves, low prostitutes, ruffians and vagabonds of every kind, flocked on to the ground, with every variety of offensive and foul behaviour. Fightings, faintings, whistlings, imitations of Punch, brutal jokes, tumultuous demonstrations of indecent delight when swooning women were dragged out of the crowd by the police with their dresses disordered, gave a new zest to the general entertainment. When the sun rose brightly . . . it gilded thousands upon thousands of upturned faces, so inexpressibly odious in their brutal mirth and callousness that a man had cause to feel ashamed of the shape he wore, and to shrink from himself, as fashioned in the image of the Devil.

The Times could not permit this maudlin criticism to go unanswered: 'We are not prepared to follow MR. DICKENS to his conclusion,' it said, in the first of three leading articles on the execution. 'It appears to us as a matter of necessity that so tremendous an act as a national homicide should be publicly as well as solemnly done.' On this occasion, as on others in which Calcraft had officiated, the solemnity of the occasion may have been a little marred by the fact that the executioner – obviously drunk – entertained the crowd with whimsical asides and mimings.

Dickens's letters made a 'great to do'; he found himself 'in a roaring sea of correspondence' about them. One reader of *The Times* regretted that Dickens had not been able to see into the rooms of Winter Terrace where, in dress-circle seats, 'men of rank' and 'men of note' wiled away the hours with champagne and cigars, and, with their ladies, used opera-glasses to study 'the dying convulsions of a murderess, just as they have criticized, through the same instrument, the postures of the ballet dancer'. This extravagant sentimentality displeased another reader of *The Times* who replied sharply: 'To object to using the same glass to look at an execution which we have used to look at a ballet is to object to a clergyman for writing a funeral sermon with the same pen which he may have used shortly before to write to his tallow-chandler for his regular supply of candles.'

Despite the solemn promise of Mr Keene, waxworks of Frederick and Marie Manning, 'taken from the life at their trial', with a cast in plaster of O'Connor, and a plan of the Manning's kitchen, were on view at Madame Tussaud's Chamber of Horrors three days after the execution. 'MADAME TUSSAUD is the artistic continuation of MR. CALCRAFT,' said *Punch*. 'When the hangman has done his work, the wax witch takes it up and beautifies it.'

Punch published a woodcut of 'The Great Moral Lesson at Horsemonger Lane Gaol', and a poem 'The Lesson of the Scaffold; or the Ruffian's Holiday'. Here are three verses:

Each public-house was all alight, the place just like a fair;
Ranting, roaring, rollicking, larking everywhere,
Boosing and carousing we passed the night away,
And ho! to hear us curse and swear, waiting for the day.

At last the morning sunbeams slowly did appear,
And then, ha, ha! how rum we looked, with bloodshot eyes and blear;
But there was two good hours at least before the hanging yet,
So still we drained the early purl, and swigged the heavy wet.

Thicker flocked the crowd apace, louder grew the glee,
There was little kids a dancin, and fightin for a spree;
But the rarest fun for me and BILL, and all our jolly pals,
Was the squeakin and squallin and faintin of the gals.

VII

James Blomfield Rush deserved his enormous infamy. He was the Victorian villain *par excellence,* a Gothic monster larger than life, too improbable for history, too wicked for melodrama, too grotesque for comedy, an unexampled blend of brutality, lechery, cupidity, cunning, stupidity, absurdity, vanity and oleaginous piety. For him, as for many of his contemporaries, it was but a short step from the chapel to the dock. 'It was his practice', said *The Times,* 'to fall upon his knees in the midst of his iniquities to implore the blessings of the ALMIGHTY and then to rise up to perfect a half-executed crime.' To his neighbours he was a godly and worthy citizen. His piety was more than a façade; he was fond of his children and he imposed on his mistress, who was also their governess, strict religious observances before and after their nightly couplings.

Like John Tawell, another godly murderer, Rush was a native of Norwich. He was a widower with a large family, and a tenant farmer heavily indebted to his landlord, Mr Isaac Jermy, The Recorder of Norwich and squire of Stanfield Hall. Rush was bankrupt. He had been ejected from one of Jermy's properties for arrears and owed him £5,000 which he had no hope of paying. He decided to resolve his difficulties by forging Jermy's signature to documents cancelling the mortgage, which was due on 30 November 1849. This made it necessary for him to kill Mr Jermy before that date. On the night of the 28th, after his customary sexual and spiritual devotions, he went to Stanfield Hall, a pseudo-Tudor moated mansion, about two miles from Wymondham, shot dead Mr Jermy and his son, and wounded the younger Mrs Jermy and a female servant. He was wearing a ridiculous Christmas-pantomime disguise of a curly wig and whiskers, and he left behind a no less ridiculous document, designed to inculpate Thomas Jermy, a seventy-year-old relative of Isaac Jermy, who had been a claimant to the estate. It began: 'There are seven of us here ... all armed' and announced that they had come to take possession of the Stanfield property. It was signed 'Thomas Jermy, the owner'. Thomas was in London when the murders took place.

Rush was soon arrested, and his mistress, Emily Stanford, gave damning evidence against him. But he retained his confidence, his godliness – and his appetite. Two days before the trial, he gave the host of the Bell Inn, Norwich, explicit instructions about his meals. For breakfast, he ordered 'anything you like, *except beef*; and I shall like cold meat as well as hot, and meal bread, and the tea in a pint mug'. For consumption during the trial he wanted 'a small sucking pig' to be served cold as well as hot, 'with plenty of plum sauce'.

Rush conducted his own defence. His behaviour in court was fantastic. He cross-examined, interjected, and orated with magnificent effrontery and magnificent irrelevance. There were indignant hisses and loud cries of 'Shame' when he asked his mistress, who was suckling one of his children and was pregnant with another, 'Have I not often told you that I could find passages of scripture that would justify our acts if we committed no other sin?' *The Times* reported that he 'was careful to elicit from his mistress . . . the fact of the strange devotional exercises by which he was in the habit of purging their connexion'. He demonstrated his virtuosity in crime by abstracting, under the eyes of a crowded court, a cheque for forty pounds from a pocket book handed up for inspection. His speech to the jury lasted fourteen hours, and has probably never been equalled for endurance, bombast and nonsensicality.

Rush's execution outside Norwich gave *The Times'* 'own reporter', who was also the reporter of the *Norfolk News*, great scope. He wrote at length of the preparations that had been made 'for rendering the execution . . . as solemn and impressive as possible'.

> For this purpose the situation of Norwich Castle and the style of its architecture are strikingly adapted. It is a fine massive structure, the principal feature of which is an immense square tower, supported by buttresses. It stands on a hill or mound, which has a commanding view of the city, with its cathedral and numerous churches . . .
>
> The drop, situated on the bridge leading from the marketplace to the castle, 'had, as may be imagined, a very striking effect!' This was heightened by an immense black flag suspended over the entrance to the Castle which, as it surged slowly in the wind, was well calculated to solemnise the minds of the spectators.

The unusual charm of the setting attracted many visitors from afar. The nobility and country gentry, with their ladies, were well represented. 'The trains from Yarmouth and other places came in loaded with passengers,' said *The Times*, 'and the population of the whole surrounding country poured towards the spot.' London 'bloods', members of the 'Swell Mob', chartered a special train to Norwich, but the police intercepted it at Attleborough and, with dubious authority, transferred most of the passengers to the next 'up' train to London. A woman who had just had a baby trudged eleven miles to the gallows.

Mr St Quentin and Madame Tussaud gratified the curiosity of Londoners who were unable to make the pilgrimage. Within a few days of the execution, Mr St Quentin exhibited models of Stanfield Hall and Rush's farm (scale three-eighths of an inch to the foot), accompanied by a dramatic guide-lecture on the crime, while Madame Tussaud had Rush in his sober black suit and patent leather boots (genuine) scowling from a dock in her Chamber of Horrors.

Punch noted that six 'human creatures', men and women, had been hanged in the past six weeks. 'How horribly eloquent have the dead walls of London become within the past fortnight!'

'Blood' – 'blood' – 'killing' – 'killing' has cried to us from all sides, men in their affected virtue pharisaically trading on the blasphemy they have denounced. This cannot be borne – will not be borne. Outraged human nature will rise and vehemently protest against a repetition of the cause of these trading horrors – against these money-changers for blood and brutalisation.

'I confess I never read these accounts of the clergymen and Calcraft performing on the same scaffold without feeling that if it were possible for the Apostles to witness such scenes they would not recognize the clergyman as one of their descendants,' said John Bright, during a debate on capital punishment in July 1850.

VIII

Those who were unable to attend notable hangings could console themselves by reading about them. 'Execution broadsheets' had enormous sales. The patient Mr Mayhew found that Rush and the Mannings topped the list of bestsellers, with 2,500,000 copies each. Sales of more than 1,500,000 copies were common. Popular gallows literature included 'Life, Trial and Execution' broadsheets and 'Sorrowful Lamentation Sheets', in which the criminal apologizes for his crime in verse:

> *'Now in a dismal cell I lie,*
> *For murder I'm condemned to die;*
> *Some may pity when they read,*
> *Oppression drove me to the deed.*
>
> *The scaffold is, alas! my doom, –*
> *I soon shall wither in the tomb:*
> *God pardon me – no mercy's here*
> *For Rush – the wretched murderer !'*

'Sorrowful Lamentation Sheets' were not known until a law was passed in 1820 prolonging the time between sentence of death and execution. 'Before that, Sir,' a street-trader told Mr Mayhew, 'there wasn't no time for a Lamentation; sentence o' Friday, and scragging b' Monday.'

'There's nothing beats a stunning good murder, after all,' the 'running patterer' told Mayhew. 'Why there was Rush – I lived on him for a month or more . . . Rush turned up a regular trump for us. Why I went down to Norwich expressly to work the execution.'

His stock consisted of *'a sorrowful lamentation'* of Rush's 'own composing' – written by a blind man in London – and 'the full, true, and particular' account of the execution, printed several days 'afore it comes off.' When a colleague, 'Irish Jem the Ambassador', said they would never again have such a windfall as Rush, the patterer told him not to despair. 'There's a good time coming, boys, says I, and sure enough up comes the Bermondsey tragedy.' The newspapers gave them too much space, and Mrs Manning's obstinate refusal to confess further depressed the patterer's market.

> When I read in the papers . . . that her last words on the brink of eternity were, 'I've nothing to say to you, Mr. Rowe, but to thank you for your kindness,' I guv her up entirely – had completely done with her. In course the public looks to us for the last words of all monsters in human form, and as for Mrs. Manning's, they were not worth the printing.

IX

Multiple executions were a robust survival from the eighteenth century. A Bow Street runner, Mr Townsend, told a Parliamentary Committee in 1816 that in the 1780s executions of 12, 16 or even 20 at a time were not uncommon. On two occasions Mr Townsend saw batches of 40 criminals executed in one day. When four murderers were hanged together at Liverpool in 1863 *The Times* pointed out that 'very many persons' would remember when 'it was only an ordinary sight to see half-a-dozen criminals suspended together in front of Newgate on a Monday morning'.

> The mercies of the law in those days were small, but as the crimes punishable with death were numerous, and as only 24 hours were then allowed to elapse between the sentence and the execution, capital cases were usually taken on a Saturday, so that the convicted offenders had the benefit of the Sunday in a day's more life. This piece of consideration threw the last work of the law into the Monday.

By 1863 multiple executions had become rare, and the elaborate arrangements for the quadruple hanging made by the Liverpool authorities reflected their sense of pride and responsibility. 'The preparations were commenced on Friday morning, and the scaffold was enlarged to uncommon dimensions,' *The Times* reported. 'It was draped with black cloth – a custom formerly observed at Newgate, until one day the funereal hangings, torn and battered with long use and frequent exposure, were blown away by the wind and never replaced.' Members of the Liverpool Town Mission co-operated energetically. For two hours before the execution they entertained the crowd with song, prayer and exhortation. 'Occasionally huzzas were raised,' said *The Times*, 'but the preachers heeded not the interruptions.' More distressing to *The Times* than the huzzas of the crowd was the levity of one of the murderers, Benjamin Thomas, a Welsh sailor, who threatened two Welsh Calvinist ministers with violence when they wrestled with him to prepare his soul for eternity. 'Oh, I shall be all right,' he said. 'Nobody can harm me. I'm fit to live in all worlds and I want nothing on earth.'

The railway companies advertised special excursion trains for the occasion. Though the execution took place on a Monday, their enterprise was well rewarded. '"Excursion" – they might have been called "execution" – trains deposited their passengers by the thousands on the fatal morning,' said *The Times*:

> Soon after 11 o'clock there arrived at the Bootle lane railway station an excursion train of 30 carriages from Bradford. The majority of the 'excursionists' were respectably dressed persons, decent-looking mechanics, women in silk dresses with expanded crinolines, and youths from 19 to 20 years of age. The struggling for places became fearful and the din of the living mass of human beings as they pushed, and shoved, sounded painfully upon the ear ... At a quarter to 12, it was estimated that there were 100,000 on the ground, and this number was increased by large arrivals of excursionists from Huddersfield and Blackburn.

Mr Hibbert later told the House of Commons that two hundred thousand people saw the execution, 'many of them having travelled night and day'.

The Times did not question the morality of the entertainment. Though 'we give a shudder', it said, 'as we read of the eagerness with which thousands after thousands pressed on towards the spot, footsore after walking and bespattered with mud', the spectacle though a 'dreadful one' could not have been averted 'without manifest wrong to society'.

Apparently readers of *The Times* agreed. Only one dissenting letter appeared. This criticized the railway companies for adopting the worldly maxim of a certain traditional Quaker: 'Get money honestly, if thou canst, but by all means, get money', and acutely pointed out that public hangings appealed to the 'grosser and more sensual passions':

> There is no use in denying the fact that 'hanging' has become a public amusement with a great portion of the nation, and holds a position analagous to the gladiatorial exhibition of ancient Rome and the modern bullfight of Spain.

Readers of *The Times* were much more interested in the problem of protecting fruit gardens from birds without interfering with what one kindhearted correspondent called the 'vested interests of rooks, magpies, jays, wood-pigeons, missel-thrushes, blackbirds, tomtits, song-thrushes, robins, sparrows and finches'.

No Liverpool merchants or shopkeepers complained about the congestion caused by the multiple hanging, but not long afterwards the Grand Jurors of Manchester boldly denounced public executions, not because they were bad for morals, but because they were bad for business. *The Times* made this objection the text for a philosophic leading-article which pointed out 'how completely the opinion of thinkers upon the subject' had changed 'of late'. Thirty years before, it said, an observer would have predicted that by 1864, 'public executions, and indeed, executions in any form, would be things of the past ... Mr THACKERAY's description of the execution of COURVOISIER and Mr DICKENS' later narrative of the execution of the MANNINGS were sentimental pleas for expediting this end.'

> But a rougher and stronger habit of thought has succeeded that time ...
> we are now tolerably well persuaded of the propriety, and, indeed, the
> necessity of executions, and the same necessity which requires that
> murderers should be hanged requires that the execution should take
> place in such a way that the public may be satisfied of the fact.

While thoroughly approving of this 'rougher and stronger' attitude, *The Times* agreed with the Grand Jurors of Manchester that public executions could be a nuisance in a busy commercial city. Then why not return to the good old practice of carrying out executions at some distance from the gaol? In the eighteenth century criminals were carted for execution from Newgate to Tyburn tree, at the junction of the Edgware and Bayswater roads, near where the Marble Arch now stands. This enabled grateful spectators to spread along three miles of streets, and gave the condemned prisoner the satisfaction of being the hero of the triumphal progress that sometimes, with stops for bowls of ale and handshakes, lasted three hours or more.

'The solemn procession in the middle of the day . . . need not be revived,' *The Times* pointed out, nor, indeed, would 'the wealthy inhabitants of Tyburnia' consent to the gallows being set up again at the old address. But, remembering, perhaps, the success of the Liverpool excursion trains, it suggested an ingenious compromise: 'In these days of railways it would be easy to execute criminals in a solitary spot, away from town, so that spectators might attend if they wished' – and, of course, if they had the price of a fare. Nothing came of this thoughtful proposal.

X

Unfortunately no memoirs of a dedicated gallows-watcher survive, and we cannot share the emotions of the enthusiast as, for example, we can share the emotions of the ardent bird-watcher. But the diary of Dr Shepherd T. Taylor, as a London medical student of the early 'sixties, shows that even among the educated, an appetite for public executions was not easily glutted. After seeing his first hanging, at the end of 1860, Taylor wrote: 'It is hardly possible to conceive a more awful spectacle . . . or one more revolting to human nature.' Yet he continued to patronize these awful spectacles for at least four years. In 1862 when Mrs Wilson, a nurse, was hanged at the Old Bailey for poisoning her friend, Mrs Soames, Taylor wrote: 'It was certainly a very gruesome spectacle, Mrs Catherine Wilson behaved very coolly, and being a stoutish woman, "fell beautiful" to use the words of an illiterate bystander.'

In 1864 Taylor enjoyed three good hangings, Joseph Brookes at Old Bailey, Samuel Wright at Horsemonger Gaol, and the five Malay pirates at Newgate. 'It was a remarkable case,' he wrote of Wright, 'in the fact that the murder, the coroner's inquest, the magisterial investigation, the trial, and the sentence, all took place in the short space of one week.' Wright was a bricklayer who lived with a woman in a lodging-house in the Waterloo road. He killed her in a drunken quarrel, pleaded guilty, had no counsel, and made no attempt to defend himself. His summary conviction was very unpopular, especially as a few months before, a well-connected young man called Townley, sentenced to death for the premeditated killing of his sweetheart, had been saved from execution because he had influential friends.

'The general public and all the newspapers without exception advocated clemency' to Wright, Taylor wrote in his diary. 'But the Home Secretary was inexorable.'

The blinds were drawn in all the neighbouring streets and the military called out in case of an attempted rescue. When the unfortunate man appeared on the scaffold, loud cries of 'Take him down! Take him down!' were heard in every direction, to which the unhappy man responded by repeated bows to the multitude. Even when the white cap was drawn over his head, he still continued bowing and was actually bowing when the drop fell.

Over a thousand police were posted and held in reserve. *The Times* reported that when the crowd yelled, hooted, and cried 'Shame', 'Judicial murder' and 'Where's Townley?' the convict 'appeared touched by the interest taken in him'. A handbill was extensively distributed in the neighbourhood of Horsemonger Gaol. It had a border in mourning and read:

> SOLEMN PROTEST AGAINST THE EXECUTION OF WRIGHT!
>
> Men and women of London, abstain from witnessing this sad spectacle of injustice. Let Calcraft and Co. do their work this time with none but the eye of Heaven to look upon their crime. Let all window shutters be up and all window blinds be drawn for an hour on Tuesday morning in Southwark. Englishmen, shall Wright be hung? If so, there is one law for the rich and another for the poor.

The belief that the law discriminated between gentleman and bricklayer was not held exclusively by the working class. Sir Fitzroy Kelly, a former Attorney-General and Solicitor-General, was shocked by the execution of Wright and the reprieve of Townley. The discrimination was clearly defined in the Criminal Court in 1850, when Robert Pate, a former lieutenant of Hussars, and the son of 'a gentleman of considerable fortune', struck Queen Victoria on the face with a stick as she was leaving the Duke of Cambridge's residence in her carriage.

Mr Baron Alderton, sentencing him to seven years' transportation, said: 'Considering who you are – the station in life you have filled – and the respectability of your connections, it is not the intention of the court to inflict upon you, as we might have done, the disgraceful punishment of whipping. We do not want to add to the disgrace of your family. We have more respect for you though you had none for others.'

When Mr G. Thompson (Tower Hamlets) asked the Home Secretary what he was going to do about these extraordinary words, Sir George Grey said coldly he did not feel justified in doing anything.

XI

Thomas Delane, who became editor of *The Times* in 1841 at the age of twenty-four and occupied the chair for thirty-six years, had a sound editorial formula: find out what the public wants and give it to them. The public, of course, were the lucky Englishmen who could afford sevenpence a day for their copy of *The Times*. But Delane knew that the clubmen of Pall Mall were as avid for gory reports of murders and hangings as the costers of the New Cut who got their ration of blood and violence from the penny broadsheets. 'You have been lucky in having so many murders,' he once wrote to his deputy. A good murder trial was worth anything up to twelve thousand words an issue and a good execution was a field-day for his most accomplished writers. Delane must have been distressed when, in 1864, the Royal Commission was set up that two years later recommended the abolition of public hangings. Meanwhile, that year, he had two splendid trials and executions to cover.

On 23 July 1863 the *Flowery Land* (Captain John Smith, master) sailed from West India Docks, Singapore-bound, with a cargo of champagne, beer, bale goods, boots and shoes. She carried nineteen officers and crew and one passenger, the captain's brother. The fourteen seamen were of many nationalities, Spanish, Greek, Turkish, French and Chinese. Bad feeling soon developed between officers and crew. The captain complained of the way the seamen worked and the seamen complained of the way the captain fed them. Some later said they were nearly starved, and given only a pint of water each a day, even in the tropics. Captain Smith was a fairly mild man but Mr Karswell, the mate, was not. While the captain was content to call his troublesome seamen 'coolies' and 'sons of bitches', the mate at times invoked the persuasion of the rope's end, and had one troublesome fellow strapped to the bulwarks, a punishment then not infrequent. The captain on this occasion interceded, but the discontent of many of the crew increased as the *Flowery Land* sailed southwards towards the Cape of Good Hope. At three o'clock in the morning of 10 September, when she was in latitude 36 S and longitude 19 W, about two thousand miles off the African coast, eight seamen murdered the captain, his brother, and the first mate. Captain Smith's body was thrown overboard to an enthusiastic cry of: 'He won't call us bloody coolies any more!' The second mate was spared because he understood navigation. He was forced to sail the ship to South America, while the mutineers helped themselves freely to the cargo. Cases of champagne and footwear were distributed round the deck and a good time had by all. Twenty-two days after the mutiny, when the *Flowery Land* was off the entrance of the River Plate, the ringleaders shared out what remained of the cargo and scuttled the ship, leaving the cook, the steward and the lamp-trimmer – all Chinese – to go down with her. As a farewell whimsy, bottles of champagne were thrown at the steward as he struggled in the water. The mutineers took ashore what was left of the wine, some green blankets, hams, and navigating instruments, and with a recklessness that can be explained only in terms of free champagne, allowed the second mate and other members of the crew to make their way to Montevideo, where they told the authorities of the mutiny. A man-of-war was sent in search of the mutineers, who were arrested and sent back to England in irons. Eight were tried for murder, and seven found guilty and sentenced to death. Two were reprieved on the eve of the execution.

The prospect of seeing five murderers on the one scaffold, and all of
them foreigners, stirred even the most jaded gallows-watcher.

In apprehension of 'an enormous crowd', 'extraordinary precautions'
were taken by the police. The whole of the space in the Old Bailey, from
Ludgate Hill to Newgate Street, and along Giltspur Street towards

Execution of the *Flowery Land* pirates at Newgate in February 1864.

Smithfield, was intersected with formidable barriers. 'If possible, all
women, and certainly all women with children in arms, will be prohibited
from entering within the barriers,' *The Times* announced. Hoardings were
erected to prevent people clinging to the ledges of buildings; it was
recalled that at an execution on the very same day of the month, fifty-seven
years before, about thirty people had been killed by the collapse of an iron
palisading on St Sepulchre's Church.

'Certain officers and men of fashion held high carnival,' said the *Morning Star*, 'and wound up a species of midnight party by feasting on the spectacle of five human beings being publicly strangled.'

The apprehension of the police was justified. 'At no time within the memory of any one connected with the prison have so many people congregated in the Old Bailey on the day preceding an execution,' *The Times* reported. 'A man residing in a small house opposite is said to have let the windows in the front of it . . . for £75. Another has struck a bargain for a single window for £25.'

Not since 1828 had five men been executed at Newgate at one time, though twice in 1829 four were hanged together. But *The Times* warned its readers to 'guard against the prejudice which is easily excited by a cheap appeal to modern sentiment'. If it were just that each man should be hanged, 'there was no injustice introduced by hanging them together'.

The Times gave a step-by-step description of the proceedings from the pinioning of each of the murderers in his cell, to the cutting down of the bodies ('almost more repulsive than the hanging'), the removal of their clothes, and the filling up of the coffins with quicklime. The portrait of Mr Calcraft was not flattering to a hangman of such repute: 'A short, thickset, shabby man, with venerable white locks and beard which his sinister face belied', who shuffled in, 'cringing with a fawning deference to all he passed'. The *Morning Star* reported that he was hissed 'just as the villain in the play is sure to be'. On the other hand, one of the murderers, who 'sprang on the scaffold with a defiant air', was cheered.

Police Inspector Thomas Kittle, who was on duty at the execution, heard two costermongers talking about it as they trudged up Snow Hill. 'So help me God, ain't it fine – five of them, and all darkies . . .' said one. His friend agreed: 'It is so, and I should like to act Jack Ketch to them . . .!, The dialogue made such a 'particular impression' on Mr Kittle that he immediately recorded it in his pocket-book.

'The gallows deter from crime!' said the *Morning Star*. 'Why, they robbed all night long up to the very foot of the gibbet!' It was the same whenever Calcraft appeared. He drew after him the desperadoes of the metropolis, not to be scared by the horrors of his calling, 'but as the expert juggler is followed by an admiring throng'.

XII

The execution of Franz Muller, in November 1864, brought a memorable year to a satisfactory climax. Muller, a young and amiable German goldsmith turned tailor, was hanged for the murder of Thomas Briggs, an elderly London bank clerk. The murder took place in a suburban railway carriage between Bow station and Hackney Wick. Briggs was killed,

robbed and thrown to the tracks in less than two minutes. The crime
evoked great public interest. In one issue *The Times* devoted twelve columns – eighteen thousand words – to its report of Muller's trial. It was
England's first railway murder, and this in part explained what Muller's
counsel, Sergeant Parry, described as the 'thrill of horror' which ran

No. 56 – Vol. II New Series   LONDON, SATURDAY, SEPTEMBER 17, 1861.   ONE PENNY.

THE ARREST OF MULLER ON BOARD THE VICTORIA.

through the land. As Parry said, it affected the life of everyone who
travelled upon England's 'great iron ways'.

But the case had other points of interest. The evidence against Muller,
though formidable, was not entirely convincing, and the clues were of a
type that Sherlock Holmes, a decade or so later, would have rubbed
appreciative hands over. They included a black beaver hat with a low

crown, not Mr Briggs's, found in the railway carriage, which the Crown claimed belonged to Muller, and a tall hat, the crown of which had been cut down, found in Muller's possession, and which the Crown claimed had belonged to Mr Briggs. Neither claim was established beyond doubt. More difficult for the defence was the fact that Muller, when arrested, had in his possession Mr Briggs's watch, which he said he had bought from a pedlar at the Docks.

Muller left for America six days after the murder was committed. He made no secret of his departure, which he had talked about many weeks before, and travelled under his own name, but to the public it was the flight of a guilty man. He travelled by sailing ship and police officers and witnesses followed him in a steamer that arrived in New York twenty days before his ship. The transatlantic pursuit, anticipating the pursuit of Dr Crippen forty-seven years later, when for the first time wireless telegraphy was used in the capture of a murderer, fuelled the mounting excitement. In news-value, Muller's arrest rivalled even the War Between the States, then at a critical stage.

The extradition proceedings were resisted with great eloquence by a New York attorney, Chancey Schaffer, on the grounds that 'a mixed or unsolemn state of war' existed between the United States and England which suspended all treaties, including the treaty of extradition. This bold plea was based on the fact that England had been supplying the rebellious southern states with ships and arms. The Confederate privateer *Alabama* had been destroyed only a few months before, and Mr Schaffer's orotund references to 'great argosies, laden with the choicest treasures of the nation', sunk with England's 'connivance and consent', evoked loud applause. Mr Schaffer said he would rather see the 'once proud island' of America become 'a sandbank for the storms of the earth to meet in conflict dire' and 'a spot for sea-monsters to fatten on' than that its supreme law should be violated by surrendering Muller to Great Britain.

Commissioner Newton of the United States District Court complimented Mr Schaffer on his able and patriotic advocacy, but rejected his submissions. If, as English newspapers claimed, Muller had possessed three or four thousand dollars, he could have bailed himself out and enlisted in the Federal Army. But he arrived in New York without a penny. On the voyage he had tried to raise a few shillings by offering to eat five pounds of German sausage for a wager.

Before Muller was brought back, his case was prejudged in the London newspapers with an outrageous contempt for justice. The German Legal Protection Society undertook his defence, and made strenuous efforts, after his conviction, to have him reprieved.

He was defended by an eminent advocate, Sergeant Parry, who suggested that one of the most important witnesses for the Crown, a

No. 59—Vol. II. New Series.   LONDON, SATURDAY, JULY 30, 1864.   ONE PENNY.

THE LATE DREADFUL MURDER ON THE NORTH LONDON RAILWAY
Mr. BRIGGS thrown from the carriage at Duckett's Canal Bridge. PORTRAIT OF THE
SUPPOSED MURDERER, FRANZ MULLER (taken from the Photograph in the possession of the Police. MULLER's late residence at Old Ford. Facsimile of the Watch, Chain,
and Box, which furnished the clue. The 'Victoria' at Sea.

cabman of dubious character called Jonathan Matthews, had been
actuated solely by the desire for the £300 reward. And he ridiculed the idea
that a light young man such as Muller could have murdered, robbed and
thrown from the carriage a man weighing twelve stone, all within two
minutes. Moreover, no traces of blood were found on Muller's clothes.
Parry contended that the crime must have been committed by two men,
and a reputable witness swore that he had seen Mr Briggs sitting in his
compartment with two other men.

Like Mrs Manning, Muller disconcerted his English public by refusing to confess, despite the persuasions of the German Lutheran minister, Dr Cappel, who attended him. For a Victorian murderer after his conviction not to emit a long, colourful and pious confession was regarded as a bit unsporting. Muller and Mrs Manning, as foreigners, may not have realized this. Even on the morning of the execution, as Dr Cappel prayed with him, he remained obdurate, and only a few seconds before the drop fell, again denied his guilt. Calcraft was getting impatient, but Dr Cappel continued his exhortations. A hurried dialogue took place in German:

Dr Cappel – I ask you again, and for the last time, are you guilty or no guilty?
Muller – Not guilty.
Dr Cappel – You are not guilty?
Muller – God knows what I have done.
Dr Cappel – God knows what you have done. Does he also know that you have committed the crime?

According to Dr Cappel, Muller then replied: '*Ich habe es getan*' ('I have done it'). As his body dropped from sight, Cappel ran down the stairs of the scaffold shouting exultantly: 'Confessed, confessed, thank God!' Whether Muller confessed remains uncertain. There was doubt about his actual words, which only Cappel heard, especially as the next day Cappel improved the text by adding the word '*Ja*' before 'I have done it.'

Tickets for admission to Muller's trial were strictly limited to the best people: ambassadors, peers, bishops, Members of Parliament, distinguished writers and artists, and 'ladies of the highest rank'. The general public had to contain its scholarly curiosity till the day of the execution. And then only people with plenty of money could enjoy the spectacle in comfort.

Mr Delane's special writers rose magnificently to the occasion. *The Times* report of the execution should be read in full by all who cling to the belief that Victorian journalism, in its loftiest spheres, was dull and unsensational. I quote a few passages from its five thousand words:

A great crowd was expected around the gallows, and, indeed, a great crowd came. The barriers to check the crowd were begun across all the main streets which lead to Newgate as early as on Friday last, and all through Friday night, and on Saturday and Sunday, a dismal crowd of dirty vagrants kept hovering around them. These groups, however, were not composed of the real regular *habitués* of the gallows, but of mere young beginners, whose immature tastes were satisfied with cat-calls in the dark, fondling the barriers, or at most a hurried scrambling throw of dirt at the police when they dispersed them. It was, however, different on

Sunday night. During the early part of the evening there was a crowd as much of loungers as of drunken men, which stood the miserable drizzle with tolerable patience, while the public-houses were open and flared brightly through the mist. But at eleven o'clock a voluntary weeding of the throng commenced. The greater part of the rough mass moved off, leaving the regular execution crowd to take their early places . . .

There were well dressed and ill dressed, old men and lads, women and girls. Many had jars of beer; at least half were smoking, and the lighting of fuses was constant, though not more constant than the cries and laughter, as all who lit them sent them whirling and blazing over the heads into the thicker crowd behind. Occasionally as the rain, which fell heavily at intervals, came down very fast, there was a thinning of the fringe about the beams, but, on the whole, they stood it out very steadily, and formed a thick dark ridge round the enclosure kept before the Debtors' door, where Muller was to die. This was at one o'clock, when the moon was bright and the night very clear indeed, and everything could be seen distinctly . . .

From its great quadrangle the sightseers never moved, but from hour to hour, almost from minute to minute, grew noisier, dirtier, and more dense. Till three o'clock it was one long revelry of songs and laughter, shouting, and often quarrelling, though, to do them more justice, there was at least till then a half-drunken, ribald gaiety among the crowd that made them all akin. Until about three o'clock not more than some four thousand or at the most five thousand, were assembled, and over all the rest of the wide space the white, unoccupied barriers showed up like a network of bones above the mud. But about three the workmen came to finish the last barriers, after the scaffold had been carried to the Debtors' door, and from that time the throng rapidly increased in numbers. Someone attempted to preach in the midst of the crowd, but his voice was soon drowned amid much laughter. Then there was another lull from any pre-eminent attempt at noise, though every now and then it was broken by that inexplicable sound like a dull blow, followed as before always by laughing, sometimes by fighting. Then, again, another man, stronger in voice, and more conversant with those he had to plead before, began the old familiar hymn of 'The Promised Land'. For a little this man sang alone, but at last he was joined by a few others, when another and apparently more popular voice gave out some couplet in which at once, and as if by magic, the crowd joined with the chorus of—

   'Oh, my,
    Think, I've got to die,'
till this again was substituted by the song of

Muller, Muller,
He's the man.'

This was all, and before the peculiar humming noise of the crowd was over Muller had ceased to live, though as he hung his features seemed to swell and sharpen so under the thin white cap that the dead man's face at last stood out like a cast in plaster. For five or ten minutes the crowd, who knew nothing of his confession, were awed and stilled by this quiet, rapid passage from life to death. The impression, however, if any real impression, if it was beyond that of mere curiosity, did not last for long, and before the slight, slow vibrations of the body had well ended robbery and violence, loud laughing, oaths, fighting, obscene conduct, and still more filthy language reigned round the gallows far and near. Such, too, the scene remained, with little change or respite, till the old hangman slunk again along the drop amid hisses and sneering inquiries of what he had had to drink that morning. He, after failing once to cut the rope, made a second effort more successfully, and the body of Muller disappeared from view.

On this occasion *The Times* seems to have had faint doubt, if not of the news value of the spectacle, at least of its propriety. It was not sure whether any human being should have passed away in such a scene. 'The gallows as a moraliser is at the best a rough one,' it reflected. And it wished that this 'last and saddest offering to man's justice could have been made less hideous'. Still, things were better than they had been, as every Victorian knew:

The time has been, and very lately too, when the dress in which a felon died, or even a cast of his distorted features, would have been worth their weight in gold. But nothing of this catering for the wretched curiosity of the gallows is permitted now.

The Times, of course, did not cater for the wretched curiosity of the crowd. It recorded facts for the incurious clubman.

Muller's photographs were sold in enormous quantities all over England, and the huge publicity he received produced a sort of execution neurosis, and what the secretary of the Society for the Abolition of Capital Punishment, Mr W. Tallack, called 'a crop of homicidal crimes'. A few days before the execution a printer's apprentice in Chancery Lane, normally a cheerful young man, brooded over it so much that he inadvertently killed himself experimenting with a home-made gallows, and a soldier charged with the attempted murder of a prostitute in Gray's Inn Road said cheerfully: 'I don't mind swinging with Muller for such a —— as her.' On the very evening of the execution, a London engineer stabbed a man and exclaimed when arrested, 'I will be hung for him as Muller was for Briggs.'

Within a few days of the execution, the drama of *Mr Briggs, or the Murder in the Railway Train*, was drawing crowded houses at a penny theatre in Dundee. One scene, which brought down the house, represented the interior of a railway carriage in which Muller was seen to attack Briggs and throw him out of the window.

IV

Mr Dickens and Mr Reynolds

I

Middle-class Victorian morality emasculated the mid-Victorian novel. But did the great Victorian writers chafe very much under the restrictions which Mrs Grundy, and her personal assistant Mr Mudie, imposed on them? Take the most representative and successful, Charles Dickens. Once, praising a French play, he wrote of 'the powerful emotions from which art is shut out in England by the conventionalities', and Jack Lindsay, in an interesting biography, presents him as a man 'who keeps trying to break through the Victorian conventions'. But he does not seem to have tried very hard. Lindsay himself points out that though Dickens might satirize the Victorian literary code in characters like Mrs General and Mr Podsnap, 'he dared not go too far in transgressing it or he would have lost his hold on his readers'. And the rewards of conformity were temptingly high for a man whose boyhood had been seared by poverty and who enjoyed worldly success very much as Arnold Bennett did – with a faintly vulgar exuberance. (He made about £10,000 out of *The Old Curiosity Shop*, written before he was twenty-eight – a sum equal to at least £50,000 today – and a few years before his death he was paid £8,000 for a hundred readings.)

Yet Dickens was no more venal than most of his contemporaries. He was incapable of writing without an audience, and the readers with whom he was most in sympathy, who, in a sense, were his collaborators, belonged principally to the middle class. He lacked the educated Englishman's appreciation of the uninhibited Greek and Latin writers, and of the robust English literary tradition from Chaucer to Fielding. In 1866, when Swinburne's *Poems and Ballads* were savagely attacked by John Morley, who, while deploring 'fat-headed Philistines' and 'poor-blooded Puritans', denounced Swinburne as 'the libidinous laureate of a pack of satyrs' with 'a mind all aflame with the feverish carnality of a school-boy', the poet replied with a formidable assault on the card-house of Victorian literary convention. The question at issue, he said, was wider than any between a single writer and his critics:

It is this; whether or not the first and last requisite of art is to give no offence, whether or not all that cannot be lisped in the nursery or fingered in the school-room is therefore to be cast out of the library... Who has not heard it asked, in a final and triumphant tone, whether this book or that can be read aloud by her mother to a young girl? . . . Never till now, and nowhere but in England, could so monstrous an absurdity rear for one moment its deformed and eyeless head . . . Literature to be worthy of men must be large, liberal, sincere; and cannot be chaste if it is prudish. Purity and prudery cannot keep house together . . . And if literature indeed is not to deal with the full life of man and the whole nature of things, let it be cast aside with the rods and rattles of childhood.

The last alliterative phrase was unfortunate in view of Swinburne's personal reluctance to cast aside at least the rods of childhood, but the manifesto as a whole, despite the clatter of rhetoric, can be read today as a vigorous and effective plea for the freedom of the artist. It is instructive to compare it with what Dickens wrote a few years later when Charles Reade's novel *Griffith Gaunt* was also attacked as indecent. Reade thought *Griffith Gaunt* was his masterpiece; Swinburne said no language could overpraise it. *The Spectator* described it as a 'noble, though somewhat rugged poem in prose' and 'a rare example of that chastity of art which can be naked . . . and yet pure' – though it conceded that some of 'Mr Mudie's heads of families' might take exception to it, for it presupposed 'that its readers live among men and women and not in a monastery'.

But so savagely was it denounced by an American critic that Reade took action for libel. Wilkie Collins and Edwin Arnold both offered to defend the book in court, and Collins asked Dickens if he, too, would be a witness.

Despite his friendship for Reade and his admiration for his work, Dickens refused. He was not prepared to plead for the artist's right to deal with 'the whole nature of things'. He was more concerned with the effect of the artist's work on the public. He said he regarded *Griffith Gaunt* as the work of a highly accomplished writer and a good man, but if he were asked as an editor if he would have passed certain passages in it, he would have to reply No.

Asked why? I should say that what was pure to an artist might be impurely suggestive to inferior minds (of which there must necessarily be many among a large mass of readers) and that I should have called the writer's attention to the likelihood of those passages being perverted in such quarters.

Apparently he would not differentiate between a good book and a book that was good for the circulation of a magazine. It is hard to imagine Balzac or Flaubert using a critical method based on the protection of a large mass of 'inferior minds' from some undiagnosed infection. But Dickens went further. He said he considered other parts of the book 'extremely coarse and disagreeable', and this was offered as a personal opinion, unrelated to the prophylaxis of people with 'inferior minds' – a class which no doubt included all the young ladies who sighed and swooned over his own novels.

Morley's frenetic attack on Swinburne – it was as hypocritical as it was hysterical for Morley enjoyed a bit of indecency over his port – appeared in the *Saturday Review*, which only a few years before had repeatedly and resoundingly denounced the infantile purity of the English novel. In a review of *Madame Bovary* printed in 1857 – the year when Dickens met his mistress Ellen Ternan, and when Lord Campbell's Act against obscene publications was passed – the *Saturday Review* had said:

. . . in considering the intentions of an author we must remember how very conventional is the standard of what is permissible to say and to write. No one would call Milton or Shakespeare immoral. Yet *Paradise Lost* and *Othello* contain passages which could not be read aloud to English ladies. Indeed, if it were not for the force of habit, the same difficulty would constantly occur in reading the Bible . . .

There are probably half a dozen scenes in it [*Madame Bovary*] which no English author of reputation would venture to insert in any of his publications; and indeed there is no subject on which we are so apt to plume ourselves as the modern purification of our light literature. But is this true? And if it is, how far does it prove that we are more moral than our neighbours? It is true, in one sense, no doubt, that our light literature is pure enough. That is, it is written on the principle that it is never to contain anything which a modest man might not, with satisfaction to himself, read aloud to a young lady. But surely it is very questionable whether it is desirable that no novels should be written except those which are fit for young ladies to read. It is not so with any other branch of literature. Theology, history, philosophy, morality, law and physical science are all studied at the reader's peril . . . Are works of the imagination, then, such mere toys that they ought always to be calculated for girlish ignorance?

But apart from the stultification of literature, there was also the question whether:

a light literature entirely based upon love, and absolutely and systematically silent as to one important side of it, may not have some tendency to stimulate passions to which it is far too proper to allude . . . it is one we should do well to take into serious consideration before we preach the doctrine that the contemporaries of Mr Dickens have made a vast step in advance of the contemporaries of Fielding.

In another discussion of the Victorian novel, the *Saturday Review* said that 'it carefully suppresses all those coarse allusions to the relations between the sexes which we find in Fielding or Defoe; but it indemnifies itself by a sort of luscious sentimentality which appears to us infinitely worse'. Quite as immoral as 'undisguised indecency' were:

> the exquisitely pathetic deathbeds of beautiful little girls – the fondling love-scenes, in linked sweetness long drawn out, and as free from passion as distilled water is from spirit – the family kissing and coaxing – the slimy apotheosis of the domestic affections.

Lord David Cecil, in his study of *Early Victorian Novelists,* comes to a similar conclusion about the immoral effect of their immoderate passion for morality:

> In the face of such exaggeration the reader's commonsense rebels . . . And as a result he begins to react against the whole moral system which leads authors to such ridiculous falsifications of the truth . . . The Victorian picture of vice, ironically enough, produced precisely the effect that its exponents hoped it would not. Far more than any sordid realist they set the reader against a high standard of chastity.

The 'standard of chastity' – or of sobriety – was not very high in the country household which Dickens described in a letter to John Forster in 1856. A friend whom he discreetly designated 'B' was sketching near Gadshill, 'not a thousand miles' from Dickens's home, when a gentleman driving

> with a lady in an open carriage, introduced himself. He was an Oxford man, and a Devonshire squire, but, for domestic reasons, not living on his estate. He invited 'B' to dine with him at a great house he had nearby. 'B' accepted the invitation, found the house had a fine library, and stayed *six months* [Dickens, not surprisingly, italicized the two words].
> The lady was a mistress, aged five-and-twenty, and very beautiful, drinking her life away. The Squire was drunken, and utterly depraved and wicked: but an excellent scholar, an admirable linguist and a great theologian. Two other mad visitors stayed the six months. One, a man well-known in Paris . . . who goes about the world with a crimson silk stocking in his breast pocket, containing a tooth-brush and an immense quantity of ready money. The other, a college chum of the Squire's, now ruined; with an insatiate thirst for drink; who constantly got up in the middle of the night, crept down to the dining room, and emptied all the decanters. . . . 'B' stayed on in the place, under a sort of devilish fascination to discover what might become of it . . . Tea or coffee never seen in the house, and very seldom water . . . Beer, champagne and brandy, were the three drinkables. Breakfast; leg of mutton, champagne, beer and brandy. Lunch: shoulder of mutton, champagne, beer and brandy.

Dinner: every conceivable dish (Squire's income £7,000 a year), champagne, beer and brandy. The squire had married a woman of the town from whom he was now separated, but by whom he had a daughter. The mother, to spite the father, had bred the daughter in every conceivable vice. Daughter, then 13, came home from school once a month. Intensely coarse in talk, and always drunk. As they drove about the country in two open carriages, the drunken mistress would be perpetually tumbling out of one, and the drunken daughter perpetually tumbling out of the other. At last the drunken mistress drank her stomach away, and began to die on the sofa. Got worse and worse, and always raving about Somebody's where she had once been a lodger, and perpetually shrieking that she would cut somebody else's heart out. At last she died on the sofa, and, after the funeral, the party broke up. A few months ago, 'B', met the man with the crimson silk stocking at Brighton, who told him the Squire was dead 'of a broken heart'; that the chum was dead of delirium tremens: and that the daughter was heiress to the fortune.

II

Dickens was the most successful English writer of his time, but the most popular was the forgotten G. W. M. Reynolds. 'Dickens, Thackeray, and Lever had their thousands of readers but Mr Reynolds's readers were numbered by hundreds of thousands, perhaps by millions,' said *The Bookseller* when he died in 1879. In an article on his life and works published eleven years before, *The Bookseller* had made a similar comparison:

It is said that Mr Reynolds has written more novels than Charles Dickens, and that, in weekly portions and complete volumes, his sensuous stories have been sold in far greater numbers, both in England and America, than the fictions of the more admired author.

'The passing away of so notorious a writer deserves some record,' said *The Bookseller*, pointing out that no notice of his death had appeared in either *The Times* or the *Athenaeum*.

Certainly Reynolds deserved mention, if not as a writer, at least as a phenomenon. A man who enjoyed for so long such enormous popularity cannot be ignored by the social historian. His neglect by the pundits of his time is easily explained: he was a violent republican and radical and he wrote of sex with a lusty and exuberant freedom unique in the popular fiction of his time. His neglect today is less understandable. No other novelist, not even Dickens, gives as good a picture of some aspects of London life in the 'forties and 'fifties.

To put Reynolds in a present-day perspective, you have to imagine the

George William MacArthur Reynolds.

gifted Mr Mickey Spillane as an active member of the American Commun-
ist Party, denouncing capitalists and congressmen at a clamant rally in
Madison Square Gardens, or Mr R. Palme Dutt challenging Ian Fleming
as England's best-selling exponent of sex, sadism and *le highlife*. For
Reynolds was not only the Spillane or Fleming of his time; he was also a
passionate and energetic Chartist when Chartism was as much a bogy to
respectable Englishmen as communism is today to respectable Americans.
The combination of serious social purpose with semi-pornography, often

flavoured with perversity, is unique in English literature, though America provides a curious parallel in George Lippard, whose novel, *The Quaker City*, published in 1844, sold 60,000 copies in the first year, and about 300,000 copies in a decade. 'It is hard to know exactly what the nature of Lippard's audience was, or precisely what satisfactions they sought in his books,' says Leslie A. Fiedler in his study of *Love and Death in the American Novel*. Like Reynolds, he offered 'a combination of sex, horror and advanced social thought' and justified his pornography as muckraking. 'He thought of his novel, stories and pamphlets . . . as weapons in the holy war of labour,' says Fiedler, with the acute comment:

> Psychologically, of course, popular radicalism has always taken advantage of the tendency of relatively naive and uneducated people to project on the upper classes which they despise the erotic and sadist fantasies of which they are ashamed, thus providing themselves with the luxury of at once indulging and disavowing their own most shamefully masturbatory dreams.

Dickens, introducing the first number of his *Household Words* in March 1850, was obviously referring to Reynolds when he denounced the 'Bastards of the Mountain, draggled fringe on the Red Cap, Panders to the basest passions of the lowest natures – whose existence is a national reproach. These we should consider it our highest duty to displace.'

But Reynolds, whether bastard, draggled fringe or pander, was not easily displaced.

III

George William MacArthur Reynolds was born at Sandwich in 1814, the son of a naval post-captain. He was at the Royal Military College, Sandhurst, from 1828 to 1830, and for the next few years travelled in Europe. In Paris he acquired a good knowledge of French literature, and met Eugène Sue, by whom he was obviously influenced. He writes of 'enjoying the friendship' during the years 1834–7 of Sir Sydney Smith, the hero of Acre, and friend of the unhappy Queen Caroline. In 1835 his first book, a three-volume novel, *The Three Impostors*, was published in London. Next year, when plump little Mr Pickwick had become a national figure, inspiring Pickwick cigars, Pickwick hats, Pickwick chintzes, Pickwick canes, and countless plagiarisms and parodies of his adventures, Reynolds was among the most successful of the neo-Pickwickians. His *Pickwick Abroad* went through many editions and was still in print when he died.

It was 'by no means an imitation or plagiarism of the original work', said *The Bookseller*, 'but rather a fanciful sketch of what Pickwick and his companions might have done, said and seen in France, Germany and Italy.' Reynolds followed this in 1839 with *The Modern Literature of France*, a critical work which showed an intimate knowledge of George Sand, Balzac, Lamartine, Dumas, and Sue. About this time, he returned to England and took charge of the 'foreign intelligence department' of the London *Dispatch*. He sympathized strongly with the revolutionary movements of Europe and, after publishing two more romances, for a time abandoned literature for politics. It was a period when the Chartist movement was evolving from theory to organization and practice, and Reynolds was active on lecture-platforms, and deputations to parliament.

In 1845 he became the first editor of the *London Journal*, one of three very successful penny weeklies, established in the late 1840s to meet a rapidly growing demand for cheap and sensational fiction. As Henry Mayhew noted, 'Works relating to Courts, potentates, or "haristocrats" were relished by a large class of readers.' They still are, of course, at least by readers of the popular English magazines, but the tone today is rather more rapturous and less critical than it was a century ago. Reynolds, while editing the *London Journal*, contributed to it a serial, *Mysteries of the Inquisition*, and published in penny numbers his long novel, *Mysteries of London*. At the end of 1846 he started his own penny weekly, *Reynolds' Miscellany*, which he conducted for twenty-three years. His fecundity was astonishing. An incomplete list of his works, published in *The Bookseller* in 1868, has more than fifty titles. *The Bookseller* points out that to list all his works it would be necessary to consult not only the British Museum catalogue but the catalogues of publishers in the United States, 'where, it is said, they are extensively read'. Most of these romances appeared first in serial form in the *Miscellany*, or in penny weekly parts, and later in book form. The most characteristic, *Mysteries of the Court of London*, was a series of eight huge novels, ranging in period from the late eighteenth century to middle nineteenth century. Each large octavo volume comprises over 400,000 words. Reynolds concluded the eighth number of the *Mysteries of the Court of London* with an instructive footnote:

Every week, without a single intermission during a period of eight years, has a Number under this title been issued to the public. Its precursor, *The Mysteries of London*, ranged over a period of four years. For *twelve* years, therefore, have I hebdomadally issued to the world a fragmentary portion of that which, as one vast whole, may be termed an Encyclopaedia of Tales. This Encyclopaedia consists of twelve volumes, comprising six hundred and twenty four weekly numbers (each weekly number contained an average of 8,000 words.) Each Number has occupied me upon an average seven hours in the composition; and therefore no less an amount than four thousand three hundred and sixty-eight hours have been bestowed upon this Encyclopaedia of Tales . . . Yet if that amount of hours be reduced to days, it will be found that only a hundred and eighty-two complete days have been absorbed in these publications which have ranged with weekly regularity over a period of twelve years! This circumstance will account to the public for the facility with which I have been enabled to write many works during the same period, and yet to allow myself ample leisure for recreation and for healthful exercise.

Despite this enormous output, Reynolds found time to start, in 1850, a radical newspaper which, under the title of *Reynolds' News*, was published in London until 1962, and to busy himself in politics and temperance work.

'He succeeded', said *The Bookman*, 'in making his newspaper the leading Radical journal, advocating republicanism, ridiculing royalty, and eagerly exposing the malpractices and crimes of the aristocracy.'

As a Chartist, Reynolds was active for about sixteen years. He made his first notable public appearance in March 1848, at a meeting in Trafalgar Square. Income tax had been raised from sevenpence in the pound to one shilling because of a war scare. The seventy-three-year-old Duke of Wellington had somehow come to the conclusion that France might invade England, though the republican government which had just chased Louis Philippe from the throne was obviously concerned with domestic problems rather than with conquest.

The fivepence-in-the-pound tax increase was very unpopular. Baron Rothschild disapproved of it as strongly as the radicals, and middle-class reformers called a 'monster meeting' in Trafalgar Square to protest. When the authorities declared the meeting illegal because it was to be held within a mile of the Houses of Parliament, the organizers abandoned it, and Chartists took over.

About fifteen thousand people assembled – pickpockets and *canaille*, or industrious artisans, according to which paper you read – and Reynolds was voted to preside. He was vociferously cheered when he acclaimed the 'glorious' French revolution and demanded that the rights of labour be recognized in England as they had been in France. But he urged his listeners to be peaceable and to show the police 'and the Government spies in plain clothes' that English workers could discuss their wrongs in an orderly manner. Despite this, there were violent clashes with the police, and many lamps, shop windows and heads were broken. When the meeting broke up, excited crowds shouting 'To the Palace!' and 'Vive la République!' followed Reynolds down the Strand to his house in Wellington Street, where he continued his exhortations from the balcony. In the evening at another 'monster meeting' on Clerkenwell Green he denounced the police for their aggressive conduct and declared that if Englishmen were forced to have recourse to bloodshed, their oppressors would have to account for the result.

Punch in a satirical account of the 'Trafalgar Square Revolution' described Reynolds as 'a literary gent from Holywell Street' – the headquarters of London's flourishing indecent book trade. The 'literary gent', said *Punch*, 'was hoisted on to the top of a balustrade where he held forth on the necessity for abolishing everything, and uniting mankind in one great elastic india-rubber band of universal brotherhood.' *Punch* was published

LADY ERNESTINA DYSART.

'Lady Ernestina Dysart', one of Reynolds's well-endowed heroines.

by Bradbury and Evans, who also published the *Daily News*, the liberal morning paper which Charles Dickens had started, but quickly abandoned.

While these stirring events were taking place, Reynolds was still turning out his long weekly instalment of *Mysteries of London*. It is typical of his method that, in the middle of an exciting episode in which an innocent young aristocrat has been inveigled into marriage with a beautiful whore, a veritable 'demon of pollution', he devotes a whole chapter to an enthusiastic account of the revolution in France, and calls on the trampled 'English Sons of Toil – oppressed, ground down by taxation, half-starved and deprived of their electoral rights' to follow the 'great and glorious' French example. And in a footnote, he reports at length his speeches at Trafalgar Square and Clerkenwell Green, 'simply for the purpose of convincing our readers that we are not afraid to proclaim in all possible ways the opinions which we have for years promulgated through the medium of our writings'. Then the adventures of the besotted aristocrat and the lovely demon continue.

A few weeks later, when London was on the verge of civil war, Reynolds helped to organize the great Chartist meeting on Kennington Common, and was one of the speakers who addressed the crowd of 100,000 or 150,000 people. On the eve of this meeting, Lord Campbell, Chief Justice of England, wrote to his brother: 'This may be the last time I write to you before the Republic.' His sombre mood was widely shared. Queen Victoria left London for the security of the Isle of Wight, and valuables were hurriedly moved from Buckingham Palace. The Iron Duke took command of 8,000 regular troops and 150,000 curiously assorted special constables – among them, Mr Gladstone and the exiled Louis Napoleon. Windows of the Foreign Office were barricaded with stout volumes of *The Times*, said to be bullet-proof. Thus the Thunderer, long the political voice of the Government, now, with happy symbolism, became its physical shield.

Chartism received a mortal wound on Kennington Common, but Reynolds, with many other idealists, rode the dying horse for many years after. In 1850 he addressed Chartist meetings in the midlands and the north. Though he abandoned Chartism in 1856, he remained politically active, and nonconformist, till the end of his life.

Reynolds' News announced the death of its founder in the same issue as it announced the death of the Prince Louis Napoleon (the ex-Prince Imperial) in the Zulu War. A French exile in England wrote:

Whilst monarchy mourns the death of its princes in diamonds, the people are compelled to deplore the loss of their friends in a more humble manner. I, therefore, assume the simple crape of the English democracy that mourns over the loss of its best champion. I may here, without fear of contradiction, express the deep-felt feelings of gratitude entertained towards him both by the young and old exiles in England. During my thirty years of banishment, on all occasions, and in every way did Mr Reynolds manifest his fidelity to the cause we all defended – the sovereignty of the people. Amongst the English press Reynolds' was the only journal that espoused the cause of those who were sent by M. Bonaparte into exile. It also had the courage to denounce in 'A letter to the Queen', the monstrosity of an alliance between a constitutional sovereign and the Man of December. It is also the only journal that sympathized with the exiles made by M Thiers, and who escaped the massacres in May. In short, the sole newspaper that maintained the principle of universal right, and boldly raised the republican banner in the country of Cromwell, as it was recognised in that of Robespierre,

I fraternally salute you,

Felix Pyat.

IV

Reynolds's plots are absurdly involved and melodramatic, and he inherits many of the tawdry trappings of the Gothic novel. But, in essence, he is a writer of considerable skill and enormous vitality, who mixes horror, sex, fact and propaganda with magnificent abandon. Between a lurid account of a squalid murder and a luscious account of a splendid seduction, you may find a severely factual account of convict-life in New South Wales, of the villainies of George IV, or the sophisticated tricks of London merchants. In his documentary passages, he is as penetrating and as painstaking as his contemporary, Mayhew, and his uncompromising denunciations of social abuses make Dickens seem a very pallid and timid reformer.

He explores the darkest recesses of London, writing with passion and authority of 'kinchin-kens' – cheap lodging houses where dozens of boy and girl thieves sleep together in filthy rooms – sweat-shops, slums, and lunatic asylums. He describes the horrors of military floggings and the brutalities of the treadmill. (In *The Soldier's Wife* published in 1850, Reynolds gives an intensively vivid account of a flogging in the British Army. *Reynolds' News* was banned in the Army that year.) And he is equally familiar with London's raffish nightlife. There are valuable descriptions of places like the Cider-Cellar, with W. S. Ross giving his famous characterization of Sam Hall, the condemned murderer ('There is no comedy in his personification . . . it is all tragedy.'); and the Judge and Jury Society, with the bawdy Baron Renton Nicholson presiding ('a man of good intellectual attainments . . . great conversational powers . . . liberality, a generosity, a kindness of heart').

Reynolds is always prepared to hold up his narrative, even at a critical moment, for a page or two of bitter comment in this vein:

> Take a bottle of cheap Port wine and let a chemist analyse it: he'll tell you it contains three ounces of spirits of wine, fourteen ounces of cyder, one ounce and a half of sugar, two scruples of alum, one scruple of tartaric acid, and four ounces of strong decoction of logwood.

> THE GAME LAWS! Never was a more atrocious monopoly than that which reserves the use of certain birds of the air or animals of the earth to a small and exclusive class . . . The game-laws are a rack whereon the aristocracy loves to behold its victims writhing in tortures.

Or to interpolate a passage such as:

Let us examine for a moment the social scale of these realms:

The Sovereign.
  The Aristocracy.
    The Clergy.

      The Middle Classes.

          The Industrious Classes.

The lowest step in the ladder is occupied by that class which is the most numerous, the most useful, and which ought to be the most influential.

The average annual incomes of the individuals of each class are as follows:

The Sovereign	.. ..	£500,000
The member of the Aristocracy	.. ..	£30,000
The Priest	.. ..	£7,500
The member of the middle classes	.. ..	£300
The member of the industrious classes	.. ..	£20

Is this reasonable? Is this just? Is this even consistent with common sense?

He is the only Victorian novelist I know who mentions the curious fact that for the greater part of the Queen's reign, men at the seaside bathed naked in front of women. Because they are persons of 'rank and wealth', he deplores their 'disgusting and scandalous indelicacies', which he presents through the eyes of a shocked young private secretary, Christian Ashton:

There were male bathers in a condition of perfect nudity within five or six yards of female bathers . . . floating on their stomachs and their backs – leaping high to dive down head foremost – or ascending the steps at the backs of the machines in order to plunge off into the sea again . . . Christian could not help observing that the ladies rambled or stood nearest to those points where the gentlemen were bathing.

V

As a deliberate pornographer, Reynolds is a spiritual ancestor of Spillane and Fleming, with an unmistakable appetite for the sadistic, as well as the normal Victorian enthusiasm for death-beds, corpses, grave-yards, and vaults. In the *Mysteries of the Inquisition*, he luxuriates in gaudy descriptions of scourging and torture. In *Wagner*, a naked woman is stretched on the rack before the eyes of her captive lover and gloating husband. In the *Mysteries of London* and *Mysteries of the Court of London*, he describes with gusto the ill-treatment of children, floggings, murders, suicides and hangings. (One of his hangmen is so devoted to his craft that he has in his bedroom a model scaffold and life-sized pinioned dummy with which he

"superb contours of her bosom"

amuses himself when he is not mercilessly thrashing his beautiful niece and humpbacked son.)

A typical chapter in the *Mysteries of the Court of London* catalogues the ingenious tortures inflicted on 'poor Hindoos' by tax-collecting officials of the Anglo-Indian Government. One young woman, stripped to the waist, her hands fastened behind her back, has 'carpenter beetles' – which bite more savagely than the English wasp – 'applied to one of her breasts'. Another, from whose 'magnificent bust' the garments are ruthlessly torn off, has her breasts crushed in a vice-like arrangement of supple sticks till she dies in agony. No doubt she was chosen for this particular torture, Reynolds comments, because of the 'superb contours of her bosom . . . firm, rounded and admirably shaped'. And he assures the reader that in his description of these, and many other no less 'diabolical tortures', there is not the slightest exaggeration.

The poverty, cruelty and evil of nineteenth-century London cast long shadows. A fascination with violence and crime is typical of much of the popular literature of the day: it is apparent in Dickens, Bulwer and Ainsworth. But what distinguishes Reynolds is the way he combines this fascination with a lush sexuality. In the pages of Dickens, no young woman ever has a body, no young man ever thinks about a bed. Reynolds's characters, male and female, are surcharged with sex. His favourite adjective is 'voluptuous'; his favourite incident, seduction. He writes uninhibitedly of attractive prostitutes and enthusiastically of rococo debauchees.

When a writer in the *Daily News* in 1847 attacked his stories for their licentiousness, he devoted a chapter of *Mysteries of London* to denouncing the 'contemptible abortion' of a paper – 'scurrilous, hypocritical and wishy-washy' – and forced it to retract its 'vile, cowardly and ruffian-like attack'. But he must have had his tongue in his cheek.

'Mr Reynolds appears to delight in carrying his heroines into the most dangerous company, and exhibiting them in the most equivocal and compromising situations,' said *The Bookseller* in 1868. And it noted that his very excellence as a writer made his immoral tales the more harmful:

> The art which makes the life of a courtezan, or an actress, a life of ease, pleasure and gay delight is an art which can only be exercised with the extremest caution . . . In too many instances this clever writer has, we regret to say, administered the poison and forgotten the remedy.

That he is not perpetually dishing out moral antitoxins is, no doubt, what endeared Reynolds to many of his readers. He is certainly not without moral purpose, but he does not accept the common Anglo-Saxon assumption that immorality means enjoying sexual relations without being married. Some Victorians carried the assumption further; they believed that it was immoral for a woman to enjoy sex in any circumstances. Dr Acton, a London physician, in a scientific work published in the 'fifties, said it was a 'vile aspersion' to say women were capable of feeling sexual desire. But at the very same time, Mr Reynolds's splendid wantons were unashamedly feeling and satisfying sexual desire. 'All the flexions of her body were the indices of her passions,' he writes of one of his Junoesque women whose uncorseted bust glows persuasively through her transparent gown. And many of his illicit lovers thoroughly enjoy themselves without coming to the uncomfortable end which Victorian literary convention demanded. The woman who 'falls' in a Dickens novel – even if, like Martha in *David Copperfield*, she is seduced by a plausible villain – finishes up as a moaning wild-eyed outcast, racked with misery and remorse. But a lusty, hospitable Reynolds girl, such as Diana Arlington in the *Mysteries of London*, marries an earl and lives happily and luxuriously ever after. In this, too, Reynolds is a more honest reporter of contemporary life than Dickens. Many Victorian aristocrats married whores, and many Victorian whores died – as they had lived – in comfortable bedrooms, unattended by any reproachful ghosts.

VI

Geoffrey Gorer, in an anthropological study of the United States, notes the 'very great erotic value' given to breasts in contemporary America. He finds they have 'almost completely replaced the earlier value given to legs'; the cleft between them is 'almost the greatest object of erotic curiosity' to the American male. Gorer attributes this apotheosis of the breast to the American's exaggerated interest in food, caused by the 'scientific' method of feeding by the clock. In such a pronouncement, anthropology seems to be about as exact a science as gallimancy. Victorian children were not fed by the clock, but Reynolds takes as scholarly an interest in breasts as any twentieth-century reader of *Playboy* and one assumes that his interest is shared by his enormous gallery of readers.

The low-cut fashions of the 'fifties, gave Reynolds and his illustrators plenty of titillatory scope. The bosoms of his heroines were described in rapturous and reiterated detail. (The word 'breast' is seldom used except as a vague male repository for tempestuous emotions.) The ideal Reynolds' bosoms are white, glowing, globular, firm, palpitating, and swelling – sculptured yet animated. They bob up and down like hydrometers registering the emotional fluctuations of their owners, or, as Reynolds puts it lyrically, swell and sink 'like the undulating motion of the sea'.

The movements of Miss Venetia Trelawney's bosom, as charted in only one volume of *The Mysteries of the Court of London*, are typical. The 'half-exposed amplitude' of her 'voluptuously grand' and 'luxuriant bust' is first noted on page 64. On page 109 her 'glowing bosom . . . swelled yet more exuberantly' to the contact of the Prince Regent's 'daring hand'. On page 120 it is 'rising grandly' above her 'exceedingly low-cut dress'. It is well displayed in another 'low-bodied' dress on page 124, and on page 172 her wedding dress allows 'transient glances' of its 'swelling volume' and 'grand contours'.

On page 246 Miss Trelawney's bust rises 'like hemispheres of polished alabaster in their well-divided contours,' yet full of 'glowing ardour, warmth and passion'. On page 283, the 'gorgeous contours' are again 'half-exposed', and her bosom, as a whole, is 'palpitating in the expectation of that deeper delirium and more frenetic whirl of pleasure into which the enjoyments of love would shortly plunge her'. (Miss Trelawney, it is explained, perhaps unnecessarily at this stage, has 'abjured all notions of prudery'.) On page 284 her abigail ventures the observations that Venetia's bust is 'the grandest, the finest, the most superb that ever woman possessed'. On page 383 her bosom 'a moment before heaving and falling with rapid palpitations, became instantaneously stilled, as if the proudly swelling globes had suddenly changed into that alabaster which they resembled'.

In the vital battle of the bulge, Venetia has two powerful rivals – Editha, Countess of Curzon, and Lady Ernestina Dysart. Editha's bosoms, though 'by no means exuberant' are 'well detached, rising in perfect hemispheres and sustaining the beauty of their proportions by their own firmness', for she wears 'neither corset nor artificial means of compression'. A wretched

"like hemispheres of polished alabaster"

bill-broker, concealed expediently in a cabinet, is quite enraptured as he observes their 'quick heavings' beneath a dress that leaves them 'more than half exposed'. In the same way the Prince Regent is enchanted by the contemplation of Ernestina's 'grandly developed' bosom, glowing in the 'unveiled luxuriance of its charms' as she bends knowingly over her harp, in a dress selected to 'display her fine form to its most exciting and sensuous advantage'. It is not surprising that a few lines farther on the Prince is devouring Ernestina's bosom with 'burning kisses', while a 'lava stream of fierce and fiery passion', boils in his amorous royal veins.

An equally ardent young commoner, 'maddened with excitement', makes a practice of allowing his 'daring hands' to invade 'the treasures of those swelling, palpitating globes, so warm with their licentious fires'. In describing such transactions, George Lippard's prose is not dissimilar to Reynolds':

The left hand of Lorimer, gently stealing round her form rested with a faint pressure upon the folds of her night-robe, over her bosom, which now came tremulously into light . . . Closer and more close, the hand of Lorimer pressed against the heaving bosom . . . Brighter grew the glow on her cheek, closer pressed the hand on her bosom, warmer and higher arose that bosom in the light . . . She felt as though she was about to fall swooning on the floor . . . her bosom rose no longer quick and gaspingly, but in long pulsations, that urged the full Globes in all their virgin beauty, softly slowly into view . . . and her parted lips deepened into a rich vermilion tint. 'She is mine!'

VII

Like Dickens, Reynolds has no faith in governments, which he sees as a conspiracy of rich against poor. He looks forward to the day when the English mechanic and the English operative have educated themselves, in spite of the neglect of their legislators; when 'holy Christian worship will cease to be regarded as an apology for endowing a Church with enormous revenues' and political administration is no longer considered 'as a means of rendering a small portion of the community happy and prosperous to the utter prejudice of the vast remainder'.

He is frank in his criticism of the Royal Family. In 1848, when it was suggested that the Prince Consort should be appointed Commander-in-Chief of the British Army, Reynolds wrote:

Prince Albert may be very resolute and very determined in worrying a poor otter with his dogs, or he may be desperately brave in firing volleys of small shot upon harmless birds; but as for his capacity or his courage to lead an army – the idea is ridiculous.

Princes had the right to be princes 'if the people are foolish enough to let them'. But when they made themselves ridiculous, it was time to speak out. 'We are inspired by no awe and entertain no solemn terror in dealing with Royalty.'

The accession of Victoria 'proclaimed the grand fact that Monarchy is a farce, since a mere school-girl can be put up as the throned puppet of the Punch-and-Judy show of Royalty':

Men are becoming too wise to maintain a throne which may either be filled by a voluptuary, a fool or a doll . . . The throne is worm-eaten . . . It is old – rickety – and good for nothing; and the magisterial seat of a President, elected by the nation at large must displace it. Monarchy falling, will drag the ancient Aristocracy along with it.

Reynolds depicts the British aristocracy, almost without exception, as selfish, cynical, parasitical and corrupt, differing only in the degree of depravity. 'Though the Aristocracy, generally speaking, are licentious and immoral to a degree, there are certain families belonging to that sphere who are more than the rest notorious for hereditary profligacy,' he writes in the *Mysteries of the Courts of London*. Thackeray, lecturing on 'Comedy and Humour' in 1852, quoted a Brighton bookseller who attributed the great popularity of this series to Reynolds's attacks on the aristocracy, and in the same year a Lancashire prison chaplain, the Rev. J. Clay, told a Select Committee on Criminal and Destitute Children that 'the demoralizing effects of these *Mysteries of the Courts of London* must be beyond anything that can be conceived'. Reynolds's work, he said, was demoralizing 'not only as regards the excitement of bad passions, but by the mischief which he intends politically. All the profligates represented in these works are persons of rank, mentioned by name.' It is true that the royal and aristocratic rakes who gambol through Reynolds's pages, appear, if not under real names, such as the Prince Regent, under very thin disguises. The Marquis of Holmesford, for example, is easily identified with the third Marquis of Hertford who was also the model for Thackeray's Lord Steyne and Disraeli's Lord Monmouth. The real Marquis, who had been a whoring companion of the Prince Regent, was very, very wealthy and very, very wicked. He owned two palaces in London – Dorchester House in Park Lane and St Dunstan's, a Decimus Burton villa in Regent's Park, where he mounted sumptuous entertainments, and maintained a harem that sometimes cost him £30,000 or £40,000 a year. With an estate worth more than £2,000,000, he could afford to be fairly generous to his girls.

VIII

The 'Marquis of Holmesford' is introduced to readers of *Mysteries of the Courts of London* as 'a nobleman of sixty-three years of age, of immense wealth', notorious for his 'unbounded licentiousness'. 'Seductions were his boast, and he frequently indulged in obscene anecdotes or expressions which even called a blush to the cheeks of his least fastidious male acquaintances.' Among these is Mr Greenwood, 'the member for Rottenborough', a successful City man and social climber. He is deputy-chairman of the fraudulant 'Algiers, Oran, and Morocco Great Desert Railway Company', of which the Marquis is chairman. After a convivial and cynical business dinner the Marquis invites Greenwood to explore the 'voluptuous mysteries of Holmesford House – one of the most splendid palaces of the aristocracy at the West End'.

Over their delicious Johanisberg, the nobleman and his guest discourse 'upon the most voluptuous subjects'. The 'old voluptuary, with one foot in the grave', explains how he fans the dim flame of his passions by devising 'truly oriental' refinements and recreations. 'Wine and women, my dear Greenwood, are the only earthly enjoyments worth living for,' he says. 'I hope to die, with my head pillowed on the naked-heaving bosom of beauty, and with a glass of sparkling champagne in my hand.' He leads his guest into a vast and lofty apartment 'furnished with luxurious ottomans

"palpitating globes . . ."

in the oriental style'. The walls are covered with luxuriant paintings, 'as large as life and unrestrained by prudery'.

> There was Lucretia, struggling – vainly struggling with the ardent Tarquin – her drapery torn by his rude hands away from her lovely form, which the brutal violence of his mad passion had rendered weak, supple and yielding. There was Helen, reclining in more than semi-nudity on the couch to which her languishing and wanton looks invited the enamoured Phrygian youth . . . There was Messalina – that imperial harlot, whose passions were so insatiable and whose crimes were so enormous – issuing from a bath to join her lover . . . There were pictures representing the various amours of Jupiter – Leda, Latona, Semele and Europa . . . all drawn in the most exciting attitudes and endowed with the most luscious beauties.

But Mr Greenwood is more interested in six 'living, breathing moving beauties', who, upon a stage at the end of the brilliantly lit apartment, engage in a rapid and exciting dance. They are dressed in a drapery 'so light and gauzy that it was all but transparent, and so scanty that it afforded no scope for the sweet romancing of fancy, and left but little need for guesses'. While they throw themselves into 'the most voluptuous attitudes', the Marquis describes them in detail. There is a nineteen-year-old fair Scotch beauty with an 'ample bust' who has been in the harem for three years; a brown-haired, somewhat stout, Lancashire girl who had been the mistress of a bishop before she removed to Holmesford House; Kathleen, an Irish girl with 'vigorous, strong, and yet elegantly formed limbs', whose drapery spreads out from her waist 'like a circular fan'; a little French girl, 'an exquisite creature – and such a wanton'; an olive-skinned Spanish beauty, 'all fire – all passion'; and Malkhatoun, 'a real Georgian,' with 'stout and plump' limbs, specially imported from Constantinople.

Mr Greenwood's mind is filled with 'an ecstatic delirium'. He escorts the plump Georgian to the supper-room, where, despite her devotion to the Koran, she joins the other girls in frequent potations of champagne. At two in the morning, Greenwood intimates his wish to retire.

Another Reynolds rake, the Marquis of Leveson, also has elaborate London headquarters for his amorous sports. Leveson House, like Holmesford House, is equipped with a number of baths – for baths in this rather hydropathic era have all the old pagan association with debauchery – and, like Holmesford House, is decorated with 'pictures and statues of such a character as to excite maddening desires even in the breast of the sternest anchorite or the coldest virgin'. One of these pictures is 'to a certain degree a copy of Rubens's splendid masterpiece, the Rape of the Sabines . . . but the copyist had so enhanced the indelicacy of the scene . . . that it burst upon the gaze like the sudden exposure of an orgie in a brothel'. As an additional help to ageing and ineffectual lechers it contains an ingenious armchair which, when a young lady sits in it, grips her wrists and shoulders in velvet-covered manacles and bands of steel, making her a helpless victim of the Marquis's will.

When the Marquis finds Miss Ariadne Varian caught in the chair, in a state of semi-nudity, 'having nothing on but the night-gear which left her neck and bosom all exposed':

> 'Beautiful girl!' exclaimed the Marquis, catching sight of her naked charms and instantaneously inflamed by the view. 'Resistance is vain! . . .'

IX

Scarcely less villainous to Reynolds than the aristocracy are the clergy. Usually his abuse is aimed at the Establishment. When he writes of the Almonry in Westminster, a squalid district of 'brothels and flash-houses', he points out that it is part of the domain endowed to Westminster Abbey:

But inasmuch as loathsome hot-beds of vice and moral lazar-houses usually produce a good rent, the Dean and Chapter could not of course think of purging a neighbourhood which yields them such large revenues.

Of another foul slum he writes:

OH! what have the myriad fat and bloated pastors done for the population that swarms in those frightful neighbourhoods? . . . If a missionary of Religion be ever encountered in such places, be well assured that he belongs not to the Established Church, but to the sphere of Dissent . . .

But even dissenters are not immune. One of his dissenting parsons begets three bastards by different servant girls and gets so drunk that he has to be carted home in a wheelbarrow. The fashionable Anglican rector of St David's, however, comes to a worse end. He is a libertine who, rising from a couch where 'visions of a most voluptuous nature had filled his sleep', abuses his host's hospitality by watching an unsuspecting girl prepare for the bath.

While 'the fires of gross sensuality raged madly in his breast' he applies his 'greedy eyes' to the keyhole. Ellen loosens the strings of her dressing-gown, and turns towards the door, revealing 'all the treasures of her bosom' to his 'licentious glance'. It is a typical Reynolds bosom, 'swelling, warm and glowing':

His desires were now inflamed to that pitch when they almost become ungovernable . . . and now the drapery had fallen from her shoulders, and the whole of her voluptuous form, naked to the waist, was exposed to his view.

The rector 'literally trembled under the influence of his fierce desires'. The door is locked and he gnashes his teeth with rage. His tremblings become more intense as he waits 'with fervent avidity for the moment when the whole of the drapery should fall from her form', but fortunately a step resounds on the stair and the 'guilty wretch' flees, full of voluptuous imaginings. Not long after, on trial for murder, he poisons himself in prison.

X

Pornography was almost a major industry in England during the middle and later decades of the nineteenth century. Cheap printing, photography, and the spread of literacy, all contributed to the boom in *erotica*, or *curiosa*, as the booksellers fastidiously described their back-room wares. When William Dugdale's premises in Holywell street were raided in 1851, police

grabbed 822 books, 3,870 prints, and 16 hundredweight of unsev
press, all 'of a most abominable description'. In 1856, when he w
for the ninth time, 3,000 books were seized. When the headquart
English photographer, Henry Hayler, whose pornographic studies
enjoyed a European reputation, were raided in 1874, police hauled away,
allegedly to destroy, 130,348 obscene photographs and 5,000 obscene
lantern-slides. In 1895 police raided H. S. Nichols's shop in Charing Cross
Road, and seized about two tons of 'obscene' literature. Throughout the
century, the holy war against pornography went on, with the watchful
Society for the Suppression of Vice constantly on the offensive.

The Society was not a Victorian invention. It had been founded in 1802
as a militant arm of the Evangelical Movement. (The Rev. Sydney Smith
called it, perceptively, 'The Society for Suppressing the Vices of Persons
whose Income does not exceed £500 per annum'.) The original committee
included the Rev. Thomas Bowdler, whose emasculation of Shakespeare
gave us the infamous verb 'to bowdlerize', Zachary Macaulay, father of the
historian, and Mr Hatchard, the Piccadilly bookseller, and the original
targets were profaners of the Lord's Day, proprietors of bawdy houses,
and promoters of illegal dances, as well as publishers of blasphemous and
obscene works. But by mid-century the Society was giving most of its
attention to pornography in its multiform guises, from the hidden 'hard-
core' *curiosa* of Holywell street to the more or less titillating publications on
open sale. Its watchdogs, themselves miraculously immune from contagion
were kept pretty busy protecting the less-favoured citizenry.

The pornographers, big and little, fought back vigorously. One of their
favourite devices, and one that still has validity, was to describe the lush
allurements of vice with the voice of outraged virtue. Thus when in 1856
Robert Martin, a Fleet Street publisher, started his penny weekly, *Paul Pry,*
'the inquisitive, quizzical, Satirical and Whimsical Epitome of Life as It
Is', he announced that its mission was 'to strip society of its baseness and
hollow cant':

> The present age is an age of shams and impositions. The game of the
> world is to keep up appearances . . . Men judge their fellows by the cut
> of the coat or the style of the hat . . . The adventurer casts his bread on
> the water, and after many efforts, he eats it in a palace or a dungeon.

'Ever watchful of the public weal', *Paul Pry* promised to review impar-
tially 'the delinquencies and shortcomings of the age' and to give 'a considerable share of its attention' to the 'Gay Women of London':

> their history, habits and haunts . . . the mode of life, income, supporters
> and connexions of the Children of Night . . . together with sketches of
> brothels and brothel-keepers, pimps, fancy men, bullies and decoys,

interspersed with recondite anecdotes of love, seduction and prostitution.

One of the early practitioners of this technique was the picturesque, bawdy, and popular scoundrel, Renton Nicholson, who in the 1840s edited at the same time a scurrilous scandal-sheet, *The Town* ('The Doings of Courtesans and Demireps of Quality'), and *The Crown*, a highly respectable high-church paper. In *The Crown* he piously denounced *The Town*, and in *The Town*, indignantly replied to his own denunciations. The advertising pages of *The Town* are instructive. They show the type of book that was on open sale in London in the first decade of Victoria's reign, as distinct from the more gamy under-the-counter stuff:

TALES OF TWILIGHT; or 'Entre Chien et Loup'; containing the adventures and intrigues of a company of ladies prior to their marriage, as related by themselves; showing the deceits practised upon men, by the artful, the prudent, the modest, and demure maidens on parting with that treasure, which never can be restored. By Madame la Comtesse de Choiseul-meuse, authoress of 'Julia, or I've saved my Rose,' 'Amelia, St. Far or the Fatal Error.' 'Eugenia, or where is the woman that wouldn't?' etc. etc., Translated from the French, and illustrated with eight fine engravings coloured.

JULIA: or I HAVE SAVED MY ROSE: Being the Amorous History of a Young Lady of ardent imagination; who, amidst the voluptuous temptations to gratify the sensual passions, succeeds in preserving her Maidenhead from destruction, By Madame H——, and authoress of 'Amelia St. Far, or the Fatal Error,' 'Tales of Twilight,' etc., etc., A new Edition, containing eight fine Plates. Price 10s. 6d.

ONANISM UNVEILED, or the Private Pleasures and Practices of the Youth of both Sexes, in all their branches, showing its insidious progress and prevalence among schools, particularly female, pointing out the fatality that invariably attends its victims; developing the symptoms, the cause of the disease, the means of cure, as regards simple gonorrhoea, etc., Translated from the last edition in French of the celebrated M. Tissot and illustrated with a fine engraving presenting the awful consequences of this revolting habit. 3s. 6d.

SAINFROID AND EULALIA; or the intrigues and amours of Sainfroid, a Jesuit, and Eulalia, a Nun, developing the gradual and imperceptible progress of Seduction of a highly educated Young Lady, who became, by the foulest sophistry and treachery, the victim of debauchery and libertinism. Translated from the French and illustrated with beautiful plates. Price 5s. 6d.

NYMPHOMANIA, or a DISSERTATION CONCERNING the
Furor Uterinus in Young and Sensitive Females, showing its dreadful
effects upon the constitution, and clearly and methodically explaining
the beginning, progress, and cause of that horrible distemper; containing also a description of the organical parts of women; a general
description of the Nymphomania, or Furor Uterinus; the cause of the
lustful, or amative Nymphomania; the degrees and symptoms of this
horrible disease on the minds of women; the history of Lucilla, a victim
to the furor uterinus, with her shameless practices; the mode of cure is
in the first and second stages of the furor uterinus, with the relief to be
expected in the third stage. To which are added, observations on the
imagination, as connected with the Nymphomania, exemplified in the
history of Julia, with an appendix, containing the most approved
remedies and recipes for this horrible disorder. Price 2s. 6d, fine plates.

The printer and publisher of these works, Henry Smith, of 37 Holywell
Street, also advertised 'Memoirs of the celebrated F. Hill. From the
original edition. Fine Plates. 3s. 6d,' and five books describing methods of
birth-control, which he commended as 'particularly interesting at the
present moment when the increasing population of the country is pressing
so heavily upon the sympathies and properties of the rich and influential
classes of England'.

Mr Smith and Mr Nicholson seem to have escaped the vigilance of the
Society for the Suppression of Vice. Mr Robert Martin was not so fortunate. He had been conducting his missionary labours for about four months,
zealously and profitably 'showing vice its own features', when the Society
prosecuted him for publishing a whimsical account of the seduction of a
servant girl, Susan, by the Right Honourable Filthy Lucre. After some
romantic preliminaries, during which Lucre asks Susan, in the current
idiom, if she will be 'good-natured' and takes her on his knee:

Susan's hand . . . held within its grasp an implement, which seemed, by
the kind way in which she used it, to have some particular interest in her
eyes. It soon possessed some PECULIAR INTEREST in her – SOME-
THING ELSE; she found its *use*, and thought, no doubt, as she lay
panting and gasping in his arms, that she never knew such an *agreeable
instrument*; or one which did such efficient work. THE DEED WAS
DONE. SUSAN entered that room a maid, and went out – ah! – 'a
virgin now no more.'

She didn't go, however, without receiving more than one specimen of this
'implement's' working capabilities. Its power was tested 'six blessed times'
on her 'little thatched cottage,' which was, each time, entered by storm, and
rifled. She did not, however, seem to object to the burglary; on the contrary,
she hailed the attacks of the 'bold robber' as a most desirable event.

And now I tell Lucre he may expect a visit in about 10 months time from a gentleman wearing a cocked hat with a little bill for 2s. 6d. a week.

Mr Martin and a bookseller, Mr William Strange, were both imprisoned in Coldbath Fields, an uncomfortable eighteenth-century Middlesex prison well equipped with oakum-picking rooms and treadmills. The Lord Chief Justice, Lord Campbell, said he was horrified by the story of Susan's seduction, and particularly by the fact that it was sold for a penny, thus, though he did not say this explicitly, making pornography available to the porter as well as the peer.

When, as a result of Susan's seduction, he introduced legislation in the House of Lords to suppress these 'licentious, obscene and disgusting penny weeklies', Mr Martin's successor on *Paul Pry* commented irreverently:

> On the Imprisonment of Mr Robert Martin
>
> *Had Fielding lived in these enlightened days,*
> *In Coldbath Fields he'd get his meed of praise.*
> *And Smollett, too, beside him would pick oakum,*
> *His moral works with glaring vice 'ud choke 'um.*
> *Dryden, and Pope, and Churchill, then might rot,*
> *And 'spuds' and 'skilly' be their constant lot;*
> *As now you see, by Campbell's law, 'tis treason*
> *To paint the manners of this saintly season;*
> *Nor satire now, nor wit, may free take wing,*
> *But slander's found in every truthful sting.*
> *The 'Cannie Scot' on oatmeal fain 'ud feed us,*
> *And by his Puritanic dictum lead us;*
> *But while the mind can bolts and bars defy,*
> *Nature will triumph o'er an ermin'd guy.*

It is possible that *Paul Pry* was subsequently suppressed, because in 1863 a very similar paper, an obvious reincarnation, appeared under the title of *Peter Spy*; changing the title of a publication was a common device to evade prosecution. *Peter Spy* proclaimed itself the 'inquisitive, quizzical, satirical and whimsical Censor of the Age' and in its first editorial, promised to 'drag Roguery from its secure retreat', to 'use the pruning-knife unmercifully' and to give particular attention to 'the bordel and bawd, dress-lodger and fancy-bleaks', and 'those sinks of abomination, the night-houses'. Supplementing this important social work, it promised articles on 'Prostitution in London, Edinburgh, Paris, Etc.,' as well as 'The Secret Memoirs of Mrs W. F. Windham' – the former *poule-de-luxe*, Agnes Willoughby.

What were the sales of these tongue-in-cheek weeklies? No figures are available for either *Paul Pry* or *Peter Spy*, each of which is represented by only one copy in the British Museum. Early in the 'seventies, however, Frederick Shove produced a threepenny weekly, *The Days' Doings*, which within two years attained a verified circulation of nearly 25,000. *The Days' Doings* was a much more elaborate production, illustrated with lively woodcuts of current events, and reproductions of gallery nudes, Mr Shove having pioneered the device of peddling pictures of fat naked women in the sacred name of art.

When *The Days' Doings*, soon after its birth, was banned from the railway bookstalls which Messrs W. H. Smith and Sons controlled, Mr Shove wrote reproachfully:

As a portion of the public, we think Messrs. Smith's prohibition is an interference with the liberty of choice: because their position as holding the bookstalls on the public roads (for such railway lines must now be considered) obliges them, in our opinion, not to consult their own individual tastes, but to supply the public with what the public wants.

Eighteen months later, when *The Days' Doings* began publication of a translation of Henri Murger's *Scènes de la Vie de Bohême*, the Society for the Suppression of Vice laid an information against Mr Shove, who was charged upon an indictment containing twenty-one counts 'with publishing an obscene, lewd, licentious and lustful libel'. The first set of counts referred to the illustrations, the second set to the translation from the French.

For the prosecution Mr Besley said that many of the woodcuts were copies of well-known paintings in public galleries and it seemed to be thought that under the veil of a love of art such pictures could be multiplied. But as Mr Justice Lush had stated in *Reg. v. Hicklin*, this was not so. It did not follow that because such a picture could be seen in a public gallery, that photographs of it could be sold with impunity in the public streets. Mr Besley then read extracts from the printed matter (*i.e. Scènes de la Vie de Bohême*) 'of undoubted obscenity' and pointed out – once more applying the economic measuring-rod, that *The Days' Doings* was far more dangerous and more calculated to deprave and corrupt the minds of the people than the most filthy photographs which were sold at high prices and with the utmost secrecy. It required only a knowledge of history, he declared, to be convinced that the sure preliminary to the downfall of a nation was the general indulgence of lust and sensuality on the part of the people.

For the defendant Mr H. T. Cole justified the pictures as less immoral than the scantily clad limbs of dancers at theatres; but Sir S. H. Bodkin, Assistant-Judge, no doubt impressed by the fearful warning that the fate of England hung in the balance, fined Mr Shove £50 on one count, and on the others bound him over in his own recognizance in £100, and two sureties in £80 each, not to exceed the bounds of common decency in the future. Should he do so, he would be dealt with most severely. The idea of boys in the public streets selling these papers was a scandal to the age, said his Honour.

Mr Shove replied vigorously. In the next issue of *The Days' Doings*, he published 'The Editor's Protest'.

As the Editor of *The Days' Doings* since its commencement, I consider I owe a duty to those artistic and literary gentlemen with whom I have the honour to be associated, to protest against the late prosecution of that paper.

I can say positively that the improper intentions attributed to us are most unjust and untrue; the character of the gentlemen who assist me with the artistic and literary matter is quite sufficient answer to this.

When the paper started, its aim was novelty – novelty in illustrating romantic, sporting, and theatrical events; there seemed to be an opening for such a venture between the jog-trot pace of the higher class illustrated papers, and the weakness of the cheaper publications of the same class.

We found this opening did exist, and in spite of an overwhelming amount of prejudice and ignorant abuse, the paper made its way – not among schoolboys and children, but among the educated middle-class; this I know from the class of persons who form the large body of quarterly and yearly subscribers we have on our books, whose subscriptions are, with very few exceptions, always renewed.

The pictures selected for illustration are always duly considered – novelty, fun, romance, etc., being chiefly aimed at. It was also our wish to engrave such Fine Art subjects as had not been produced in newspaper form before, and to procure photographs and other legal works to copy from.

Speaking from my own opinion of artistic matters, I utterly fail to see any illustration in our paper one whit an exaggeration upon what one actually sees in real life. In fact, after reading the morning papers, or looking into a photographic shop window, I have been astonished how tame our illustrations were.

The protest appeared in the last issue of *The Days' Doings*, dated 17 February 1872. The following week it was metamorphosed into *Here and There*, which 'the editors' introduced in a haughty manifesto:

. . . they leave the improved paper to speak for itself, and are confident that they will largely increase their list of subscribers amongst the sensible class of persons who are not frightened at the sight of a lady's leg.

V

Salvation Below Stairs

I

Mr Reynolds had a rival in fecundity, if not in popularity: Mrs Clara Balfour. The British Museum catalogues more than seventy works from her unflagging pen. But whereas Reynolds's aim was to castigate the high and titillate the low, hers was to reconcile the low to their uncomfortable lot as servants of the high. This she did in a spate of messianic novels, in which workers are counselled, under threat of divine displeasure and horrible punishment, not to question their station in life, but to adorn it with hard work, church-going, cheerfulness, humility and gratitude.

The often-proclaimed belief that the rigid stratification of society, from peer to pauper, had been ordained by the Almighty, was very comforting to the peer, and was supposed to offer similar comfort to the pauper. Mrs Alexander gave poetic expression to it in her *Hymns for Children*, published in 1848, which went through sixty-two editions before the end of the century:

> *The rich man in his castle,*
> *The poor man at his gate,*
> *God made them high or lowly*
> *And ordered their estate.*

Speaking at a Harvest Festival in 1871, the vicar of a Kentish rural parish expressed the same thought in prose, when he said: 'God has appointed from the very first, that there should be different grades of human society, high and low, rich and poor, and it is not for the rich to boast or the poor to complain.' And he warned his applauding audience of the horrors that had beset France since its people had tried to upset God's order of things by Revolution.

One of Mrs Balfour's publishers, Mr S. W. Partridge of Paternoster Row, was fired by a messianic purpose similar to hers. He specialized in cautionary and inspirational tales with titles such as 'The Rod and Its Uses', 'Brands Plucked from the Burning', 'No Gains Without Pains', and 'How Paul's Penny Became a Pound'. He also published a magazine remarkable even in an age of specialized journalism, titled *The Servants' Magazine, or The Friend of the Household Workers*. This was a continuation of a magazine that had begun in 1838, under the title of *The Servants' Magazine and Female Domestic Instructor*, and under the auspices of the London Female Mission. A preface to the first issue had defined its purpose:

95

Times are changed since the great bulk of female servants were unable to read . . . Servants are now fond of reading, and this is well; but it is of vast importance that what they read should be adapted to promote their real welfare, to render them useful in their station, more contented with the arrangements of a kind Providence which has placed them in it, and more alive to those hallowed principles which alone can prepare them for the engagement and happiness of heaven.

Mr Partridge amplified this text in a rather sombre foreword to the first issue of *The Servants' Magazine*, which appeared on New Year's Day, 1866:

This Magazine is the successor the one hitherto known as *The Servants' Magazine and Female Domestic Instructor*. Changes have been made, with a view of affording useful, profitable and entertaining reading for all classes of servants, both *male* and *female*, and the occupants of cottage homes in town and country. Most villagers' children are obliged to leave school at an early age – the boys going to work, and the girls to service – or perhaps to help their mothers, where there is a large family of young children. It is not, then, surprising that the generality of servants have so limited an amount of education; but, in *these* days, it is their own fault if they do not grow wiser as they grow older.

After the day's work is done, most have one leisure hour, and many servants have more. This time is often given to smoking, drinking, idle talk, or novel reading, all of which are more or less injurious; and the time wasted might be wisely appropriated to improvement in writing, and in reading what is worth remembering . . .

We wish all the readers of the *Servants' Magazine* a very happy New Year. We also ask them seriously to consider whether they are nearer *Heaven* this New Year's day than they were at the last. All are nearer Eternity; but, unfortunately, all are not in the narrow way that leads to everlasting life . . . God alone knows how many of the readers of these lines will see January 1st, 1867. Flee then, O reader, if you have not already fled, to *your* Saviour, the Rock of *your* salvation, for He died for *all*.

According to a sermon preached to female servants by the Rev. W. B. Mackenzie, of Holloway, and quoted approvingly by Mr Partridge, there were then more than a hundred thousand female servants in London alone, 'more than one for every house', and another fifteen thousand always in search of a job. 'It is one of the greatest earthly mercies which God gives to Christian families, to have servants who sincerely fear and love Him,' said Mr Mackenzie. But he was concerned with the fate of these fifteen thousand who were 'continually out of place'.

Many are insidiously entrapped into vicious sins, which are sure to spread their infection into the kitchens or into the guileless nursery of their next situation; others, from scanty and exhausted means, try first

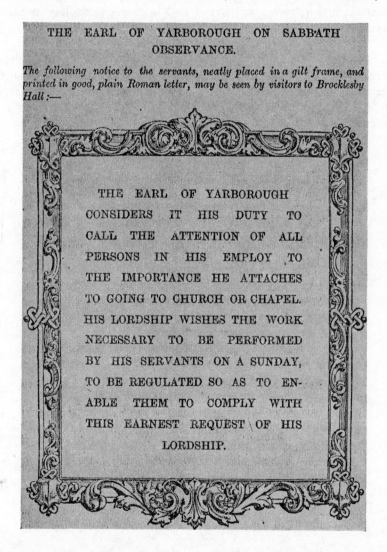

THE EARL OF YARBOROUGH ON SABBATH OBSERVANCE.

The following notice to the servants, neatly placed in a gilt frame, and printed in good, plain Roman letter, may be seen by visitors to Brocklesby Hall:—

THE EARL OF YARBOROUGH CONSIDERS IT HIS DUTY TO CALL THE ATTENTION OF ALL PERSONS IN HIS EMPLOY TO THE IMPORTANCE HE ATTACHES TO GOING TO CHURCH OR CHAPEL. HIS LORDSHIP WISHES THE WORK NECESSARY TO BE PERFORMED BY HIS SERVANTS ON A SUNDAY, TO BE REGULATED SO AS TO EN-ABLE THEM TO COMPLY WITH THIS EARNEST REQUEST OF HIS LORDSHIP.

to support themselves by the wretched system of pledging their few articles of clothing, and are soon forced to hide their shame and desti-tution in some squalid and obscure dwelling; while numbers of once happy domestic servants fall victims to the most fearful wickedness, inveigled, deceived, stupefied, ruined, then flung, as objects too low for pity, as worthless weeds, left to rot as the very refuse of society. Out of 159 cases of female degradation of the most profligate kind, which were investigated for a society, in last year, 114 were found to have been formerly *domestic servants*; 96 had once been scholars in Sunday Schools.

Besides reports of uplifting sermons, *The Servants' Magazine* published poetry, short stories, and useful hints. All are severely didactic. What the poetry lacks in lyricism is made up for by the importance of its message – that, in serving your earthly master well, you are greatly pleasing your Heavenly Master:

THE CHRISTIAN LAD

If I find a kind master, I do not much care
What calling I find, if here, or if there;
Whether in-doors, or out-doors, in country or town,
If my master but smile, at no work will I frown.

I'll try to be dutiful, faithful, and true,
Whether making a coat or repairing a shoe;
If wheeling a barrow, I'll wheel it along,
As merrily O! as if humming a song.

I'll whistle away as I curry my nag,
Nor complain, if sometimes at late work I may fag,
Though but for my lantern it all should be dark;
Nor grumble if called to be up with the lark.

If sent on an errand I'd go like a hare,
And be back ere my master had thought I was there;
Be ready and waiting for something to do,
Help the gardener to weed, or the farmer to sow.

I'll carry my load with an air and a grace,
With a spring in my foot and a smile on my face;
If sawing a plank, I will saw it with glee;
Let drones play or idle, I'll work like a bee.

My master shall see that I look for reward,
Not only from him but from Jesus, my Lord;
And when here, on earth, all my service is done,
May Jesus, my Master, welcome me home.

THE SERVANT-MAID

Though servitude's my destined lot,
And I am doomed to roam
Far from my native peaceful cot,
Far from my friends and home.

Yet ever be His bounty blest,
Whose hand bestows my food;
I know what He appoints is best,
And must be for my good.

If God saw fit to make me great
He would not this deny;
And while I'm in a meaner state,
He will my wants supply

Ordain'd this humble state to fill,
Though destitute of wealth,
I can't be poor while I have still
Contentment, peace and health.

Let virtue be my early choice,
Let Jesus be my guide.
I'll hearken to religion's voice,
And give up all beside.

Then let each murmuring whisper cease,
Each earth-born care subside,
I'll rest upon the word of grace,
For God will still provide.

THE SONG OF THE TIRED SERVANT

One more day's work for Jesus
One less of life for me;
But Heaven is nearer
And Christ is clearer
Than yesterday, to me.

One more day's work for Jesus,
Yes, a weary day;
But Heaven shines clearer
And rest comes nearer,
At each step of the way.

CONTENTED JOHN

One honest John Tomkins, a hedger and ditcher,
Although he was poor, did not want to be richer;
For all such vain wishes to him were prevented
By a fortunate habit of being contented.

Though cold were the weather, or dear were the food,
John never was found in a murmuring mood;
For this he was constantly heard to declare,
What he could not prevent he would cheerfully bear;

'For why should I grumble and murmur?' he said;
'If I cannot get meat, I'll be thankful for bread;
And though fretting may make my calamities deeper,
It never can cause bread and cheese to be cheaper.'

If John was afflicted with sickness and pain,
He wished himself better, but did not complain,
Nor lie down to fret in despondence and sorrow,
But said that he hoped to be better tomorrow.

If any one wronged him, or treated him ill,
Why, John was good-natured and sensible still;
For he said that revenging the injury done
Would be making two rogues where there need be but one.

And this honest John, though his situation was humble,
Passed through this sad world without even a grumble;
And 'twere well if some folk, who are greater and richer,
Would copy John Tomkins, the hedger and ditcher.

Mr Partridge offers his readers some 'friendly Hints on Dress':

A gown should never be made in that fashion which is suitable only for the mistress, perhaps made after the same pattern, which is a liberty some servants are too apt to take – a profusion of ribbons on the cap and flowers in the bonnet, are out of character; long drop earrings are likewise very unseemly – they have a disreputable appearance. It is almost surprising that rings are not put upon the fingers; so little distinction seems to be made in the dress of maids and their mistresses; and they are, many of them, so tenacious of being interfered with, or spoken to on the subject, that they have been made to leave a good place on this account. This is a great weakness, as well as great ignorance; and it is to be regretted that many articles of clothing are so cheap as to hold out a temptation to dress in appearance beyond what is becoming. Flowers, likewise are so cheap and plentiful, that for the small cost of *fourpence* or *sixpence*, the face may be almost imbedded in roses and heart's ease.

It is a painful sight, and this folly in finery needs an amendment; indeed, it reflects no credit on a mistress who allows these things. Let a servant's dress be neat and respectable, suitable to her station and the wages she receives; but to be very dirty in her working-dress and very fine and gaudy on the Sunday, or when she has a holiday, is altogether unbecoming, neither ought it to be tolerated. The love of dress is often ruinous in its consequences. No prudent working man would think of marrying a young woman who spends all her money in dress. His weekly earnings would fall very short of supplying fine clothes for a wife; it requires the greatest management and prudence to supply necessary food and fuel for a family; and if extravagant habits are fostered in service, they run through the character and conduct in afterlife, to the no small discomfort of many a hard-working honest man.

There are useful hints, too, in the correspondence columns. 'I take the liberty to send you a hint . . . if you think it worth inserting,' writes 'A':

There is a box on my sister's kitchen plate-shelf called a Forfeit-box: it was placed there by the Cook, and each of the servants has agreed to put a halfpenny in the box, if not up at the proper time. The mistress has kindly joined the party! The box is now very heavy, and what is to be done with the money? It is to assist in sending to the poor heathen the knowledge of Him who has stirred up the heart of a benevolent servant to remember those who are in bonds, as bound with them. Reader, go and do likewise.

The Servants' Magazine also printed a notice designed to hang in a cook's quarters:

> NEVER CHANGE YOUR PLACE
> UNLESS THE LORD CLEARLY SHOWS
> YOU IT WILL BE
> FOR YOUR SOUL'S GOOD.

II

How successful were the salvational labours of Mrs Balfour, Mr Partridge and their colleagues? The evidence suggests that they often laboured in vain. The author of *My Secret Life* discovered early in his secret life 'that

George Cruikshank

"It's my Cousin Mum!"

servants were fair game'. They were 'proud of having a gentleman to cover them', and if the gentleman were the son of the house, they would not risk their position and their 'character' by informing on him. 'I have now had many servants in my time,' he wrote, 'and know no better companions in amorous amusements.' He claimed a total tally of 'something like twelve hundred women . . . of eighty or more different nationalities, including every one in Europe except a Laplander'. Of servants he wrote appreciatively:

> They have rarely lost all modesty, a new lover is a treat and a fresh experience to them . . . No one will . . . give more of herself than a lass who says 'I couldn't get out before – I'm sorry you had to wait – I must really be back by ten.'

Servants were the largest single group in Victorian England, and the 'young master' often learned more of the facts of life from the kitchen-maid than from the governess.

'Female servants are far from being a virtuous class,' wrote Henry Mayhew, in his *London Labour and the London Poor*, published in 1861. 'In small families', he explained, 'the servants often give themselves up to the sons or to the police on the beat or to soldiers in the park; or else to shop-men whom they meet in the streets.' Maidservants were then 'more commonly known as Dollymops'. Mayhew deplored their 'suicidal decking in flowers' – suicidal, because 'flattered by the attention of the eldest son or some friend of his staying in the house, the pretty lady's maid will often yield to soft solicitation'.

During the Christmas holidays of 1871–2, three Wellington schoolboys, living in Surbiton, seduced – or were seduced by – a fourteen year-old serving-maid. When they came back to school, the eldest had a venereal disease; all three were expelled by the headmaster, Edward White Benson. The boys' parents protested and, despite Benson's opposition, the two younger boys were reinstated by order of the Governors. The Rev. C. W. Penny, an assistant master who had been tutor to one of the boys, commented that the Governors – who included the second Duke of Wellington, the Duke of Richmond, Earl Stanhope, and Lord Eversley – 'had acted like a pack of cynical, hoary, old sinners, who looked upon youthful immorality . . . as a sort of childish complaint, like measles'. Indeed, as Mr David Newsome says in his *History of Wellington College*, the most interesting feature of this incident was the attitude of these 'intensely aristocratic Wellington Governors'. Their indifference to the behaviour of the boys was, he says rightly, 'a nice indication that the oppressive moral code of the Victorian middle-class had not penetrated the ranks of the aristocracy' – especially when the girl in the case was only a serving-maid.

III

Female servants were not subject to tax, but, under *Act 32.33 Vict. C.14,* 'Persons Keeping Male Servants, Carriages, Horses or Mules, or wearing or using Armorial Bearings, or exercising the Trade of a Horse Dealer' were subject to these annual duties:

	£	s.	d
For every Male Servant		15.	0
For every Carriage with 4 or more wheels or weighing 4 cwt or upwards	2.	2.	0
For every carriage with less than four wheels or having four or more still weighing less than 4 cwt		15.	0
Horse or Mule		10.	6
For Armorial Bearings – If painted on, or affixed to a carriage	2.	2.	0
If otherwise worn or used	1.	1.	0
Every Horse Dealer	12.	10.	0

A notice setting out these duties was 'to be affixed to Church Doors' throughout the kingdom.

VI

Boys Will Be Girls

I

When Oscar Wilde was sent to gaol in 1895 for homosexual practices, there was a tendency to link his downfall with the *fin-de-siècle* cult of Decadence, absinthe and Sin with a capital S. 'Beauty had existed long before 1880,' said Max Beerbohm; 'it was Mr Oscar Wilde who managed her *début*.' In the same mood it might be said that homosexuality had existed long before 1895; it was Mr Oscar Wilde who managed its *débâcle*.

Boulton and Park are not very important names in the roll-call of eminent Victorian homosexuals – a roll-call that includes John Addington Symonds, Edmund Gosse, Walter Pater, Edward Fitzgerald, John Gray, Edward Lear, Lionel Johnson, Simeon Solomon and William Johnson – who changed his name to Cory when he had to leave Eton because he loved his pupils too well. But the case of Boulton and Park is still of considerable interest, not because it shows that homosexuality was fashionable in the London of the early 'seventies but because it shows with what extraordinary tolerance it was viewed. It was not, of course, till 1885 that the notorious 'blackmailers' clause', under which Wilde was sentenced to two years' hard labour, was smuggled into the Criminal Law Amendment Act. This clause, which made homosexual acts between consenting males in private a crime, was not repealed till 1967.

II

Two fashionably dressed defendants stepped nonchalantly into the dock at Bow Street Police Court on Friday, 29 April 1870. One wore a cherry-coloured silk evening dress trimmed with white lace, bracelets on bare arms, a wig and plaited chignon. The other, whose hair was flaxen and in curls, wore a dark green satin dress, low-necked and trimmed with black lace, a shawl of the same material round the shoulders, and white kid gloves. The former was Ernest Boulton, the twenty-two-year-old son of a stockbroker, and the latter, Frederick William Park, a twenty-three-year-old law student, son of a Master in the Superior Courts, recently arrived from Edinburgh. Both were living at 13 Bruton Street, Berkeley Square. With them in the dock, but more conventionally attired, was Hugh Alexander Mundell, twenty-three, of 158 Buckingham Palace Road, the son of a barrister. All were charged before Mr Flowers with frequenting the Strand Theatre with intent to commit a felony. According to *The Times'* report:

William Chamberlain, detective of the E. Division, stated that he saw the prisoners Boulton and Park on Thursday evening come out of 13 Wakefield-street, Regent-square. It was about 8 o'clock, and they were accompanied by a gentleman. They had on satin and silk dresses and

248   THE DAYS' DOINGS.   [MAY 13, 1871.

The original caption reads: 'THE BOULTON AND PARK TRIAL – THE COM-
MENCEMENT OF THE STORY. THE SALOON OF THE SURREY THEATRE. "They
were dressed as men. I took them to be women from their manner and appearance. I
entered into conversation with them, and I asked them if they would like to go behind
the scenes."'

wore chignons. Their arms and necks were bare. A cab was called, into which the three got, and they were driven to the Strand Theatre. Witness called another cab and followed them. When they arrived at the lobby of the theatre they were met by Mundell and another person. Witness entered the Theatre and saw them go into a private box. He waited in the refreshment bar. During the evening Boulton and Park entered that compartment by themselves and ordered some brandy, which they drank. One of them entered the ladies' cloak-room and desired an attendant to pin up some lace that had fallen from his skirts. When this was done he remunerated her and went with his com-panion back to the box. Witness communicated with Superintendent

Thomson and Sergeant Kerley, and they apprehended the prisoners on leaving the theatre. The fourth person who was with them made his escape.

Superintendent Thomas added that he had watched the prisoners in their private box at the theatre, where they were repeatedly smiling and nodding to gentlemen in the stalls.

When evidence of arrest had been given, the prisoners were remanded. Mundell was released on bail, but Boulton and Park were taken away in a prison van, still wearing their elegant *ensembles*, to the raucous satisfaction of the great crowd that had assembled outside the court. Next day, reported *The Times*, which had quickly got its sensation-hungry teeth into the story, the court and its approaches were literally besieged by the public:

The case excited unusual interest probably owing to the notoriety acquired by certain young men who, for years past, have been in the habit of visiting places of public resort in feminine attire, and who have been occasionally turned out or compelled to retire to avoid the consequences of the public indignation excited by their presence when detected.

The crowd outside the court was immense, completely blockading the thoroughfares occasionally. There appears to have been an impression abroad that the prisoners would be again placed at the bar, according to the usual custom, in the costume in which they were arrested. Much chagrin was experienced when the two young men stepped into the van like any ordinary delinquents, and the yelling with which they were saluted may have been partly intensified by the disappointment of the crowd.

Mr Poland, who prosecuted, announced that the charge against Mundell would be withdrawn, as he appeared to have been the dupe, rather than the ally, of the other prisoners. With the permission of the court, he would be placed in the witness-box to give evidence against Boulton and Park, who were now charged with personating women at public places for unlawful purposes. The court amiably concurred, and Mr Mundell entered the witness-box. He told the court that he had first met Boulton and Park a week before, in the Surrey Theatre. They were attired like gentlemen, but his attention was drawn to them as women in gentleman's attire:

My curiosity was excited and I followed them when they left the theatre during an interval in the performance. They went to a public-house, and returned to the theatre. They went out again after the next act of the play and I followed them. They said in a joking manner, 'You are following us.' I was in company with a gentleman, and we replied, 'Yes, we are.' They did not return to their seats, but leant over the back of the circle. I got into conversation with them, and eventually asked them if they would like to go behind the scenes. I obtained the permission of Mr Shelley, the lessee, and took them behind. We remained there about a quarter of an hour. They said as they had lost the thread of the story of the play (*Clam*) they should like to see it again. I said I should be very happy to accompany them, and we fixed to go together on the Tuesday following. We walked together as far as Waterloo-bridge, and there parted. I had 'chaffed' them about their being women, and told them that they ought to swing their arms a little more to look like men [A laugh] . . . I arranged to join the prisoners in their private box the next Tuesday, and I went to the theatre on that night accordingly . . . I arrived at the theatre first. The prisoners came shortly afterwards in female costume. Park invited me into his private box, and we all walked in together. I had taken some flowers with me, and I presented one to each defendant. I then went out to fetch some pins to enable them to pin the flowers to their dress.

At the theatre he had asked for 'Mrs Graham's' box, that being the name Park went by. He knew Boulton as 'Stella'. Park went by the name of 'Jane'. He believed Boulton to be a woman, but had some doubt about Park.

Mr Poland – Tell me, did you treat the defendants as women of the town?
This question was objected to.
Mr Poland – Well, how did you treat them?
Witness – I treated them as women, and made certain advances to 'Stella' (Boulton), which were repelled. I might have gone further, but the arrival of the other man kept me off. I had repeatedly asked them where they lived. Boulton did not give me his address.
Mr Poland – Had you made any proposal to Stella?
Witness – I had. I asked her when I could call and see her, and where?

On the third day of the hearing, *The Times* reported that there was 'the usual rabble' outside the court, but inside, the tightly packed audience included 'many persons of rank, besides many literary and theatrical personalities, who were probably admitted by personal application to the authorities'.

From the evidence of many witnesses, including Henry Holland, 'Mrs Graham's' brougham driver, George Smith, a former beadle of the Burlington Arcade, Ann Empson, a lodging-house keeper of 46 Davies Street, Berkeley Square, Francis Cox, a former auctioneer of Leadenhall

Street, and John Reeves, the staff superintendent at the Alhambra, in Leicester Square, it appeared that Boulton and Park for some two or three years had appeared in public places dressed as women, and with painted faces; at the Alhambra, at the Surrey and Strand theatres, at the Casino de Venise in Holborn, in Brunswick Square, in the Burlington Arcade, in the Haymarket, at Haxtell's Hotel in the Strand, and at the Oxford and Cambridge boat-race. They promenaded the Haymarket and Regent Street late at night making acquaintances. They had been seen with as many as twenty men, all with painted faces.

Mr George Smith said he had known Boulton for about two years as a visitor to the Burlington Arcade, 'painted very thickly with rouge and everything else on'. (The Burlington Arcade, built in 1819 by Lord George Cavendish on the boundary of Burlington House, was a favourite promenade for whores and their customers. A writer in the *Saturday Review* in 1871 called it the 'Western counterpart of an Eastern slave-market'. As beadle, Mr Smith would have worn an impressive livery, and carried a brass-topped staff of office.) On one occasion, said Mr Smith, Boulton had said to him, 'Oh! you sweet little dear' – a fact which Smith had communicated to the policeman on duty. He had twice ejected Boulton from the Arcade for winking at men, and making a noise with his mouth, 'as women would to entice them'. Mr Smith imitated the sound.

When Mr Smith, who had been seven years in the police force before becoming a beadle, was asked by Mr Straight, counsel for Park, why he had left Burlington Arcade, he replied spiritedly:

I left the Arcade through quarrelling with another beadle. He had said that I received some money for liquor from a gay lady, and what if I did? Some of them, although gay, are very respectable, and if a lady offered you half-a-crown wouldn't you take it? [Roars of laughter] I may have taken money from girls a hundred times. I am too much of a man to threaten to eject women from the Arcade unless they paid me money. I was asked to resign, through the other beadle reporting me, and I did resign. He is now dead. My object in taking money from the women was to get a drink. I have had a few glasses to-day. A gentleman in court gave me a shilling. I decline to say who it is. He has nothing to do with the police. I could not get back to the metropolitan police if I wanted to. I should not object to a situation if the Treasury would give me one.
Mr Straight – I should think they would not.
Witness – I don't think it a disgrace to have taken money for a drink. Everybody does it. I am not ashamed of it.
Mr Straight – You do not appear to be ashamed of anything.

Though the court was over-crowded and oppressively hot, the

distinguished audience listened attentively as Inspector Shenton of the E.
Division related what he had found when he searched two rooms in 13
Wakefield Street, Regent Square, which Boulton and Park sometimes
occupied: letters, photographs, jewellery and an extensive wardrobe of
women's dresses and toilet articles. Doggedly, the Inspector itemized the
articles, providing posterity with a comprehensive guide to what the well-
dressed young homosexual wore in the 1870s:

> Dresses: Mauve satin, trimmed with blonde lace; white corded rep
> silk, trimmed with white lace, pink satin, and tulle; white glacé, trimmed
> with blue satin and lace; a white Japanese silk, pink stripe, trimmed
> with white lace and swans-down; green cord silk; violet glacé silk and
> white lace; black satin, trimmed with mauve satin; blue and white
> satin, piped with white satin; mauve rep silk and green satin; blue satin
> tunic, pink tarlatan, muslin, camlet costume, cambric running, gray
> moiré antique, etc. Also a number of skirts and petticoats, in tulle, tarlatan,
> white frilled cambric, white book muslin, frilled, check, plain, coloured
> petticoats, crinoline, etc., a list of cloaks, jackets and bodices, opera-
> cloaks, shawls, ermine jacket and muff, crimson velvet and tunic, about
> four dozen pairs of ladies kid boots, shoes, etc., seven chignons, (of
> various kinds and colours) two long combs, ten plaits, one gray beard.
> Mr Flowers. – The gray beard can hardly be called part of a woman's
> costume.
> Mr Poland – It may be part of a disguise.

The list also included curling-irons, sun-shades, six pairs of stays, one
low crossover, two tulle falls, chemisettes, garters, drawers, five boxes
of violet powder, one of bloom of roses (rouge), silk stockings, eight
pairs of gloves, one bottle of chloroform, artificial flowers, and a great
quantity of wadding, used apparently for padding. There was found
also some articles of male apparel, and it was computed that the things
seized were over £200 in value.

On the fourth day Mr Flowers was inclined to give the defendants bail.
He said he did not feel justified in detaining them week after week for
what appeared to be a bailable offence. Mr Poland thereupon announced
that he would read some of the letters addressed to Boulton, the disclosures
in which, he said, would convince Mr Flowers that the defendants should
not be allowed bail, 'because of the extreme – the almost unparalleled
gravity of the charge'. One of the letters read:

Edinburgh, April 20.

My darling Erne – I had a letter last night from Louis which was
cheering in every respect except in the information it bore that he is to
be kept a year or so longer in the North. He tells me that you are 'living

in drag'. What a wonderful child it is. I have three minds to come up to London and see your magnificence with my own eyes. Would you welcome me? Probably it is better that I should stay and love and dream of you. But the thought of you, Louis and Antinous in one, is ravishing.

Let me ask your advice. A young lady whose family are friends of mine is coming here. She is a charmingly-dressed beautiful fool, with £30,000 a year. I have reason to believe that if I go in for her, I can marry her. You know I should never care for her, but is the bait tempting enough for me to make this further sacrifice to respectability? Of course, after we were married, I could do pretty much as I pleased. People don't mind what one does on £30,000 a year, and the lady wouldn't much mind, as she hasn't brains enough to trouble herself about much beyond her dresses, carriages, etc.

What shall I do?

You see I keep on writing to you and expect some day an answer to some of my letters. In any case, with all the love in my heart.

I am, yours etc., John.

Mr Poland explained that the term 'drag' was a slang phrase employed in certain circles to mean 'wearing women's clothes'. He could give evidence of this fact if necessary. Mr Flowers was still undecided, but after a short adjournment, in which he saw another letter which had not been read in court, he announced that it was of so grave a nature that it left him no alternative but to refuse bail. Again, *The Times* reported, 'the court was densely crowded throughout the inquiry by a class of persons very superior to the ordinary visitor to be seen at Bow street.'

When the court sat next, still 'filled to repletion', the charges against the defendants, originally a common charge under the Vagrancy Act, had been amended to the more serious form of 'conspiring to incite others to commit an abominable offence'. Despite this, reported *The Times*, 'they appeared to be as cool and collected as on each former occasion, although looking somewhat the worse for their three weeks' confinement in prison'.

Mr Francis Cox described a meeting with Boulton at the Guildhall tavern, in August or September 1868. Boulton, who was lunching with Mr W. H. Roberts, of Moorgate Street, and Lord Arthur Clinton, was dressed as a man but Mr Cox formed the opinion, from his manners and conversation, that he was a woman:

Among other things he said, 'I suppose you young City birds have fine fun in your offices, and have some champagne there.' I said, 'You had better come and see.' They all accompanied me to the office, and we had some champagne. I treated Boulton as a fascinating woman. During their stay Lord Arthur Clinton went into the outer office, and appeared to be jealous of me. [A laugh] While he was away, Boulton went on with me in such a flirting way that I was induced to kiss him, never suspecting that he was a man. Shortly after this Boulton complained of being chilly, and my business partner wrapped up his feet in a table-cloth.

At a subsequent meeting at Evans's famous supper rooms in Covent Garden, the disenchanted Mr Cox, having discovered that Boulton was a man, went up to him and Lord Arthur Clinton and said: 'You ———

A RETROSPECT OF THE BOULTON AND PARK CASE.—From Bow Street Station to the Van,' April 10th, 1870.

infernal scoundrels, you ought to be kicked out of this place.' But they took no notice. In cross-examination, Mr Cox said he had held a commission in the Army, which he sold for £2,500; he had lived in the colonies; he had been secretary of the Civil Service Club; he had lost a large sum of money in his auctioneer's business, and was then living on his means.

Two young ladies who lived together at 12 South Bank, Regent's Park, and whose social or economic status was not defined, Miss Marie Cavendish and Miss Agnes Earle, told of a ball they had attended at Haxtell's Hotel shortly before the boat-race. The ball was given by Mr A. Westropp Gibbings, who received his guests in a lady's evening dress. Boulton was dressed in a white satin dress with tulle and pink roses, and Gibbings in mauve silk. Miss Earle said she was in the ladies' retiring-room when she discovered the defendants were men. A lady fainted and fell upon the bed.

The next witness, Ann Empson, was one of those sharp-tongued, irrepressible, irreverent London landladies, a stock figure of novelists and playwrights, unawed by rank or authority, the haughty autocrat of her domain of third-floor backs. One can imagine her tossing her head as she addressed the court:

I let my drawing-room floor to Lord Arthur Clinton in December, 1868. He occupied the rooms two weeks. I know the prisoners. The one nearest to me [Park] visited Lord Arthur, and had chops and bitter beer. I complained to Lord Arthur that he had brought a woman to my house. He said it was a man. I complained of it as an abuse of my latch-key. After he had gone I examined the drawers and boxes, and I found Boulton's shirts, some women's clothes, powder, rouge, etc., and a quantity of his letters in my room. Both prisoners were at Lord Arthur's lodgings. I made them help me down with some boxes when they left, and they said, 'I never wish to see your house again'. I said, 'And I'll take care you never do.' I turned them out because I had only let my lodgings to Lord Arthur Clinton. Before Lord Arthur left I had bought a bed for Boulton, whom he represented as his cousin. He slept with Lord Arthur on the night when he came in women's clothes. Lord Arthur left because he owed me money besides £10 which I had lent him in ready cash, and some of which was given to Boulton. I stopped Lord Arthur's boxes and Boulton's shirts for the money due to me. I knew they were Boulton's shirts because his name was upon them. They were in Lord Arthur's box. I cannot say which of the two prisoners is Boulton, but I believe it is the nearest one [pointing to Park]. It is very difficult to say, seeing them now dressed as men and without the powder, chignon, etc.

Cross-examined – My debt was contracted after Lord Arthur's bankruptcy, therefore I am not in the schedule. The total amount of my bill was £20. 10s. 8d. I had £5 out of it when I went to him and Boulton at Evans' Hotel.

By Mr Flowers – I was surprised, after purchasing a bed for Boulton, to find that Boulton slept with Lord Arthur Clinton, and the new bed was never used.

Mr Straight – When you say 'Boulton', do you still refer to Park – the one nearest to you?

Witness – Yes, that is the one. It was the one with the golden hair.

Mr Straight – Have you been drinking this morning?

Witness – I could not speak so well as I do if I had.

Mr Flowers – You had better answer the question.

Mr Straight – Have you been to a publichouse to-day?

Witness – On my oath I have not. I have not had any drink at home. A policeman brought me here in a cab, but I don't know who it was. I was never married. It might have been better for me if had been, unless I married Lord Arthur or Boulton [A laugh].

Superintendent Thomson said that Ann Empson had given him about two thousand letters and papers. Some were signed 'Fanny Winifred Park', others 'Fanny' or 'Fan'. In one, thanking Lord Arthur Clinton for a birthday present, Park wrote:

> I cannot echo your wish that I should live to be a hundred, though I should like to live to a green old age. Green, did I say? Oh! *ciel*, the amount of paint that will be required to hide that very unbecoming tint. My 'campish undertakings' are not at present meeting with the success they deserve. Whatever I do seems to get me into hot water somewhere; but *n'importe*, what's the odds as long as you're *rappy*?
>
>   Believe me, your affectionate sister-in-law
>
>   Fanny Winifred Park.

In another, also to Lord Arthur Clinton, he apologized for interfering in matrimonial squabbles between Clinton and 'Stella' Boulton:

> She may sometimes treat you brusquely, but on the other hand see how she stands up for your dignity and position. . . . As to all the things she said to you the other night, she may have been tight, and did not know all she was saying, so that by the time you get my answer you will both be laughing over the whole affair, as Stella and I did when we quarrelled and fought down here – don't you remember, when I slapped her face? Don't think me unkind, dear . . .

In another, inquiring about a broken umbrella, he asked Lord Arthur, 'Is the handle of my umbrella mended yet? If so, I wish you would kindly send it back to me, as the weather has turned so showery that I cannot go out without the dread of my back hair coming out of curl.'

'During the reading of these letters,' reported *The Times*, 'the audience in the body of the Court appeared to be exceedingly amused, and the prisoners themselves smiled occasionally':

> Certain expressions of endearment addressed by one man to another, caused such an outburst of laughter that Mr Poland rose and begged that such unseemly demonstrations might be checked, observing that to him it was a matter of surprise that a body of Englishmen could regard an inquiry of such grave importance in such a spirit. The learned

magistrate remarked that it was certainly 'no laughing matter,' but neither the admonition of the Bench nor the repeated remonstrances of the chief clerk and officers of the court had any appreciable effect upon a certain portion of the public.

The first witnesses for the defence were medical men, one of whom, Dr Frederick le Gros Clark, F.R.C.S., an examiner of the University of London, testified that he saw 'nothing to suggest that the young men had been guilty of such an offence as that implied'. When Dr Clark added that Boulton's appearance differed in no respects from hundreds whom he had examined, there followed what *The Times* described as 'a most indecent manifestation of applause expressed by stamping and cheering' and Mr Flowers 'entreated that such ebullitions of feeling be restrained'.

The medical men were followed by young Mr Gibbings, the host of the ball at Haxtell's Hotel, who also gave his address as 13 Bruton Street, Berkeley Square. He had come from France to give evidence. 'His appearance in the witness-box was regarded with intense curiosity, and created quite a sensation in court,' said *The Times*:

> The young man stepped into the witness-box without any sign of diffidence, and gave his evidence with remarkable clearness and self-possession. His voice and manner were decidedly effeminate. He spoke with a slight lisp, and with an air of simplicity and candour which impressed the Court materially in his favour. He appeared to regard the modern pastime of 'going about in drag' as perfectly harmless, and repudiated with indignation the notion that he was being made the dupe of others, or was in any way implicated in the nefarious transactions sought to be established by the prosecution.

Gibbings said he was twenty-one years of age, and had been educated by many private tutors and at Repton. He had been in the habit of dressing in female attire since he dressed as a girl for a charade six or seven years before. Since then he had frequently dressed as a woman and had acted female parts in amateur performances. He had played Lady Teazle, Mrs Mildmay in *Still Waters Run Deep*, Mrs Chillington in *The Morning Call*, Mrs Honeyton in the *Happy Pair*, Helen in *The Hunchback*, and many other trifling parts. He had asked about twenty people to his ball, but the number swelled to about forty-five. He invited six real ladies 'in order that nothing might be said or suspected about the party'. Before the ball he had gone to the boat-race in a brougham with Mr Cumming, both dressed as women, wearing false hair, chignons, stays, ladies' boots, etc. 'Our faces were painted and powdered,' he said. 'When gentlemen dress as ladies they must employ some such means of disguising themselves.' Gibbings's evidence was designed to show that his association with Boulton and Park was based simply on a common interest in amateur theatricals. 'The reason for my giving a ball was to gratify many of my friends who had seen me act and who wished to learn how I could sustain the character in a private room,' he said. 'I invited Mr Boulton because I had heard of his musical talent and thought he would be a great acquisition at my party.' But he admitted that he had gone out three times with Boulton in female attire, that he had slept with another of his guests, Mr Thomas, in the same bed, and that he and Thomas jointly rented the room in Wakefield Street 'chiefly to keep my dresses and wigs there'. However, he insisted, all the female dresses were originally made for theatrical purposes. 'If I saw the things I could point out which of the dresses were mine and which were Boulton's or Thomas's. Two out of the six stays were mine. None of the *chignons* were mine.'

Mrs Louisa Peck, of 26 Southampton Street, Strand, who had let her drawing-room floor to Lord Arthur Clinton, and her servant, Eliza Clark, both gave evidence that they had never seen anything improper in the behaviour of Lord Arthur, or of Boulton and Park, who sometimes stayed with him. Eliza Clark said she used to accuse Mr Boulton of being a female, but he passed it off as a joke. 'I heard him sing. He had a woman's voice,' she said. 'I thought he was a woman all the time he was here. . . . The hairdresser called to dress Boulton's hair, but not every day.' Miss Clark finished her evidence with a tribute to her mistress. 'I am still with Mrs Peck and very comfortable,' she said.

The last witness for the defence was another of Mrs Peck's tenants, Mr Arthur Gladwell, a dealer in works of art, who told the court that Boulton was always dressed as a gentleman, except once when he and Park went out in evening dress with Lord Arthur Clinton. 'I understood they were going to some theatrical entertainment in the West End,' he said.

Mr Besley (for Boulton) said that the gross charge of conspiracy imported into the case at an advanced stage of the inquiry was wholly unworthy of the Crown. The court was asked to believe that these young men were guilty of a crime under the imputation of which no man could live, upon the merest conjecture, without evidence of a single date or fact, in the absence of any possible motive, and upon the interpretation of letters which might have been written in a foolish freak or by an absolute lunatic. The young men were well connected, had means of their own, or were too amply equipped by their parents, to indulge in these foolish and indiscreet freaks, and in those amateur theatrical enterprises to which alone the depositions pointed. The habit of assuming women's clothes for these purposes may have led to their feminine epithets to each other, but it was monstrous to assume criminality upon such flimsy pretences.

Mr Straight (for Park) said that the young men, after being hunted down by the police, and brought into court eight times in succession, were now to be charged with a capital offence and conspiracy upon evidence such as, he ventured to say, had never before been relied on in a court of justice. He concluded by entreating the magistrate, if he resolved to commit at all, to indict the defendants on the minor charge of misdemeanour only, and to restore them to the liberty to which they had been so long and unjustly deprived by accepting bail.

Unmoved by these pleas, Mr Flowers committed the prisoners for trial for the capital offence, for conspiring to incite, and for the common misdemeanour, without bail. Park appeared to suffer from nervousness, and almost fell back into his chair. Boulton evinced no emotion whatever. 'An immense crowd had filled the street all day,' said *The Times*, concluding its very detailed report of the trial, 'and the prisoners saluted them on entering the van by waving their hats.'

III

The letters found in Ann Empson's lodging-house led to warrants being issued for the arrest of Lord Arthur Clinton, the thirty-year-old third son of the Duke of Newcastle, and of five others: John Safford Fiske, an American merchant in Edinburgh and a former American consul at Leith, Louis Charles Hurt, a clerk in the Post Office, Martin Luther Cumming, William Domerville, and C. H. Thompson. But only four defendants appeared in the Court of Queen's Bench, before the Lord Chief Justice and a special jury, on 9 May 1871: Boulton, Park, Fiske and Hurt. Lord Arthur Clinton had nobly committed suicide, and the others had ignobly gone into hiding. (There was no inquest on Lord Arthur, two co-operative doctors having stated that he had died from exhaustion resulting from scarlet fever, aggravated by anxiety.)

It was more than a year since the arrest of Boulton and Park; Fanny had grown 'whiskers' in gaol and Stella 'a slight moustache'. The evidence was largely a recapitulation of that given in the police-court, but the defence called an important new witness, Ernest Boulton's mother.

Again the court was crowded with celebrities, and again *The Times* gave a lengthy and uninhibited report of the proceedings, though not quite as uninhibited as the reports of two of its contemporaries. 'We do not desire to report more than is really necessary,' it explained. Among the celebrities was the brilliant but ill-starred homosexual artist Simeon Solomon, then an intimate friend of Swinburne's. (Swinburne dropped him three years later after Solomon had been convicted of an offence in a public lavatory.) 'There were some very funny things said but nothing improper except the disgusting and silly medical evidence, of which I heard very little,' Solomon wrote to Swinburne. '*Reynolds* publishes everything they say and the D.T. [*Daily Telegraph*] does nearly the same.' At the lunch adjournment

Solomon went to a near-by restaurant and found Boulton, Park and Hurt eating with one of their solicitors. He joined them. 'Boulton is very remarkable,' Solomon wrote. 'He is not quite beautiful but supremely pretty, a perfect figure, manner and voice. Altogether, I was agreeably surprised at him. Of course, they will be acquitted.'

The superintendent of the Alhambra and the beadle of the Burlington Arcade both now remembered that Boulton and Park were given to 'chirruping' at one another. The beadle admitted that he had received as much as a sovereign at a time from 'gay ladies' and did not turn them out because they were the 'best supporters' of the Arcade.

The Lord Chief Justice – Were you ordered to turn out these women? The Witness – My Lord, we were bound to use discretion (Laughter). A tradesman would say to me if I turned a lady out, 'Why, you've turned out one of my best customers.' (More laughter).

The defence took the bold line that the whole business was a joke. Thus, addressing the jury on Boulton's behalf, Mr Digby Seymour said that folly was not crime, and culpability was not legal proof:

However culpable it might be for men to go about in women's clothes, it was not for that the prisoners were now being tried. To do so might be a foolish joke – an outrage upon decency if they liked, – but there was no evidence of the conspiracy that was charged in the indictment. He would prove out of the mouths of certain actors he would produce the taste that existed for private theatricals, and the fact that it was common amongst performers to use both off and on the stage, the language they had used when on it, and also assume the names of the characters in which they had appeared when they met or communicated by writing; and as Lord Arthur Clinton and Boulton had performed on the stage the parts of husband and wife, that fact would account for the expressions such as 'matrimonial squabble' and the like in the letters.

Mrs Boulton said that from about his sixth year her son had shown an extraordinary *penchant* for personating female characters. Sometimes he would dress as a parlour-maid, and he had even waited upon her own mamma at the table without being recognized. In fact, when he left the room, her mamma had said, 'I wonder, having sons, that you have so flippant a girl about you' (Laughter). Lord Arthur Clinton and her son had performed together at the Egyptian Hall, at Chelmsford, Brentwood, Scarborough, Southend and other places. Lord Arthur, when he was the Member for Newark, had once acted in private theatricals in her house. Her son, who had a fine soprano voice, always played female parts. 'His success was something wonderful. Bouquets were thrown on the stage.' She knew nothing of the Wakefield Street address, or of her son walking about London dressed as a woman. She allowed him about £1 a week pocket-money.

The Lord Chief Justice, in a dispassionate summing-up, expressed strong disapproval of the form in which the case had been brought before the court, a form which 'manifestly operated unfairly and unjustly and oppressively against the parties concerned'. As for Hurt and Fiske, they should have been tried in Scotland, if at all. Gross injustice had been done

them. The administration of justice was seriously embarrassed by the proceeding. He did not, however, condone the conduct of Boulton and Park, which was sufficient, he said, to stamp them with the deepest disgrace, although they might not have had any felonious intention. Their going, for example, to the ladies' rooms in theatres and other public places was an offence which the legislature might justly visit with corporal punishment.

The jury took fifty-three minutes to return a verdict of 'Not Guilty' on all counts. There were loud cheers and cries of 'Bravo!' Stella Boulton fainted and had to be revived with water. Fanny Park, as Mr William Roughead put it in his account of the trial, 'fortified by whiskers, never turned a hair.'

The Times, which devoted its first leader to the imminent fall of the Paris Commune, moralized at length on the Boulton and Park case in another leader. It expressed 'a certain feeling of relief' at the failure of the prosecution. 'A victory for the CROWN would have been felt at home, and received abroad, as a reflection on our national morals.' The verdict should be accepted as clearing the defendants of the odious guilt imputed to them:

> Those who know most of life are least easily startled by the wildest extravagances of conduct or sentiment, and the experience of all ages tells us how frail is the banner of self-respect against the infatuation of youthful vanity.

But *The Times* deplored the fact that youths of respectable parentage should habitually frequent streets and public places in women's clothes, 'practising all the petty art of prostitutes'. Though sympathizing with the disgust and indignation of the Lord Chief Justice, it did not agree with his suggestion that their behaviour called for corporal punishment. And it warned Englishmen of the danger which was not so remote as some imagined:

> The rising generation is probably, not more dissolute or idle, but there is good reason to fear that it is more effeminate than its predecessors, and such effeminacy is wont to spread very rapidly. If there is any real lesson to be learned from the recent contest between France and Germany, it is that Parisian manners have weakened the fibre of French character. We believe the really typical character of the English gentleman to be still pure, noble, and robust; but we regard it as nothing less than shameful that masquerading so indecent and unmanly should have been tolerated – nay encouraged – so long, until the police intervened.

VII

Girls of the Period

I

The Victorian myth, the cosy vision of a people virtuous, prosperous and contented, has been nourished by that curious nostalgia for the 'good old days' that infects every generation. An inevitable comparison is between the virtues of the past and the vices of the present.

This practice of lamenting the lost innocence of an earlier day was noted by Seneca about two thousand years ago: 'The corruption of the present times is the general complaint of all times,' he wrote. 'It has ever been so, and it will ever be so; not considering that the wickedness of the world is always the same as to its degree, though it may change places, perhaps, and vary a little in the matter.'

Translated into folk-philosophy, this lament recurs in such timeless observations as: 'The world gets wickeder and wickeder'; 'The world isn't what it used to be'; 'When I was a boy, things hadn't come to this pass'; and 'We shall never see such times again.' These four examples, which might have come over your radio last night, were quoted by Douglas Jerrold in 1843, in an article comparing the reigns of Elizabeth and Victoria. 'Since the builders of Babylon were scattered,' said Jerrold, 'these thoughts have been voiced in every language.' They were thus voiced in *The Ladies' Magazine* of 1800:

> Young women of to-day live in a perpetual round of amusement. They go about in perfect freedom. Their sole occupation is to walk, and drive, and amuse themselves with dancing. They read the most improper books, and the foam of a poisonous philosophy falls from their lips.

And the gates of Hell were still yawning for the young in 1868, when a female Savonarola, Mrs Lynn Linton, wrote disapprovingly in the *Saturday Review* of the 'Girl of the Period'. Her articles aroused great interest, and the phrase 'Girl of the Period' was current for many years, as 'flapper' and 'Bright Young Thing' were to be generations later:

> Time was when the stereotyped phrase 'A fair young English girl' meant the ideal of womanhood ... a creature generous, capable and modest; something franker than a Frenchwoman, more to be trusted than an Italian, as brave as an American but more refined, as domestic as

a German and more graceful. It meant a girl who could be trusted alone if need be, because of the innate dignity and purity of her nature, but who was neither bold in bearing nor masculine in mind. . . . We prided ourselves as a nation on our women. We thought we had the pick of creation in this fair young English girl of ours, and envied no other men their own. We admired the languid grace and subtle fire of the South; the docility and childlike affectionateness of the East seemed to us sweet and simple and restful; the vivacious sparkle of the trim and sprightly Parisienne was a pleasant little excitement when we met with it in its own domain; but our allegiance never wandered from our brown-haired girls at home. . . . This was in the old time, when English girls were content to be what God and nature had made them. . . . The girl of the period and the fair young English girl of the past, have nothing in common save ancestry and their mother tongue; and even this last the modern version makes an almost new language, through the copious additions it has received from the current slang of the day.

The girl of the period is a creature who dyes her hair and paints her face, as the first article of her personal religion; whose sole idea of life is plenty of fun and luxury; and whose dress is the object of such thought and intellect as she possesses. Her main endeavour in this is to outvie her neighbours in the extravagance of fashion. No matter whether, as in the time of crinolines, she sacrificed decency, or as now, in the time of trains, she sacrifices cleanliness. . . . The girl of the period has done away with such moral muffishness as consideration for mothers, or regards for counsel and rebuke.

It was all very well in old-fashioned times, when fathers and mothers had some authority, and were treated with respect, to be tutored and made to obey, but she is far too fast and flourishing to be stopped in mid-career by these slow old morals. . . . Nothing is too extraordinary and nothing too exaggerated for her vitiated taste. . . . If a sensible fashion lifts the gown out of the mud, she raises hers midway to the knee. If the absurd structure of wire and buckram, once called a bonnet, is modified to something that shall protect the wearer's face without putting out the eyes of her companion, she cuts hers down to four straws and a rosebud or a tag of lace and a bunch of glass beads. If there is a reaction against an excess of Rowland's Macassar, and hair shiny and sticky with grease is thought less nice than if left clean and healthily crisp, she dries and frizzes and sticks hers out on end like savages in Africa.

What the demi-monde does in its frantic efforts to excite attention, she also does in imitation. If some fashionable *dévergondée en evidence* is reported to have come out with her dress below her shoulder-blades, and a gold strap for all the sleeve thought necessary, the girl of the period follows suit next day and then wonders that men sometimes mistake her for her prototype ...

The imitation of the demi-monde in dress leads to something in manner and feeling, not quite so pronounced perhaps, but far too like to be honourable to herself or satisfactory to friends. It leads to slang, bold talk, and fastness; to the love of pleasure and indifference to duty; to the desire for money before either love or happiness. . . . The girl of the period envies the demi-monde far more than she abhors them. She sees them gorgeously attired and sumptuously appointed, and she knows them to be flattered, fêted and courted with a certain disdainful admiration of which she catches only the admiration while she ignores the disdain.

II

Miss Jemina Rowland was an attractive girl of sixteen when in 1856 she left her mother's respectable cottage at Needham, Sussex, and took a job as a barmaid in a Windmill Street café, living in the Cavendish Hotel near by. Four years later she was the mistress of a luxuriously furnished mansion in Upper Westbourne Terrace, with an establishment of servants and an expenditure of £1,200 to £1,500 a year. The fairy prince of this familiar Victorian transformation scene was a wealthy young man of undisclosed occupation called Poynder, who met Miss Rowland in her café soon after her arrival in London, and invited her to the Argyll Dancing Rooms. Mr Poynder did not himself dance, so he arranged for a young man to take her round the floor while he sat at a table and sipped a drink. To the lively strains of a polka his proxy told Miss Rowland of Mr Poynder's great wealth and merits. She was sufficiently impressed to take supper with Mr Poynder in the Haymarket, and then to accompany him to his home where, rather precipitately, she was shown into a bedroom. Though surprised, she remained. No niggardly seducer, Mr Poynder made a down payment of several sovereigns, and next day sent her a refresher of fifty pounds. But Jemina was not to be, in Arthur Symons' phrase, merely 'the Juliet of a night'. The chance romance of the bar burgeoned into an amiable relationship in which Mr Poynder was as generous as he was affectionate. For seven years, under the homely title of 'Mrs Prince', Miss Rowland lived, as she put it, 'luxuriantly', sometimes in a comfortable house, sometimes travelling with her lover, who made her frequent presents of £50 or £100. Once he gave her a parcel which, he said, contained railway shares worth £10,000 and would yield her an income of £500 a year for life. She gave them back, saying that she did not understand such things, whereupon Mr Poynder said he would arrange the matter some other way.

Mr Poynder did not always take Jemina with him on his excursions out of London, but when he was away he punctiliously wrote to her every day, and Jemina, no less punctiliously, preserved every letter she received. Once, during his absence in Scotland, she took herself to the Exhibition of 1862, and wandering through *'the long laborious miles of Palace, lo! the giant aisles rich in model and design,'* apostrophized by Tennyson, met a middle-aged gentleman who bought her an ice, told her she reminded him of his late wife, identified himself as the mayor of 'a big town in the north', and offered to marry her. Miss Rowland dutifully referred the proposal to Mr Poynder who urged her to reject it. At the same time, he asked her to return certain of his letters and promised to give her £2,000 with which to buy a house, and a weekly allowance of £6 or £7. She returned the letters, but the promises were not kept, and in 1864 she sued him at the Guildford Assizes for £10,000. She was then, according to the *Morning Post*, 'an accomplished young woman of 24'. Sergeant Parry, opening the case, said she had been a most beautiful girl, and was a most beautiful woman, adding gallantly that he felt it 'a pleasure to represent her'.

Some of the letters that Miss Rowland had retained, described by Sergeant Parry as the 'most harmless', were read in court. They did not reveal Mr Poynder as a correspondent of conspicuous brilliance:

My dear Jess [one read] – I was not able to come to town. The carte-de-visite is the best you have had taken, but the position is not quite satisfactory – it does not show your figure.

Another, which moved the court to some laughter, was:

Dear Jess – I have been at Newberry at a ball, where I saw three heiresses, one £30,000, the second £50,000, the third £80,000, the last very ugly and dear at any price.

Miss Rowland had no evidence to support her claim, but after counsel had conferred with Mr Baron Martin it was agreed to dispose of the case without a verdict and pay her £1,000 and costs. Mr Hawkins, Q.C. (the future Baron Brampton), who appeared for Poynder, recommended the settlement because he said there should be the utmost liberality in such cases.

The *Daily News* drew some instructive conclusions:

The political doctrine of supply and demand applies to human society as well as to vulgar commodities. Here is a careless youth flush of money in the streets of London. His passions were to be gratified and if money could purchase gratification he was willing to spend it. Here was a good-looking girl living, perhaps, in wretched plight in some country village, not without ambition or some consciousness of her personal charm . . .

It is very well to tell such a young girl that virtue is its own reward, and that flatteries which are showered on her will only deck her for the tomb. The history of leaders of the demi-monde are known here. They are the common talk. The Opera and the Park bear combined witness to the fact that she has a career before her, and that like many others she may attain wealth and occupy a high position. . . . Perhaps her passions are naturally strong and difficult to control; so at length, with a wild burst of delight, she plunges into the sea of London life. . . . As long as there are Poynders there will be Jemina Rowlands. . . . These are the facts of our civilization, neither few nor rare, and it would be foolish to suppose that immorality will not increase when it leads to wealth and pleasure, and when even our Courts of Justice can be employed to extort its rewards.

III

The disappearance of Miss Elizabeth Canning, who vanished from her mother's house on New Year's Day, 1753, and returned four weeks later, half-starved and half-naked, with a sensational but untrue account of her experiences, provided eighteenth-century London with its most contro-verted mystery. The story of Miss Jane Newell's disappearance, a little more than a century later, if it lacks the sauce of incertitude that gives the Canning case its rare flavour, is still of interest as a mirror of mid-Victorian life.

Miss Newell began her career as a ballet-girl at the Olympic Theatre when she was fifteen. As she matured into a graceful and accomplished dancer, she received occasional engagements with the Italian Opera Company at Her Majesty's, and at times earned twenty shillings a week. Between engagements she rested at her mother's lodgings in Stangate Street, Westminster Road. Mrs Newell was a widow with two daughters younger than Jane, whom she supported by shirtmaking. One day towards the end of January 1859 she called at the Lambeth Police Station and told the magistrate, Mr Norton, a sad story. Her daughter Jane had been missing for a week. She had been out of work for some time, and had become so depressed that on the night of her disappearance she had said: 'Oh! Mother, what are we to do for the four months I am to be out of a situation? We had better take a pennyworth of something that will put us out of our misery. We had better be in Heaven than in this wretched state.'

Weeping copiously during her recital, Mrs Newell said she had been vainly inquiring at Scotland Yard, Bow Street and several other police stations, and now appealed to Mr Norton for assistance. Her daughter, she assured him, was a young lady of the strictest moral conduct who had refused the presents and advances of several persons. She was confident that the child had not been guilty of any dereliction of moral rectitude.

Mr Norton was moved by the mother's distress. He handed her a half-sovereign from the poor-box and sincerely hoped that with the powerful assistance of the press her daughter would soon be found, and would be able to give a satisfactory account of her absence. Next day, Mr Cave, lessee of the Marylebone Theatre, called at the Lambeth Court and announced that, though he had a full company, he would give Miss Newell an engagement should she return. He handed over ten shillings and sixpence for Mrs Newell. The magistrate also received a letter from Mr E. T. Smith of the Theatre Royal, Drury Lane; it contained two sovereigns and expressed satisfaction that numerous readers of the public journals (including the Dean of Carlisle) would now realize that artists of the ballet 'continued as virtuous on the stage as in any other situation'. Mr Smith, too, offered Miss Newell a place in his company. Other sympathizers sent sums of money from two shillings and sixpence to two pounds, and Mrs Newell called again and told Mr Norton that a gentleman had paid her a visit to say that he had seen a person exactly resembling her missing daughter near Soho Square the night before; she was with two women, one of whom appeared to be French.

Three days later, Mr Norton received a letter signed 'James Brown, fireman at Her Majesty's Theatre', saying that Jane had called at that establishment and taken away her practising dress, explaining to Mr Brown that she had been married for three weeks and was living in St James's Square. While Mr Norton and the readers of the journals (including the Dean of Carlisle) that had given some space to the problem of Miss Newell's whereabouts were still absorbing this report, Miss Newell presented herself at Lambeth Court, accompanied by her mother.

She gave Mr Norton this account of her absence:

On the evening of Wednesday week, I left my mother with a letter to deliver to a lady in Soho Square, and in passing over Westminster Bridge, I met Emily Hobbs, a young woman who used to belong to the Drury Lane Ballet. . . . She asked me where I was going and I told her to a lady in Soho Square, and she then asked me to go with her and see a lady friend of hers, and if I did so, she would afterwards go with me to Soho Square. She asked me if I had an engagement, and I told her that I had not and that I was very much troubled in my mind at not having one. She told me to keep up my spirits, and took me into the Red Lion public house in Parliament Street and gave me a glass of sherry.

Mr Norton: Was one glass of sherry all the drink you had?

Miss Newell: Yes, Sir, she wanted me to take another, but I refused to take it. We then got into a cab and drove to the house of her lady friend, No. 5 Somerset Terrace, St. George's Road, Pimlico.

Mr Norton: What is the name of her lady friend?

Miss Newell: Mrs Ellis, Sir.

Mr Norton: State exactly, or as near as you can recall, what took place when you got to that person's house.

Miss Newell: Miss Hobbs had some conversation with Mrs Ellis, which I did not hear and Mrs Ellis said she could not let me go – that I had a long way to go, and it was so late. She told me I was to make the house my home, and that I must not be so low-spirited.

Mr Norton: What was the cause of her saying that?

Miss Newell: Because I told her I felt so unhappy for want of an engagement, and about my mother; and she said I could do better for my mother by stopping with her than by being at home. She said I should be her companion, and that she should treat me with the greatest kindness, and I stopped there.

Mr Norton: Who were the occupants of the house?

Miss Newell: Mrs Ellis and her little boy; Miss Stanley, a dressmaker; a footman and two female servants.

Mr Norton: What became of Miss Hobbs after she took you to this house?

Miss Newell: She went away almost immediately, saying she should call again, but I have not seen her since.

Mr Norton: Were you allowed an apartment to yourself?

Miss Newell: Oh yes, Sir, a very nice apartment indeed.

Mr Norton: What is Mrs Ellis? What account did she give of herself?

Miss Newell: She said her husband, who was a gentleman, had gone to Australia.

Mr Norton: Was she not in the habit of receiving the visits of gentlemen?

Miss Newell: Yes, Sir; three gentlemen called there at different times while I was there.

Mr Norton: Were you introduced to these gentlemen?

Miss Newell: No, Sir; they saw Mrs Ellis in the drawing-room, but I was not introduced to them.

Mr Norton: Did Mrs Ellis say anything to you about receiving the visits of gentlemen?

Miss Newell: Yes, Sir: she told me I was to see gentlemen, and that by doing so, I could do better for mother than being at home.

Mr Norton: When was it she said this?

Miss Newell: On Friday night.

Mr Norton: You were then in the house 10 days; are you sure she had not said so before?

Miss Newell: Yes, Sir, quite sure.

Mr Norton: What was your reply to her?

Miss Newell: I told her I should not consent to see gentlemen on any account; and she then said she should not ask me, and that I should be her companion.

Mr Norton: How was it you remained one hour in her house after making so base a proposition to you? I find that you did not leave until Sunday (yesterday) evening.

Miss Newell: I could not get out with the leave of Mrs Ellis; she said I must not go out without her.

Mr Norton: How used you to spend your time while there?

Miss Newell: At crochet work principally.

Mr Norton: Were you out at all while there?

Miss Newell: Only once, and then I accompanied Mrs Ellis to Brompton to purchase a bonnet.

Mr Norton: Can you account to me in any way how it was you had not communicated with your mother all the time you were at this house?

Miss Newell: On the Thursday, the day after I left home, I wrote a letter to mother, and gave it to the servant girl to put into the post, but mother never got it. On Saturday last I asked Mrs Ellis's leave to go to Her Majesty's Theatre, thinking I might hear of mother there, and on my going I asked for my practising dress. The fireman told me there was a long account in the papers about me, and mother making an application to the magistrate, and he gave me a newspaper containing the account. I was very much frightened and showed Mrs Ellis the paper on my return home.

Mr Norton: How was it you did not return to your mother on the Saturday evening, after leaving the Opera?

Miss Newell: Because Miss Stanley, the dressmaker, was with me, and Mrs Ellis told me I was to return. So she did on Sunday evening and said mother might come.

Mr Norton: I must repeat that I wonder you could remain one hour under the roof of a person who made the base proposals to you that Mrs Ellis did. Are you prepared to declare before me and in the presence of your God that nothing of an improper character took place between you and any of the gentlemen visiting the house while you were there?

Miss Newell: I do most solemnly declare it, Sir, nothing has taken place.

Mr Norton: Well, I sincerely hope that such is the fact.

When this examination was finished the stage manager of the Adelphi said he was authorized to offer Miss Newell an engagement. Mr Norton said other managers had also made offers; he intended to go on with the investigation of the case; and should she come scathless out of the inquiry, as he hoped she would, she should be left to accept the best offer. Money was still coming in from sympathizers. This would be withheld until the matter was thoroughly sifted.

Mr Norton then issued a summons for Mrs Ellis and Miss Hobbs to appear before him. The summons on Mrs Ellis was served by an officer called Waghorn, but Miss Hobbs could not be found. Next day Mrs Ellis, a 'middle-aged person, expensively dressed', attended at Lambeth Court, accompanied by a male friend and her solicitor, Mr George Lewis. Mrs Ellis, who said she was not married, told the court that when Mr Waghorn called, she had explained to him that Miss Newell had not been brought to her house by a woman at all; she had been recommended by some Brompton friends as a lodger, and nothing improper took place while she had been at the house. Mr Norton asked Mr Lewis if he had any objection to giving the names of the parties? Mr Lewis said none whatever, but he would rather withhold them for the present, adding ominously: 'Your worship will very soon see how shamefully you have been imposed on by this artful girl, Jane Newell, and her mother.' Mr Waghorn said Mrs Ellis told him Miss Newell had been brought to her house by a gentleman whom she did not know.

Jane Newell was then called into the witness box. She gave her age as seventeen last birthday. *The Times* reported she was tall for that age, 'of a good figure, with rather fair complexion, and dark hair and eyes', and noted that 'her manner while making her statement on the day before was rather forward, but her tone and manner yesterday was decidedly pert'.

Mr Norton: Before making your statement yesterday, I cautioned you in the most solemn manner not to state anything but that which was positively true, and I now ask you in the same manner whether all you have stated is true?

Miss Newell: It's all true but one thing. I was not taken to Mrs Ellis's by Emily Hobbs, though I met her after leaving my mother, and had a glass of sherry with her, as I stated yesterday.

Mr Lewis: Pray, young woman, reflect a little, and again consider the question put to you by his worship. Recollect where you slept, and with whom you slept, on the Wednesday night after leaving your mother, and before you went to the house of Mrs Ellis at all.

Miss Newell: (hastily) Well, I slept with a lady.

Mr Norton: I want you to state what became of you after you had seen Emily Hobbs.

Miss Newell: I went to the Adelaide Gallery and asked Mr Smith who keeps the rooms there to pass me in to see the Ethiopian performances, and he did. I remained there until 10 o'clock. Mr Smith asked me to go to see a lady friend of his, and took me, with a friend of his, Mr Lee, to sup at an oyster-shop in the Strand. He next took me to the house of his lady-friend, next door to his rooms at the Adelaide Gallery, and there I stopped the night. We sat up until near 3 o'clock conversing and I slept on the sofa. Mr Smith slept in the same house upstairs. I breakfasted with him and the lady next morning.

Mr Norton: Had you known Mr Smith before?

Miss Newell: Yes, Sir, for some time.

Mr Norton: Was Mr Smith aware that you had a mother, and lived with her?

Miss Newell: Yes, Sir. On the Wednesday night I stopped so late he would not let me go home.

Mr Norton: Why not go home on the Thursday morning?

Miss Newell: Having stopped out all night I did not like to do so.

Mr Norton: What took place when Mr Smith took you to the house of Mrs Ellis?

Miss Newell: He went in first, and he told me after he had been there for a few minutes to ring at the bell. I did so, and was admitted by a servant into the dining-room, and was then taken to the drawing-room, where I saw Mrs Ellis and Mr Smith, and she asked me how I liked the house. I had the room to myself. On the Friday week following, Mrs Ellis asked me if I had been in the habit of seeing gentlemen, and I said no, and she said if that was the case, I should not.

'The Smith here indicated,' says *The Times* report, 'and who sat at the attorney's table with the utmost composure, is a person of at least 50 years of age, with a face covered with hair, and dressed like a gentleman. He received from the worthy magistrate a rebuke for his conduct which met an echo in the heart of every well-thinking individual present, as the applause, which could not be checked by the officers for some moments, was unmistakable; and Mr Smith in a few moments sneaked out of Court.'

As the cross-examination of Miss Newell continued, 'she was obliged to make the most damnatory admissions' as to her moral character. She admitted that she had written to Mrs Ellis the morning before, offering to go back to her house, and that Mrs Ellis on the previous Sunday had entreated her to go home, but that she had gone instead with Mrs Ellis and another lady to a dinner-party given by a French gentleman in Camden Town. Mr Lewis then handed in a letter she had written to Mrs Ellis:

My dear Mrs Ellis – I returned home to my mother last night. I told her that a young woman brought me to you, and that you had taken care of me, and that I left your house as pure as when I came, and if any inquiries should be made I hope you will say the same. I will be sure to come and see you tomorrow afternoon or Tuesday. I must conclude with my kind love. I shall stay with you altogether, with my mother's consent.

Mr Lewis asked after this whether it was necessary for him to proceed further. If so, he had the keeper of an improper house near Leicester Square who would be able to satisfy His Worship that the girl had for a very considerable time been a frequenter with different men of her house, and further, she could show that, he might say for years, she had supported her mother and other members of the family by prostitution.

Miss Newell's spirit was not crushed by this series of disclosures.

'You are wrong, Sir,' she cried angrily. 'It has not been many months, and I am not ashamed to say that I did so to support my mother. I needn't be a prostitute because I have been allowed a guinea a week by my seducer, the gentleman near Brunswick Square.'

Mr Norton: Do you solemnly swear that you have not had an intimacy with any person but Mr Smith?

Miss Newell: I do.

Mr Lewis: Do you understand the magistrate's question, and if so, do you mean to swear that you have not had improper intimacy with gentlemen while you lived at Mrs Ellis's?

Miss Newell: (after a moment's reflection) Well, Mrs Ellis introduced them to me, and she had half of what they gave me. The first gentleman she introduced, she said she should settle with him. I had intimacy with that gentleman, and Mrs Ellis gave me a sovereign immediately afterwards. I might have had intimacy with six or seven gentlemen altogether while there, and understood that those gentlemen paid as much as £2 and £3 each, but I only received the half of it.

Cross-examined by Mr Lewis, Miss Newell admitted that her first seducer was a musician called Cummings residing in Henrietta Street, Brunswick Square. This person courted her and promised her marriage, and she was in the habit of meeting him in his house, with the knowledge of her mother. She admitted she had spent an evening with him while living at Mrs Ellis's, and had an opportunity of then going to her mother, and also admitted that she had been in the habit of attending the Portland dancing rooms with Mrs Ellis, and that one night she left there in company with a gentleman in a cab, and remained out all night with him, and also admitted she had attended a masquerade at those rooms on Friday night in the character of a page and paid for the dress she then wore.

Mr Lewis: Now I want you to look at this gentleman sitting here, and tell me whether you did not sleep with him on the night you left home?

Miss Newell: I did, and Mr Smith induced me to do so.

Mr Lewis: You slept with him in his own bed and not on the sofa, as you have sworn to His Worship just now?

Miss Newell: I did; but I say again he made me do so.

This was the end of the inquiry. The summons against Mrs Ellis was dismissed. Mrs Newell (who had made a great uproar when Jane acknowledged she had slept with Mr Smith), declared she had not been aware of the slightest misconduct by her daughter. Mr Norton was sceptical about this, and refused to hand over the money until he had heard the wishes of the donors. Most of them requested him to divert it to the poor-box. What Mr E. T. Smith of the Theatre Royal (or the Dean of Carlisle) thought about the whole business was not disclosed. But there was a curious sequel in the Lambeth Police Court a week or so later. A 'respectable tradesman' from Regent Street waited on Mr Norton with Jane Newell and her mother, and asked permission to make a short statement. At the earnest solicitation of a number of his customers, he had interested himself in the Newells. He had visited them in their lodgings in Stangate Street, where he found them almost without furniture, with a bundle of rags for beds. These sufferings were being endured amid 'a number of the most liberal, but dishonorable offers', all of which had been scorned. No less than thirty-seven had been thrown into the fire:

> Finding that as much as £10 had been offered Jane for her consent to meet certain persons, and that such offers were treated with contempt, when ten shillings received in charity would have been a perfect godsend, he relieved them, and asked that all future letters be forwarded unopened to him. This was done, and he then held in his hand as many as 20 of a very singular character.

Jane's *réclame* brought her not only this profusion of pen-friends, but also so many personal callers, 'some of them in carriages', that she and her family had been obliged to leave their residence and change their names. The respectable tradesman of Regent Street was satisfied that she desired to obtain an honest living, and had decided to bind her to a business which would soon provide this. After Mr Waghorn had confirmed Jane's change of heart, Mr Norton handed her five pounds out of the seven pounds that he still held.

(Mr William Cummings, tenor vocalist of the Temple and Westminster Abbey, wrote to *The Times* to point out that he was not the musician called Cummings referred to in the case.)

VIII

Husbands and Wives

I

'Girls have been educated to be either drudges or toys beneath man or a sort of angel above him,' said Thomas Huxley. Sociologists of the Victorian era have counted the drudges and novelists have described the angels. Not so much notice has been taken of the toys – the luxurious mistresses, the elegant harlots, the rough-and-ready whores, who existed in such great numbers in nineteenth-century England. Victorian wives were more often drudges than angels, sometimes a blend of both. The Blessed Damozel was kept pretty busy filling the nursery, or the cemetery, with ten-pound babies as earnests of her husband's potency and position. And as a wife she had a much lower status than a Roman matron. A century ago a man could legally keep his mistress in broughams, brocades and champagne, on money owned or earned by his wife.

II

Though they disagreed on other doctrinal points, Saint Peter and Saint Paul agreed that wives were inferior to their husbands, and ranked, in the hierarchy of the home, little higher than maidservants. Many middle-class Victorian men who shared this Christian belief chose wives of lowly social status who would not be likely to question the dogma of male superiority. But, so that the bride from the wrong street would not disgrace him, the husband often put her through a rigorous course of domestic training before she was permitted the privilege of sharing his bed.

In 1866 when Mr Baring-Gould was an energetic young clergyman of thirty-two, he met a dark, pretty girl called Grace Taylor. She worked at Poppleton's mill in Horbury, and wore the traditional outfit of the mill girl, clattering to work on clogs, with a crimson kerchief tied under the chin and a tin can swinging in her hand.

Mr Baring-Gould decided that if these symbols of her inferior station were discarded, and she were taught to wear shoes, speak English something like his, and handle a knife and fork correctly, she would make him a suitable and undemanding wife, according to the recipe of the Apostles. Miss Taylor agreed to his refurbishment plan. She was sent for two years to friends of Mr Baring-Gould's in York who patiently groomed her for the altar. She returned to Holford in shoes, and with a sufficient gloss of gentility to enjoy the honour of being Mrs Baring-Gould for forty-seven years, in the course of which she bore the eminent folk-lorist sixteen children. (The family proliferated so rapidly that it was said Mr Baring-Gould sometimes failed to recognize its younger additions.)

III

At least Mr Baring-Gould was reticent about this project for transforming a mill-girl into a clergyman's wife. But one of his contemporaries, Mr Benjamin Riley, a manufacturer of Desborough, Leicestershire, seized with a similar idea, published his plan at length in the *Midlands Free Press*, and solicited the approval of his respectable neighbours for it. 'At first sight', he confessed, 'this appears extraordinary, foolish and unwise.' But he reassured the good gigmen of Desborough that the marriage – for which, naturally, 'God's blessing' had been arranged – would not take place until his bride, Mary Anne Paine, had been satisfactorily reconditioned: 'Of course,' he explained, 'to unite myself to this young woman now would be very foolish indeed; I having been favoured with a good education and cultivation, she is an uncultured factory girl.' The programme of raising Miss Paine to Mr Riley's cultivated level was carefully worked out. It began with travel:

> Wishing her at once to see Desborough was only a small portion of the world, and in order to fill her with new ideas, she passed through London, and also through a large railway-station in the south to Worthing, on the sea-coast, under the charge of our kind friends, Rev. S. Drakeford and Mrs Drakeford; this rapidity of movement I thought advisable.

After this instructive Grand Tour, Miss Paine was to be installed in a home to be 'a little initiated into the habits and manners of middle-class life'. During this period she would be encouraged by 'a very voluminous correspondence' from Mr Riley himself, and a lady, 'a member of the Christian church', would be employed to teach her 'to play fairly well on the harmonium, also to read the French language with ease, to write it freely, and to speak it with tolerable fluency'. Nine bilingual Christian ladies had already applied for the job. Mr Riley estimated that the educational process would take about a year.

Mr Riley had entered into a sort of matrimonial treaty with his future wife, the terms of which were unambiguous. One clause, for example, definitely resolved the eternal problem of the unwelcome relative-in-law.

> The terms of our engagement are numerous, and are placed before her in an extensive correspondence on my part. For the present it must be

obvious she can do no more than follow my directions implicitly, for it is not the uncultured factory girl, but the moderately cultivated young lady of the future I design uniting myself to.

I shall feel a pleasure, according to the terms of our engagement, in her visiting her family as often as she pleases, but it is understood they are not to visit her unless asked.

The *Saturday Review* expressed the hope that the 'modest and sensible' gentleman would be as candid in writing of the future as he had been about the past. 'His post-nuptial experiences, if disclosed in the same delightfully frank spirit, will be perfectly invaluable.' Unfortunately posterity has not been permitted to peep through the heavy curtains of Mr Riley's cultivated double-bed.

IV

Mr Benjamin Riley is a figure of high comedy. Mr Thomas Hopley, who too took a Pauline view of wives, also had profound and passionate beliefs about the creation of perfect children, the education of boys, and, predominantly, about his own piety, importance, and infallibility. The complex of these convictions produced in this Eastbourne school-teacher a real Victorian monster beside which the synthetic Mr Wackford Squeers glows in an aura of benevolence and compassion.

'Is it to be wondered that persecution fascinates and obscures the mind of the best of men?' asked Lord Houghton. 'Fancy the united pleasures of the exercise of cruelty and the satisfaction of the love of truth.' Sadism, in fine, has no more fertile breeding-place than the heart of the reformer who is convinced that he is at least the junior partner of God. Mr Hopley, like Mr Riley, had no doubt about his intimate relations with the Deity.

Miss Fanny Cobb, daughter of a gentleman of independent property, was seventeen when she met Hopley in 1854. He was a 'highly educated' private tutor of about thirty-three, who accepted resident pupils at his house on the Grand Parade, Eastbourne. He told Miss Cobb of his plans to open a model establishment where his highly individual theories of education could be put into practice. He also told her that he desired to make her into a 'model wife', and was prepared to put her through a course of training that would transform her, within five or six years, into a companion worthy of him. Miss Cobb, who seems to have lived the sheltered, enervating life of the typical middle-class girl of the time, did not resent Mr Hopley's proposal. She was, in her own words, 'fascinated by him'.

They were married in July 1858. On their wedding night Hopley said he did not intend to treat her as a wife. He wanted his children to be 'second Christs' and he did not consider she was yet fit to be their mother.

A few days later, however, he changed his mind about some aspects of Fanny's fitness, and moved into her bed. Within three months she was pregnant. Meanwhile, Hopley had begun his course of training. He made his wife learn lessons and music and treated her, in all respects but one, as a young child. Rules for her guidance on almost every occasion were drawn up, and she was made to learn these and constantly refer to them. The slightest infraction of one of these rules, or any inattention in her studies was punished by Mr Hopley 'with barbarity'. When she was a few months pregnant she made a mistake repeating a lesson and was struck a blow on the head so violent that she was stunned. Four months before the child was born, Mr Hopley knocked her down to emphasize a spelling mistake she had made. Sometimes he varied his educational methods by spitting in her face and kicking her in the back.

'In my first confinement I had no nurse or medical man to attend to me,' Mrs Hopley said. 'My husband said it was not necessary and that it would be indelicate to have a medical man.' The child was born in the presence of the cook and the housemaid. Five days after, Mr Hopley insisted on taking his wife for a drive in his fly, accompanied by the child in a fish hamper. When the child was a fortnight old Mr Hopley began to beat it often. He also struck his wife on the head while she was suckling. It was discovered about this time that Mr Hopley's first-born, instead of being a second Christ was an idiot. He blamed this on Mrs Hopley's mismanagement and continued to beat both mother and child. 'He used to say I was not fit to say my prayers with him every night,' said Mrs Hopley, 'and that I every day flew in the face of Almighty. He used to call me a fiend, a demoness, a beast, a fool and a ——.'

In April 1858 Mrs Hopley's second child was born, again without doctor or nurse. Mr Hopley began beating it frequently before it could walk. In November 1860 a third child was born. How long Mrs Hopley would have continued her training for model wifehood is impossible to conjecture; her studies were abruptly interrupted in July 1860 when Mr Hopley was sent to prison to serve a sentence of four years' penal servitude.

Among Mr Hopley's pupils was a fifteen-year-old boy, Reginald Cancellor, whose father was a Master of the Court of Common Pleas, one of these 'persons of high rank of life', said the *Annual Register*, 'willing to pay a large sum of money for the best instruction of their children, with the accommodation and treatment suitable to their position and prospects'. Mr Cancellor selected the Hopley academy as 'a private school of the highest class, conducted by a scholar of high attainments and irreproachable character'. The fees were correspondingly high, £180 a year.

Young Cancellor was a difficult pupil, obtuse or obstinate or both, and Mr Hopley, in the intervals of assaulting his wife and beating his babies, attempted to thrash him into an appreciation of the curriculum. One night in April 1860 Mr Hopley summoned Cancellor to the pupil room and began to flog him with a rope and a pointed walking-stick, occasionally varying the technique by poking the point of the stick into his pupil's thighs. The flogging continued for two hours. Mr Hopley then dragged the boy up four flights of stairs and resumed the indoctrination. Next morning Cancellor was found dead in his bed. The body was carefully covered over; it had white kid gloves on its hands, and long stockings drawn up far over the thighs. Mr Hopley suggested that the boy had died from heart disease and asked a visiting doctor for a certificate so that an immediate burial could be arranged. But, again to quote the *Annual Register*, 'mysterious stories of midnight shrieks and bloodstained instruments of punishment began to be whispered around'.

There was an inquest, which from Mr Hopley's point of view was very satisfactory. The finding was that there was 'no evidence to show the cause of death'. Again Mr Hopley wanted to dispose of the embarrassing corpse and get back to training his wife and his surviving pupils, but by now the 'mysterious stories' had reached the ears of the dead boy's brother, the Rev. J. H. Cancellor, who insisted on viewing the body in the schoolmaster's presence. At the sight of the body, which had the appearance of 'a human creature who had been mangled by an infuriated and merciless assailant', Mr Hopley clasped his hands and said: 'Heaven knows I have done my duty by that poor boy!' And he told Mr Cancellor that he prayed with his brother before he left him.

Despite his protestations, he was arrested and charged with manslaughter. He made a lengthy statement to the magistrates in which he said that 'he was as innocent of the charge as any person in the room', and he was very surprised when he was committed for trial.

It became apparent that the purveyors of the 'mysterious stories' were Alice Deacon, housemaid, Ellen Fowler, nursemaid, and Fanny Holland, cook of the Hopley household. 'The narrative of these uneducated women', said the *Annual Register*, 'told the tale of horror with a dramatic force beyond the reach of art.'

Alice Deacon said she heard Mr Hopley and Master Cancellor in the pupil room about a quarter to ten. 'I heard him beat him. I waited up till nearly eleven to take Master Cancellor a candle to his bedroom . . . He cried when he was beating him and sometimes ran around the room. It continued on and off from a quarter to ten to nearly half-past eleven. Master Cancellor went to his bedroom about eleven thirty or twenty minutes to twelve. It seemed by the noise they made going upstairs that Mr Hopley was either carrying or pushing him up.' Next morning Alice went about her duties with an acuity worthy of the yet-uncreated Sherlock Holmes. 'I saw blood on the carpet on the pupil room,' she said. 'It seemed as if it had been powdered and rubbed . . . After I had done that room, I went up to Mr Hopley's dressing-room and I saw in a chair a pair of trousers and drawers. The left leg of the drawers had been washed out and was wet. One sock was also wet and the other sock had marks of blood on it. They were Master Cancellor's. In Mrs Hopley's bedroom I saw that the two dusters had been washed out . . . There was a sheet in the dressing-room with marks of blood on it . . . At a quarter-past eight Mr Hopley rang his dressing-room bell and called me in. He told me that he had been to Master Cancellor's bedroom and had found him dead and that he and Mrs Hopley had made him comfortable and put on a clean nightshirt.'

Ellen Fowler, who occupied a room on the fourth floor next to Cancellor's, heard Mr and Mrs Hopley going about the unusual process of making the corpse comfortable. She told of the beating in the pupil room, the noisy ascent of pupil and master, the continued beating in the bedroom: 'I heard my master say "Now do, there is a dear good boy". Master Cancellor was saying his tables and master said "And four". Master Cancellor answered him. He beat him again and he cried, screamed and groaned. Then there was silence. At a quarter-past twelve, Mrs Hopley came into Ellen's room, ostensibly to open the window and wish her good night. When she left she locked the door after her.' Ellen then heard 'a constant running up and down stairs, sluicing of water, and emptying of basins'.

The three doctors who had performed the post-mortem on Cancellor translated the story into anatomical terms . . . the cellular membranes under the skin of the thighs reduced to 'a perfect jelly' . . . extensive bruising on arms, legs, thighs on front and back surface . . . two leg wounds an inch deep covered with sticking plaster . . . muscles of one leg torn from the bone.

The jury had no difficulty in giving a verdict. 'Neither the pertinacious courage of Sergeant Ballantine nor the keen-sighted impartiality of the Chief Justice could discover a single flaw in the chain of evidence,' said the *Saturday Review*, and it expressed the quaint hope that 'the poor little fellow died bravely under the lash without disgracing himself by an exchange of unmanly blandishments with the cruel hypocrite who was torturing him into his grave'. 'Not discipline but murder', was the comment of *The Times*.

With unabated messianism Hopley continued his missionary labours from his cell in Lewes gaol. With the assistance of his wife he issued an extraordinary pamphlet, *Facts Bearing on the Death of Reginald Cancellor, with a Supplement and Sequel, by Thomas Hopley, F.S.S. Author of 'Lectures on the Education of Man': 'Helps towards the Physical, Intellectual and Moral Elevation of all Classes of Society': 'Statistics of Wrongs that Cry for Redress', etc.* He expressed no contrition for having beaten his pupil to death but gave a long account of the idyllic life at his academy:

We at Eastbourne worked together and played together. With marbles, balls, kite-flying, jumping, wrestling, blindman's bluff, I have always made myself one of them. . . . The boys find bird-nests, and they watch for the hatching of the eggs, and note the growth of the young birds, but never take them. . . . The pupils are instructed never to inflict unnecessary pain on the smallest insect; never to destroy a worm or a beetle, unless it be to add to their entomological collections or to study the wonders of nature.

He justified the destruction of Cancellor on educational and religious grounds and described the 'Model Educational Establishment' he proposed to set up when he was free, with himself as 'the model Christian Master', and his wife, married and educated by himself for this express purpose, 'the model Christian Mistress'.

Cancellor was flogged to death, it transpired from Hopley's published account, because of his sluggish response to a mathematical questionnaire:

The answers which were expected:

Ques. How many figures are there? Ans. Nine, ten, if we call *nought* a figure.
Ques. Which of these denote even numbers? Ans. 2,4,6,8.
Ques. Which denote odd numbers? Ans. 1,3,5,7,9.
He had then to count as follows:
2,4,6,8,10 etc., up to 100;
And then 3 and 3 are 6, and 3 are 9, and 3 are 12 and 3 are 15, etc., up to 100;
And then 4 and 4 are 8, and 4 are 12, and 4 are 16, etc., up to 100.
After the evening prayer, I again tried patiently at intervals to win him to his better self . . . I then said to my wife, 'I know I ought to hesitate no longer, but determine that Reginald shall not go to bed till he manifest a return to duty but,' I added, 'I fear if I so resolve he may keep us till very late' . . . I kept my word and went on till it was enough. He said everything he had to say perfectly and rapidly.'

Of the final session in the bedroom, Hopley wrote:

He sat down doggedly on the bed next his own and refused to undress. . . . From time to time I had pointed out to him how he was punishing me, and entreated him to let me leave off so painful a duty . . . But nothing had availed but stripes. And now he sat doggedly on the bed, wilful as ever. It would not have been right to leave him thus. It seemed necessary to meet firmness with still stronger firmness: 'My boy, is not all this enough. Have you not learned that I will have my way? If you do not immediately begin to undress, bitter grief as it will be to me, I will go downstairs and get the stick; and if you do force me to bring the stick up here, I will make you say your lessons over again . . .' He would not move, and I left the room to perform my promise. He would not say his lesson, and I punished him. He still refused, and I punished him again. I was not angry for one moment. I was full of affliction for the boy, and keenly alive to my own painful position . . . at the sacrifice of much time and feeling and energy . . . I punished him again . . .

When Hopley looked at the boy he had killed, he was satisfied that he had pleased his Maker, 'and so, through all my grief for the poor boy's pain, I felt happy – happy, though sad, in the consciousness of having acted rightly.' When the mess had been cleaned up, he went down to the dining-room, and placidly studied some architectural designs for his Model Establishment, after which he retired and slept 'peaceably and soundly'.

The *Saturday Review* said there was 'something inexpressibly shocking in the greasy, unctuous religious pretensions' of the author. *Punch* was even more outspoken:

A TORTURER'S PLEA

One Hopley, ruffian, usurping the sacred name of Teacher, recently flogged a child to death and is undergoing a righteous sentence for his crime. For some reason, he is permitted to make a plea in print against his punishment. His plea is as loathsome as his crime. He has the effrontery to urge that in beating REGINALD CANCELLOR to death, he HOPLEY, the Brute, was but following a System which has been strenuously maintained by religionists. And he cites cases in which the most cruel punishments have been persevered in by Christian parents, until exhausted and tortured children have been compelled to beg Mercy. His argument is that we, the Wiser and Stronger, are entitled to use our strength against others until they admit our wisdom. We are content to admit the man's propositions, and we call for the adoption of his system. Outraged English society says in its wisdom, 'It is wicked to torture children.' Hopley refused to admit this. Well, outraged English society happens to be stronger than HOPLEY. Let his system be enforced. Is there a Cat and Nine Tails in the gaol in which he is doing penance?

Hopley emerged from gaol in 1864, with his belief in his own rectitude and his passion for pamphleteering equally unimpaired. 'God will help the right!' he cried in court when his wife applied for a judicial separation on the grounds of cruelty. He pleaded denial and condonation and addressed the judge at great length on his plans for his ideal school. When the jury found both cruelty and condonation proved, Mrs Hopley left

England and Mr Hopley wrote another pamphlet, which he dedicated to Lord Brougham: *A Cry to the Leading Nation of the World for Justice and for the Souls of My Wife and Children.*

V

'Men of the highest rank marry women of infamy even, not to say of extreme low birth,' wrote J. Shebbeare in his *Letters on the English Nation,* in 1756. A writer could have said this with equal truth about the English nation in 1856, or later. The nineteenth-century English aristocrat, contemptuous of middle-class values, might choose his wife from the lowest ranks of society; looks were often more important than lineage. Havelock Ellis argues that the aristocracy constantly renewed itself by this form of natural selection. Certainly, the dignified pages of Burke and Debrett are adorned with the names of many pretty girls who in the nineteenth century took the golden road from harlotry, or at least, high-kicking, to high society. The spectrum ranges from Sophia Dubochet, sister of the most famous of Regency whores, Harriette Wilson, and herself a fashionable daughter of the game, who in 1811 married Lord Berwick, to Connie Gilchrist, the skipping-rope dancer, who in 1892 married the Earl of Orkney.

When the Australian writer Henry Lawson visited London in the 'nineties, he found it a city of 'splendid harlots and squalid brutes'. His native land, of course, produces better wool than wantons. In the history of international harlotry, no Australian name compares with that, say, of Cora Pearl, the red-haired trollop from Plymouth who conquered Paris – and two princes – with her bedcraft. Yet one girl from Down Under deserves recognition: Miss Kate Walsh graduated from the streets of London to the nuptial chamber of an English earl, and played the leading role in what *The Times* enthusiastically described as 'perhaps the most extraordinary case ever tried in the Divorce Court'.

She was the daughter of an Australian journalist. Her early life is obscure. In her teens she was living in England with a circus-proprietor named Cooke. When she left him to become a part-time chorus girl and – to use the stately archaism of *The Times* – 'courtesan', she assumed the *nom de lit* of Kate Cooke. She was good-looking, vivacious, and dressed well. Soon she was one of the principal attractions of the Casino de Venise in High Holborn. This dance-hall was perhaps London's liveliest night-house of the 'sixties. With its elegant marble ballroom, its band of fifty performers under the baton of Mr W. M. Packer, its well-stocked American bar, and its modest admission fee (on normal nights) of one shilling, the Casino offered many consolations to the tired Victorian business-man, the jaded Victorian husband, the troubled Victorian bachelor.

Not the least of these was the galaxy of splendid harlots who held court each night beneath the Casino's hundred glittering crystal chandeliers. Their acknowledged queen was Miss Mabel Grey, a haughty brunette who, partnered by a favoured man-about-town, led the company in quadrilles, but never condescended to a waltz or polka. Mabel Grey, a one-time London shop girl, had also worked in a circus and may have met Kate Cooke under the big top. They were close friends when Kate joined the Cytherean court at the Casino de Venise.

Miss Cooke had enjoyed many generous protectors when, towards the end of 1870, she was introduced to the Honourable Henry Fitzroy, known as the Earl of Euston. A handsome young man of twenty-one who was said to look like one of Ouida's magnificent guardsmen, he was the heir of the Duke of Grafton. Miss Cooke was twenty-three.

There is a tradition of gallantry in the Fitzroy blood, for the first Duke of Grafton was Lady Castlemaine's second son by Charles II and the third Duke, having picked up his mistress, Nancy Parsons, in the streets, displayed her proudly among his fellow noblemen at Ascot. The young Earl became infatuated with Miss Cooke. He moved her from her lodgings in Montpellier Place to a discreet villa, which he shared with her for about six months. At the end of this companionate period, in May 1871, they were married quietly at the parish church of Worcester. The Earl embellished the licence with a settlement of ten thousand pounds which he possessed in his own right. Miss Cooke signed the register as a 'Widow'. It transpired that when she was about sixteen she had been married at St Mungo's church, Glasgow, to a commercial traveller called George Manby Smith.

Though the prelude had been satisfactory, the marriage was not a success. The Duke and Duchess of Grafton did not welcome the young Countess as a daughter-in-law and the Earl found he was no longer popular in the drawing-rooms of Belgravia. He lived with Kate, in a mood of fading compatibility, for about four years, when he left her.

The countess resumed her old life, setting up house with a betting man, and her husband made the traditional pilgrimage of the aristocrat who had lost caste. In 1875 he went to Australia, and became A.D.C. to the Governor of South Australia; in 1881, he returned to England.

The Duke of Grafton, who had never been happy about his pretty daughter-in-law, set his agents at work to find some way of upsetting the marriage. They began by investigating her relations with George Manby Smith, and found that she had sworn in a County Court, where she had been sued for debt, that Mr Smith had been drowned on the way to Australia when the S.S. *London* foundered in the Bay of Biscay in 1866. If this

were correct, she had truthfully described herself as a widow when she
married the Earl. The agents inspected the last passenger list of the *London*
and found among the drowned the name of George M. Smith. This
seemed conclusive, but they tenaciously followed the inquiry and discovered with some satisfaction that it was not the George M. Smith who
had married Miss Cooke. It was a George Muslin Smith, whose widow
was alive and willing to give evidence. Then what had happened
to George Manby Smith? If he had been alive in 1871, Miss Cooke's
second marriage was bigamous, and the Earl was released from his
mésalliance.

With unlimited money to spend on the quest, the Duke's agents tracked
Mr George Manby Smith to New Zealand and persuaded him, despite his
reluctance, to return to England as a witness in an action for a decree of
nullity. Mr Charles Russell, Q.C. – a future Lord Chief Justice – whose
brief was marked with a fee appropriate to the eminence of his client,
appeared for the Earl. As Mr George Manby Smith and Mrs George
Muslin Smith were waiting to give evidence, Mr Russell opened the case
with understandable confidence, though like many other observers, he
may have been puzzled by the aristocratic calm with which the Countess
listened to his address. Her composure was explained when her counsel,
Mr Inderwick, Q.C., rose to cross-examine Mr Smith:

'You married my client at Glasgow?'

'Yes, sir.'

'You described yourself as a bachelor?'

Smith nodded, but he did not look happy and Inderwick fixed him with
a devastating stare:

'Was that true?' he barked. Smith hesitated.

'You were, in fact, a married man? Isn't that so? You had a wife living
at the same time? You had deserted her, and it was because you feared
that she might discover you were a bigamist and have you arrested that
you deserted my client?'

'I didn't desert her. We agreed to separate, and we parted friends.'

'But the suggestion first came from you? Come, had you a wife living
when you married Lady Euston?'

Smith was dogged. 'I had not,' he answered.

But it was apparent, as the cross-examination went on, with Smith still
trying to deny he was a bigamist, and Inderwick pressing him vigorously,
that the case was collapsing.

'Supposing I proved that your first wife lived for four years after that
bogus marriage of yours to Lady Euston, would you be surprised?'

'I would.'

'Very well, then.' Inderwick was enjoying himself now. 'You may stand
down. I have another witness to examine.'

Into the box, with the eyes of the court upon him, stepped a middle-aged man. He was the brother of the first, and only legal wife, of George Manby Smith. He swore, unshakeably, that his sister had been alive when Smith married Kate Cooke in 1863. Mr Inderwick then produced a copy of the real Mrs Smith's death certificate. The date on it was 1867. The proof was conclusive that Smith was a married man when he went through the form of marriage with Kate Cooke. The judge announced coldly that Lady Euston was still the lawful wife of the Earl. The petition must be dismissed with costs.

Lady Euston was granted a handsome allowance and enjoyed it till her death in 1903, the coronet of a countess fixed immutably on her brow.

VI

Another graduate of the Casino de Venise was Miss Val Reece; hers is one of the most picturesque of the rags-to-riches, or whore-house to manor-house, sagas. She was born Valerie Susie Langdon, and was a pantomime girl at the Surrey Music Hall, and a barmaid at the Horse Shoe tavern in Tottenham Court Road, before she was attracted by the glitter of the Casino de Venise, under the imperious leadership of Miss Mabel Grey. Here, on the dance-floor, she met Sir Henry Meux, third and last baronet, whose seat was Theobald's Park, Waltham Cross, Hertfordshire, and whose immense wealth came from brewing. Sir Henry came of age in 1877, and the following year married Miss Langdon, described by her enthusiastic obituarist in *The Times* as 'a very beautiful young woman, perhaps slightly older than himself'. Sir Henry settled on her at marriage twenty thousand pounds a year, and Lady Meux entered gracefully into the life of the English country gentlewoman.

Theobald's Park was one of England's most historic homes. It had been given to James I by the Cecils in exchange for Hatfield House, and the main entrance consisted of old Temple Bar, which was moved from the Strand in 1879, where it had marked the boundary between the City of London and the liberty of Westminster, and on which, for over a century, the heads and limbs of traitors had been displayed. 'Within the grounds,' said *The Times*,

Lady Meux constructed for the use of her numerous guests, a swimming bath, Turkish bath, racquet court, and roller-skating rink. She also built a museum for the mummies and other Egyptian relics on which she spent much money in collecting. In the house itself were fine collections of old silver and of Nelson relics, including his sword. Among the pictures were two portraits of herself by Whistler. Her jewels, especially her ropes of pearls, were famous.

Lady Meux rode to hounds, raced under the name of 'Mr Theobald's' and had the high distinction of breeding the winner of the 1901 Derby, Volodyovski. At Sir Henry's death in 1900 she became one of the richest women in England, with an income of about fifty thousand pounds a year. Perhaps because of her first-hand experience behind the bar, she proved to be an accomplished business-woman and, as the largest shareholder in Meux's Brewery, for many years successfully directed its affairs. At the outbreak of the South African war she demonstrated her patriotism by donating a battery of artillery to the nation, at a cost of twenty thousand pounds. When she died in 1910 *The Times*, in its lengthy obituary, listed the properties she had owned: Theobald's Park; Sheen House, at East Sheen; the Dauntsey estate in Wiltshire, bought forty years before for about a million pounds; a town house, 41 Park Lane; and an old château at Sucy-en-Brie, about fifteen miles from Paris. In her will she left twenty thousand pounds to her foster-mother, but little to the members of the Meux family, because they had snubbed her.

Rose Wilson, yet another old girl of the Casino de Venise, became Lady Verner. Belle Bilton, of the Canterbury Music Hall, married the Earl of Clancarty. Mademoiselle Marguerite Steinheil, in whose arms the French president Faure expired romantically, married the sixth Baron Abinger. Stick a pin at random in your Burke and you are likely to find a transmogrified trull.

VII

At the British Legation in Dresden in August 1862 Mr Travers Twiss, Q.C., was married to twenty-two-year-old Marie Pharialde Rosalind Van Lynseele, who was stated to be the orphan daughter of a Polish major-general. Twiss, who was then fifty-three, was one of the most brilliant and versatile lawyers of his time, equally distinguished in international, civil, ecclesiastical and admiralty law. For many years he occupied the chair of international law at King's College, London, resigning to become Regius Professor of Civil Law at Oxford. In 1851 he was one of the commissioners for the delimitation of the frontiers between New Brunswick and Canada, and subsequently served on royal commissions dealing with such diverse problems as the management of Maynooth College, marriage law, rituals and rubrics, neutrality, naturalization and allegiance. He was commissary-general of the City of London, vicar-general of the province of Canterbury, commissary of the archdeaconry of Suffolk, and a prolific writer on many subjects, from archbishops to sea law.

Soon after his marriage, Twiss was appointed Admiralty Advocate-General, and in May 1863 his wife was presented at Her Majesty's Drawing Room at St James's Palace by Lady Rutherford Alcock. Five years later,

Twiss was appointed Queen's Advocate-General and knighted. In 1869 Lady Twiss again had the honour of being presented at Court. But on 19 April 1872 London society – or that portion of it that read the *London Gazette* – was staggered to learn that the Lord Chamberlain had cancelled Lady Twiss's presentation at Court. A few days later, Sir Travers resigned his Advocate-Generalship and all his other appointments.

The events that led up to this unexampled social eclipse began on 29 April 1869, when an elderly London solicitor named Alexander Chaffers wrote to the Lord Chamberlain complaining about Lady Twiss's presentation, and stating that she had misconducted herself in London before she married Twiss.

The Lord Chancellor dutifully made inquiries, and was satisfied that there was no truth in the allegations. Chaffers brooded over this for nearly two years and, on 4 April 1871, called at the Bow Street police station to make a statutory declaration which read:

I, Alexander Chaffers, of 89 York-road, Lambeth, in the county of Surrey, gentleman, do solemnly and sincerely declare as follows:

1. I have been for several years past well acquainted with Sir Travers Twiss, Kt. of 19, Park-lane, in the county of Middlesex, Queen's Advocate, and Dame Pharialde, his wife.

2. The said Travers Twiss was married to Pharialde Van Lynseele in August, 1862, at Dresden, in the Kingdom of Saxony.

3. The said Pharialde Van Lynseele is a native of Belgium, and resided in London for several years previous to 1862, and always went under the name of Maria Gelas. In April, 1859, the said Maria Gelas was in lodgings at 12, Upper Berkeley-street, Connaught-square, and continued to dwell there until the month of September, 1859, when she removed to and took a house in South-street, Thurlow-square. In 1860 the said Maria Gelas took a house in Neville-terrace, Brompton, where she resided until March, 1862.

4. My first acquaintance with the said Maria Gelas was on Friday, 15th April, 1859, when I spoke to her in Regent-street between 9 and 10 o'clock in the evening, and accompanied her to her lodgings in Upper Berkeley-street, where I remained with her a couple of hours and gave her a sovereign.

5. I subsequently visited the said Maria Gelas very frequently, and constantly passed the whole night with her.

6. In the summer of 1859 I frequently saw the said Maria Gelas at Cremorne gardens, sometimes alone and sometimes in company with another foreign prostitute.

7. On the 18th August, 1858, the said Maria Gelas informed me of her intimacy with the said Travers Twiss, and on the 27th August,

1859, the said Maria Gelas informed me that the said Travers Twiss had agreed to keep her as his mistress, and allow her £5 a week.

8. I have frequently seen the said Maria Gelas at the Argyll-rooms, different music-halls, in the Haymarket, and at the Holborn Casino. On one occasion I saw the said Maria Gelas dancing at the Holborn Casino with her hair all hanging down her back, so misconducting herself that the master of ceremonies was obliged to speak to her.

9. The said Travers Twiss regularly visited her, the said Maria Gelas, and kept her as his mistress from August, 1859, to March, 1862. In March 1862, the said Travers Twiss sent the said Maria Gelas to Dresden, where it was arranged she was to remain until the following August, when the said Travers Twiss was to join her and be then married.

10. Previously to the said Maria Gelas leaving London in March, 1862, the said Travers Twiss gave her four promissory notes for £500 each, and I make this solemn declaration conscientiously believing the same to be true, and by virtue of the provisions of an Act made and provided.

Declared at the Police-court, Bow-street, in the county of Middlesex, this 4th day of April, 1871.

A. Chaffers.

Ten months later, Chaffers appeared at the Southwark Police Court, before Mr Benson, to answer a charge of 'maliciously publishing defamatory libels upon Sir Travers Twiss ... and Lady Twiss, with intent to extort money'. He conducted his own defence. Mr Poland, who prosecuted, in a lengthy opening lasting nearly two hours said that previous to her marriage in 1862, Lady Twiss

had known the defendant in business transactions, and when Sir Travers and his lady returned to London in 1863 they met defendant in the Botanical Gardens, when he congratulated her ladyship in the marriage. After that began the defendant's persecutions. He wrote to Lady Twiss in 1864 for money, demanding £150. Sir Travers' solicitor paid him £50, and he gave an acknowledgement in full of all demands. He sent other letters, and brought sham actions against Lady Twiss for alleged slanders...

Determined to carry out his malicious persecutions, Chaffers had made the statutory declaration at Bow Street Police Court, to the effect that Lady Twiss had led an immoral life in London under the name of Marie Gelas, Mr Poland declared.

On the second day of the hearing Mr Poland asked for an adjournment because the Government required him at Bow Street to prosecute the young man who, the previous evening, had made an attack on the Queen.

Many witnesses, whom Chaffers declined to cross-examine, flatly contradicted his story. They swore that in 1859 and 1860, when the future Lady Twiss was alleged to have misconducted herself with Chaffers, she was either living with her guardian in Brussels, or with her governess Marie Gelas in London, where she moved in good society, including that of Mrs Twiss, the mother of Sir Travers. It was impossible, they said, for Marie Gelas, 'a little dark woman with a turned-up nose', to be mistaken for Miss Van Lynseele.

Chaffers submitted Lady Twiss to a pitiless cross-examination, taking her almost day by day, and night by night, through the years of 1859 and 1860. Hour after hour, she gave a categorical denial to his detailed questions:

Have we not been intimate for years? – No.

On Friday, the 6th of May, 1859, did I not remain all night with you in Upper Berkeley Street? – No.

Mr. Benson – You had better ask her generally on that point.

The Defendant – I have reason to ask her. Did not another woman come and sleep in the same bed with us? – No.

Did you not tell me that Dr Twiss had agreed to keep you, and allow you £20 a month, and that he could not allow you any more, as he had had great expenses during the past year? – No.

On Thursday, the 3rd of November, 1859, did we not dine together, and did you not tell me that Dr. Twiss's last mistress, Agnes Willoughby, had cost him £8,000 besides property she had taken from Park Lane? – No.

[Agnes Willoughby was one of London's top-ranking harlots. She kept a string of high-class hunters, rode in Hyde Park, and followed the Queen's staghounds in Buckinghamshire. In 1861 she married the eccentric William Frederick Windham, of Felbrigg Hall, Norfolk. The marriage lasted two months.]

Did you not get in a passion with me on the 19th August, and smash my white hat? (Laughter) – No.

On Friday evening, the 9th of March 1860, did we not go to the Holborn Casino, and you misconducted yourself, so that the master of the ceremonies spoke to you? – No, I did not go with you to the Argyll Rooms and remain with you that night.

Did you not go with me to Courtrai in September 1860, and did we not have a bedroom, No. 15, overlooking the Grand Platz? – No, never, how can you say so.

Did you not use to call me 'Bébé' in South Street, and Sir Travers Twiss, 'Bonhomme'? – No, never.

Did you not speak to me in indecent French language while you were in South street? – No, I did not.

On Wednesday, the 10th of March, did you not throw a teacup at my head? – No.

At one point Mr Benson said if he could prevent any torture to the witness he would willingly do so, but he could not stop the questions being put. It was a unique case, and he could not exclude evidence. He urged on the defendant not to go through every day in the year. At another point, he interrupted Chaffers with the curious observation: 'You are asking questions over and over again about what occurred years ago. She has nothing to refresh her memory. You, I suppose, have a diary. She swears that she did not see you on any of the days you have named.' As the inquisition went on he interrupted again to say: 'I object to these questions. You are going on day by day, and there must be a limit to them.'

Chaffers was unmoved, and continued his questioning. On the seventh day of the hearing, after he had demanded that the Archbishop of Canterbury, the Lord Chamberlain and the Bishop of London be subpoenaed, he finished his cross-examination and announced that he would call eight or nine defence witnesses. Next day *The Times*, which had devoted up to three columns an issue to its report under the fixed heading 'EXTRAORDINARY CHARGE OF LIBEL', changed its heading to 'EXTRAORDINARY END TO AN EXTRAORDINARY CHARGE', and announced that the case had come to a 'most extraordinary and painful conclusion'.

The court was densely crowded, and the magistrate was informed that the learned counsel was in consultation with the solicitors for Sir Travers and Lady Twiss. After half an hour's delay the magistrate and his chief clerk left the court, and returned in a few minutes. Mr. Poland at the same time taking his accustomed seat in the court . . .

Mr. Poland, addressing the magistrate, and apologizing for the delay that had occurred, said – I may state that since I was here yesterday Lady Twiss has determined not to appear again in court, and she has, I am informed, left London. I am, therefore, reluctantly compelled to abandon this prosecution, as it would be idle to proceed without her evidence. I have thought it right to come here myself to make this announcement, painful and annoying as it is to me and to the gentlemen who instruct me. I much regret, Sir, that your valuable time . . . has been so much taken up with a case ending in this way . . . I will add that I only became aware this morning that it would be necessary to adopt this course.

The announcement created much excitement and surprise. 'I have no option but to say that the defendant, who has been charged with crimes of deep dye, must be discharged,' said Mr Benson. He then delivered a typical judicial homily of the period in the course of which he said:

This exceedingly unlooked-for termination of the proceedings against you leaves me no choice but to give you the benefit of all that feeling of want of confidence in their case which has induced the prosecutors to announce their intention of appearing here no more. I do not remember in the history of any Criminal Court a result so demoralizing as I am afraid the result of this trial may be to those who look at it superficially or hastily. I fear that to the vulgar, uneducated mind your escape to-day may convey an impression that a libel, though malicious, is justifiable if it is true. I only hope that everybody who sees you walk forth a free man to-day will consider well the subject, and not come to that conclusion. With regard to what you said of the conduct of that woman – that unfortunate woman, whose courage, after having been brave for a few days, has failed her, who has shrunk from meeting the frightful charges, which, perhaps, some former connexion with or knowledge of her in early days has enabled you to make – she has gone. But you, for your conduct in this case, making it necessary that steps should be taken against you, and for your behaviour in your defence, will possibly for the rest of your life be an object of contempt to all honest and well-thinking men. (This remark elicited considerable applause in court.) I have nothing more to say to you except warn you not to imagine that you may further persecute these unfortunate people – the husband wrapped in distress and shame through some weakness in his wife's evidence which may have been concealed from him, and the woman shrinking from the fearful publicity consequent upon again facing a court of justice and submitting to the ordeal to which you subject her. I warn you not to renew or repeat the frightful tyranny which some knowledge you may have enables you to exercise over her. Above all things, let me warn you not to think you will be acquitted by the verdict of any civilized society of the gross misconduct of which you have been guilty because there may be some vestige of truth in the assertions you have made.

'We have great regret'; said *The Times* on 21 March, 'in announcing that Sir Travers Twiss has placed in the hands of Mr. Gladstone the resignation of his offices of Queen's Advocate and that he has also resigned the Ecclesiastical offices held by him under the Archbishop of Canterbury and the Bishop of London.'

Seven months later, the implacable Chaffers was again before Mr Benson in his Southwark court, but this time as a complainant applying for warrants or summonses against Lady Twiss and Louisa Harrison, her former maid, for perjury: 'they having sworn at this court . . . that Lady Twiss was not Madame Gelas'. Chaffers called two witnesses by Crown office subpoena, *The Times* reported, 'but as they could not give any positive evidence, Mr. Benson declined to accede to his proposition. Mr. Chaffers left the Court in rather an angry mood'.

Sir Travers Twiss devoted the rest of his life 'exclusively to juridical science and scholarship'. He edited *The Black Book of the Admiralty*, a reconstruction from manuscript fragments of medieval maritime law, and other legal classics. He acted on Law Reform committees, assisted the King of the Belgians in drafting the constitution of the Independent Congo State, and compiled a great treatise on *The Law of Nations*. He died in 1897. The secret of Marie Gelas died with him.

IX

The General and the Draymen

I

'One of the "Privileged Sights" of the metropolis is a visit of inspection to the vast Brewery of Messrs Barclay, Perkins and Company, in Southwark, which we may characterize as the largest establishment of its class in the kingdom, or, indeed, in the world,' said the *Illustrated London News* in a special article in 1847. 'Privileged sight' meant that it could be enjoyed only by a letter of introduction. 'A large proportion of the foreigners of distinction who visit London avail themselves of such permission to inspect the gigantic brewery', the article continued. 'Thus, among recent entries in the visitors' book, kept at the counting-house, we find the names of Ibrahim Pasha, and Prince Louis Napoleon; both of whom were highly gratified with what they saw of the vastness of individual enterprise in this country.'

Barclay and Perkins's Brewery was not only vast – it covered about twelve acres of land, immediately adjoining Bankside – it was also historic. The site of Shakespeare's Globe Theatre was within its walls, and in 1781 Dr Johnson, on behalf of his friend Mrs Thrale, who had inherited the brewery from her husband, auctioned it to Robert Barclay for £135,000, after telling an inquiring buyer: 'Sir, we are not here to sell a parcel of boilers and vats, but the potentiality of growing rich beyond the dreams of avarice.' (Johnson was a little disappointed when he received only two hundred pounds for his eloquent salesmanship.)

Early in September 1851 a foreigner of dubious distinction arrived in London and, through appropriate diplomatic channels, expressed a desire to inspect the famous brewery. He was his Excellency Baron Julius Jacob Von Haynau, late commander of the Austrian forces during the war with Hungary. In April 1849 Hungary, then part of the Austro-Hungarian Empire, had declared itself an independent republic. Hungarians fought heroically for their freedom and were overwhelmed only when Russia, curiously anticipating the events of 1956, intervened. Haynau was responsible for the brutal repressions that followed: mass hangings, imprisonments and floggings. Among the patriots flogged by his orders were many women, an atrocity which aroused some indignation in England – mainly, of course, among middle-class Radicals, Chartists and workers. When Haynau's visit was announced, George Julian Harney, a fiery and often-imprisoned Chartist, urged in his paper, the *Red Republican*, that the General should not be allowed to disembark, but that if he were allowed to land, there should be a 'manifestation of public opinion'. It was left to Barclay and Perkins' draymen to make the historic manifestation.

On 4 September General Haynau, 'unusually tall and slender, with grey

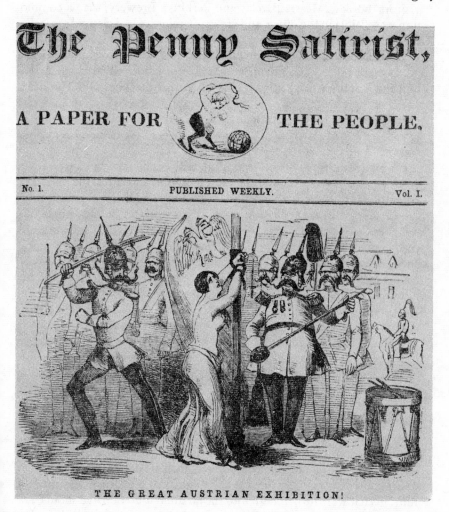

THE GREAT AUSTRIAN EXHIBITION!

moustachios of extraordinary length, a sallow meagre face, deepset eyes, and bushy grey eyebrows', with his nephew and an interpreter, presented his compliments and his invitation (arranged by the Foreign Office) to the keeper of the visitors' book in Barclay and Perkins' counting-house. After signing their names, the visitors began their tour of inspection, accompanied by a guide. Within minutes it became known all over the brewery that the man with the mustachios was the notorious Austrian general, and, as *The Illustrated London News* reported:

... it appears that no sooner had the Marshal written his name in the visitors' book at Messrs Barclay and Perkins's Brewery, than a commotion was visible in the office, and ere many minutes had elapsed several of the clerks and collectors were seen to leave the brewery hastily, and in a short space of time the carters, draymen, and others from the opposite premises of the establishment, with a host of labourers from the neighbouring Borough-market, congregated outside the gates of the brewery. Some of them were armed with long carters' whips and others had long cane brooms. The General had been shown over most of the departments, and had arrived at the stables, when the series of assaults commenced.

On his escape from the brewery, and, with his nephew and interpreter, reaching the street, they were met with the most fearful yells and execrations from the mob who had collected outside the gates. Some of the carters, who were in waiting with their heavy whips, cried out, 'Oh, this is the fellow who flogged the women, is it!' and instantly commenced lashing him with all their might. The marshal then quickened his speed, but the mob, which had considerably increased crowded round him, and all that could get near him were kicking, and pushing him, and crying, 'He's a murderer; give it to him!' 'Down with the Austrian butcher!' 'Shove him into the river.' With some difficulty he contrived to reach the corner of Bankside, when he was knocked down, and an attempt was made by the more excited of the populace to drag him away. His nephew and interpreter, however, managed to keep hold of him, and again got him upon his legs. He then made another effort to get away between his attendants. The mob, however, followed him up, and lashed, pelted, and hooted him most furiously. Several gentlemen who witnessed the attack made an attempt to protect the Marshal, who seemed to be fast sinking from exhaustion and ill-usage, while his interpreter implored the mob not to kill him. Two young men in the service of Mr. Winter, the ironmonger, in Bankside, met the men, and endeavoured to restrain them, but in vain. Another rush was made at him; his hat was thrown high into the air amid loud derisive shouts, and his clothes nearly torn off his back. By this time the party had reached the George, on Bankside, and in the confusion the General succeeded in getting from the mob, and running into the house. The nephew and interpreter remained at the door as long as it was practicable; they, however, were soon compelled to seek shelter inside, the mob beating them and rushing up-stairs. In an instant, the lower part of the house was filled by the mob, while hundreds collected in front. Loud were the cries – 'Out with the butcher!' 'Drag the murderer out!' 'Down with the wretch!' Several men scaled the front of the house and got into the front-room windows. The nephew and interpreter were found on the landing, but the object of their fury was nowhere to be seen. In a few moments a loud yell proceeded from the back part of the premises; some coalheavers had discovered the Marshal crouched in a dust-bin attached to the house. By the hair of his head they dragged him out, shouting, 'We have got the Austrian woman flogger!' This announcement was received with almost frantic cheers by the mob outside the house, and the Marshal was being dragged along the passage into the streets, when his cries attracted the sympathy of some strangers, who, with the aid of his nephew and interpreter, succeeded in getting him from the grasp of his assailants, and in locking him up in one of the bedrooms, while others stood sentry at the door, and prevented it being forced. On the arrival of the police, the fury of the mob was quelled: the inspector, on entering the house, found the General seated on the edge of a bed, much exhausted, and complaining severely of the pain he endured from the injuries inflicted upon him. Under the protection of a strong body of police, he at length ventured to make for the Thames police galley that was lying at the foot of the stairs fronting the George. Getting safely into the boat, it was rowed to Waterloo Bridge. A cab was then procured, and the exhausted Marshal was then conveyed to Morley's Hotel, Charing-cross. When he took his departure from Bankside, he was greeted with yells, and his hat was thrown into the river after him.

During the remainder of that day, the General was confined to his bed at his hotel. On Friday, he was still suffering from the injuries he had sustained. He was visited by several of the Austrian nobles and others resident in London; and, in the course of Friday night, he took his leave.

It has been mentioned that the firm of Barclay and Perkins had suspended the whole of the hands employed on the establishment. Such, however, is not the case. Although the firm greatly regretted the occurrence, they did not see that any good would result by their adopting such a course. And in order that the excitement may be allayed in every possible manner, the signature of General Haynau, in the visitors' book, has been obliterated.

According to another account, a truss of straw weighing 36 lbs was dropped on the General's head, and he was dragged along the road by his moustache – or what was left of it after a drayman had tried to cut it off.

Her Majesty the Queen was not amused by the spirited reception given to her distinguished guest, nor by the perfunctory and provocative apology which her difficult Foreign Secretary, Lord Palmerston, in answer to a request from the Austrian *chargé d'affaires* in London, sent to the Austrian Government. Palmerston, though apparently indifferent to the struggle of the Hungarians for independence, privately sympathized with them and in his note he suggested that a person with Haynau's reputation would be well advised to avoid exposing himelf to public

VIOLENT DISPLAY OF POPULAR INDIGNATION AGAINST THE AUSTRIAN MARSHAL HAYNAU, AT BANKSIDE.

indignation in England. The Prime Minister, Lord John Russell, writing to the Queen, said he regarded this as 'derogatory to the honour of the nation, as if no one could be safe in this country, who was obnoxious to the public feeling'. The Queen echoed Russell's disapproval, but the note had already been sent, with the offending paragraph, before the draft was submitted to him. The Home Office instructed the police to trace the leaders of the 'ruffianly attack', but without success. General Haynau did not accept the invitation to come to England to identify his assailants.

But Haynau was not without defenders. *The Times* and the *Morning Chronicle* had indignant editorials about the assault and one *Times* reader recalled in his justifications that the noble Duke of Wellington had also flogged women – during the war in Spain. Another, who signed himself 'An Old Officer', and who 'blushed for the character of his countrymen', advised the General how to behave if he again came into collision with an English mob:

> I have been in such collision myself, alone, with 200 English savages yelling around me, and I can therefore assure the General, from experience, that if he had planted himself and his aides-de-camp against the wall of Barclay's Brewery, and shown a determined front, and taunted his cowardly assailants with their numbers, and singled out any three opponents (one a piece) he would in all likelihood have been met with a cheer, and been speedily released, by the respectable proprietors of the establishment, and he would at least have escaped his ignominious flight, and I might have been saved the blush with which, as an Englishman, I pen this note ...

'Let public writers say what they please,' said the *Penny Illustrated London News*, 'Haynau is not much worse as a woman-flogger than many American shareholders, who are daily permitted to walk these streets and to sit at the tables of our citizens.'

It is to the credit of *The Times* as a newspaper that, despite its editorial disapproval, it gave a full report – more than a column of small type – of the public meeting convened by the 'National Democrats' in Farringdon Hall, Snow Hill, to acclaim 'the noble conduct of the workers employed at Barclay and Perkins' brewery, in having given expression to the feeling felt towards the assassin and woman-flogger, Haynau, by all true Englishmen'. The hall was crowded, with 'a sprinkling of women'. Among the speakers was Frederick Engels. The meeting which began with the singing by a Hungarian 'in a stentorian voice' of the Italian *Marseillaise*, was punctuated by cheers for the brewery men and groans for Haynau.

The chairman, Mr J. Pettie, invoking the names of Lord Byron and General Buyon, said it was the duty of Englishmen to show their hatred of foreign despotism. Mr D. W. Ruffy said that the blood-stained Austrian, instead of General Haynau, ought to be called General Hyena (loud cheers), and warned Barclay and Perkins that there was not a man who would not pledge himself never to drink a drop of Barclay and Perkins' beer if they dared to persecute their men (loud cheers). There was only one place fitting for Haynau, namely the depths of Hell.

Mr Harney said that the meeting was composed of those who, enemies of slavery, were resolved not only to free the black, but to strike the fetters from the white. A leading spirit which distinguished modern democracy from all other democracies was its fraternal spirit. They felt sympathy for all their fellow-men without distinction of country, culture, colour or creed. They were told that Jesus Christ came 1800 years ago to preach the gospel of fraternity, but if the gospel of brotherhood was preached by Him, it was reserved for present times to be carried into practice, and that not by kings or princes, not even by bishops or archbishops, not by your highly respectable moral classes of the community, but by the denounced and execrated party commonly designated Red Republicans (cheers).

After the French *Marseillaise* was sung by the Hungarians, 'Citizen

THE BED-ROOM IN WHICH MARSHAL HAYNAU WAS CONCEALED.

Engels', introduced as one who had fought for freedom in many lands, and who wore a long beard, assured the meeting that Haynau, having had a broomstick broken on his back, having been dragged through the streets by his moustachios, had been brought into contempt not only with all nations but with his own class. As a German, Engels thanked the brewery men for what they had done to his countryman. (Cheers).

Mr Brown asked rhetorically, if Haynau had been put into the vat, who would have drunk the beer? Had he been thrown into the Thames, all the fish would have been poisoned. His very breath was poisonous. He had the form of a man but all the fiends of hell were centred in his heart. The man who struck him with a broom ought to be honoured no less than the man who dragged him up by the beard from the dustbin. At the end of an impassioned speech, Mr Brown cleared up misapprehensions about the conduct of the landlord of The George. When Haynau asked to have some brandy, the landlord, to his honour, had said, 'I'll be damned if he have any brandy here!'

A resolution was put and carried unanimously. It read:

'That all the peoples of the earth are brethren; that the infliction of tyranny and cruelty upon any country is an outrage; that Italians and Hungarians command the sympathy, and their Austrian oppressors the hatred of the people of the united kingdom; that foremost among the Austrian tyrants in Italy and chief among the Austrian savages of Hungary stands Marshal Haynau, the military murderer, executioner, and woman-flogger [groans]; that the aforesaid Marshal Haynau is the enemy of the human race, outlawed by the voice of the people and amenable to popular justice; and that therefore the humiliating punishment inflicted upon that miscreant on the occasion of his visit to Barclay and Perkins' brewery was honourable and praiseworthy to the administrators thereof; and this meeting declares the brewery workmen and the high-spirited men and women who assisted in chastising the Austrian deserve well of their country and are entitled to the thanks of the friends of freedom and justice throughout the world.

The meeting closed with three more groans for Haynau, and three groans for *The Times* and *Morning Chronicle*, three cheers for Kossuth and Hungary, three cheers for the glorious French Republicans, three cheers for the German, Italian and Polish patriots, and 'an equal number, given with great enthusiasm, for Barclay and Perkins' workmen'.

From Scotland, where he was engaged in the royal and ritualistic slaughter of deer, Prince Albert, Victoria's philosophic husband, wrote to his mother, the Dowager Duchess of Coburg: 'We in London have in the Haynau demonstration also had a slight foretaste of what an unregulated mass of illiterate people, *le peuple souverain*, which like to be accuser, witness, judge, executioner, all in one, can do . . .' The Prince was happy to get away from these sombre speculations to tell of the 'altogether primitive, true-hearted and without guile' people of the Highlands: 'Yesterday the Forbeses of Strathdon passed through here . . . they drank to the health of Victoria and the inhabitants of Balmoral in whisky (*Schnapps*) but as there was no cup to be had, their chief, Captain Forbes, pulled off his shoe and he and his fifty men drank out of it.' The Prince also reported that the deer were so wild and elusive that he 'only brought down four, and this after infinite trouble'.

ESCAPE OF MARSHAL HAYNAU IN THE POLICE GALLEY.—SEE NEXT PAGE.

Barclay and Perkins' draymen were acclaimed in many broadsheets. One of the most popular was this Catnach ballad, written by Mr Eversom:

GENERAL HAYNAU AND BARCLAY & PERKINS' DRAYMEN

Good people, pay attention, pray,
Just now to what I have to say
Of what was done the other day,
    By Barclay & Perkins' Draymen.
There was a chief well-known to fame,
General Haynau was his name,
Who a tyrant's favour sought to gain
By causing grievous sorrow and pain.
By blood and slaughter, fire and sword,
He did commend his Cossack horde,
Till Freedom's blood like water pour'd;
    Sing Barclay & Perkins' Draymen.

Hit him, kick him up and down,
  Box him, knock him round and round,
Out of his hat break the crown,
  Cried Barclay & Perkins' Draymen.

When fair Hungary prostrate lay
Beneath a tyrant's despot sway,
And many mourn'd the fatal day;
  Oh! Barclay & Perkins' Draymen.
Her bravest sons he put to death,
Her fairest women by the lash
Had their flesh cut from living flesh!
While freedom to the earth was dash'd,
By this monster man in human shape.
But you shall quickly know his fate,
He got his desert at any rate,
  From Barclay & Perkins' Draymen.

  Hit him, etc.,

One day he went to have a stare,
At where we English brew our beer,
And met a warm reception there,
  From Barclay & Perkins' Draymen.
Out on the tyrant all did cry;
How you would laugh to see him fly,
To cut his lucky he did try,
But soon found out 'twas all my eye.
One collared him by his moustache,
And one with mud his face did wash,
Another roll'd him in the slush,
  Did Barclay & Perkins' Draymen.

  Hit him, etc.,

One let down upon his head
Straw enough to make his bed,
One pulled his nose till it was red,
  Did Barclay and Perkins' Draymen.
Then out of the gate he did run,
And now there was some precious fun,
A rotten egg he got from one,
For all did cry — yes, every one,

To show how we loved such a brute,
Who women flogged, and men did shoot,
For trying tyranny to uproot.
  Oh! Barclay & Perkins' Draymen.

  Hit him, etc.,

At length he found a place to hide,
All at the George by Bankside,
But not till they'd well-tanned his hide,
  Barclay & Perkins' Draymen.
Let this to tyrants a lesson be,
Not to crush fair liberty,
Or like Haynau they'll have to flee
And not get off so well as he!
Then for Barclay's men we'll give a cheer,
May they live long to brew our beer,
And from their masters nothing fear,
  Barclay & Perkins' Draymen.

  Hit him, etc.

Punch, which seized on the Haynau incident with huge enthusiasm, contributed its own ballad:

BARCLAY AND PERKINS' DRAYMEN, NEW VERSION

General there was on Austria's side,
  A Baron who ruth did lack, man,
He hang'd brave soldiers, and – tan his hide!
  He wallopp'd the female back, man.
Whether he ever did much in fight,
  Is more than I'm able to say, man;
But I know that he nearly got killed outright,
  By Barclay and Perkins' Draymen.

Our Baron bold, who whopp'd the fair,
  Of hanging who had the knack, man
Came over here to England, where
  He could have no ladies to whack, man
For gibbet and halter in vain he sigh'd,
  At hanging unable to play, man,
So in quest of amusement, a visit he tried
  To Barclay and Perkins' Draymen.

The British Draymen's blood boils high
   On woman a whip if you crack, man;
It makes him mad – the reason why –
   'Tis the act of a dastard black, man.
Accordingly his fury rose,
   When the Baron came in his way, man
And his eyes flash'd fury and 'Butcher, here goes!'
   Swore Barclay and Perkins' Draymen.

The Baron was seized with blue despair,
   And his teeth like mill did clack, man;
Cries he – 'Vere shall I ron? ah vere!
   To esgabe vrom deir addack, man?'
'You blood-stain'd thing! we'll make you feel
   Though you may be dead to shame, man!'
So, though in language less genteel,
   Cried Barclay and Perkins' Draymen.

Says they, 'If truly our mind we tells,
   Your skull we should like to crack, man;
For really your name so nasty smells –'
   And so they went at him – smack! man.
You can't think how my heart it pains
   To have such things to say, man;
They pelted the Baron with mud and grime,
   Did Barclay and Perkins' Draymen.

The Baron at running tried a match;
   They followed him in a pack, man,
Crying, 'Down with the Butcher!' and 'There goes Old Scratch!'
   That scratched the lady's back, man!'
They tore his clothes and they punch'd his head,
   Until he look'd not like the same man,
While he, like a hunted hyaena, fled
   From Barclay and Perkins' Draymen.

With frantic speed down-street he flew,
   With the mob upon his track, man,
And a ginshop door he darted through,
   To hide in a two-pair-back, man
'This here land', cries the crowd, 'is free,
   We'll teach you the ladies to flay, man';
'And don't show your face here no more among we,'
   Says Barclay and Perkins' Draymen.

The New Police came just in time,
   ('Tis said that they're sometimes slack, man),
And rescued him cover'd with bruises and grime.
   And carried him off in their smack, man.
With rage and fear he did glare and grin,
   Says they – 'You are well away, man';
'And don't let us catch you here agin,'
   Says Barclays and Perkins' Draymen.

X

Pranksters and Playboys

I

In one respect, Dickens's London was still like Boswell's London. Throughout the metropolis were 'accommodation houses', varying from the strictly functional to the gilded and elegant, in which at any hour of the day or night you could transact your business with a peripatetic whore. The tireless amorist of *My Secret Life* describes one which he patronized early in his sexual odyssey:

> It was a gentleman's house, although the room cost but five shillings: red curtains, looking-glasses, wax lights, clean linen, a huge chair, a large bed, and a cheval-glass, large enough for the biggest couple to be reflected in, were all there.

Another such establishment, the economics of which he discussed with the manageress, had only eight rooms, 'two mere closets', yet it often took twenty pounds a day, 'and sometimes much more'.

In another respect early Victorian London was close to the London of the Regency. There were, indeed, eccentrics like the Yorkshire squire, Sir Tatton Sykes, who until his death in the 1860s, wore the long, high-collared coat, the chokers, frills, and mahogany-topped boots, of the Regency. And, as his grand-nephew, Christopher Sykes, writes, 'he preserved to the last the more revolting vices of the brutal age which produced him'. He once savagely flogged his schoolboy sons because he found the 'unmanly frippery' of toothbrushes in their baggage. Many of Sir Tatton's contemporaries behaved as if Prinny were still holding revel in the Pavilion. The spirit of the Regency bucks, with their love of violent horse-play and unfeeling practical jokes, and their contempt for tradesmen who expected to be paid, lingered on well into the nineteenth century, sanctioned by the inviscerate English respect for wealth and rank. Behaviour that would have earned a young bootblack imprisonment, or a whipping, was dismissed in a young baronet as high spirits.

II

Henry de la Poer, 3rd Marquis of Waterford, who died in 1859 after falling from his horse, lived like an eighteenth-century mohock. He was an assiduous collector of knockers and bell-handles wrested from the houses of sleeping citizens, and an inveterate prankster and practical joker. One of his earliest japes was to break into Eton, after a heavy boat-race dinner, by removing a panel from the great doors, and perilously creeping along a narrow ledge, to carry off the headmaster's birches and flogging block. In this brilliant *coup* he was assisted by two other Old Etonians, Lord Alford and Mr J. H. Jesse. The block was made the official seat of the president of the 'Eton Block Club', membership of which was limited to old boys who had been birched at least three times – not a very exclusive condition.

The Marquis was a redoubtable boxer, and was also given to smashing clocks on club mantelpieces with his naked fist. He once tried to bring a high-mettled horse into a police court to disprove a charge of furious driving. Because he had been jostled in an overcrowded railway-carriage, he took a chimney-sweep, in all his sooty regalia, into a first-class carriage to discourage others from entering. He used to rush around the Haymarket in shabby clothes with large joints of meat under his arm. He astonished a constable who was politely questioning him because of his dishevelled appearance, by taking out a large knife and apparently hacking off a finger which he threw into the gutter. It was a bloody blade-bone acquired at the market for such an emergency.

His favourite haunt in his younger days was Mother Emerson's night-house in the Haymarket. Mother Emerson was a notable character in London's night-life. Her pleasure-dome, which dispensed girls and grog till early in the morning, was originally called The Turk's Head, but as a compliment to her best customer she changed its name to The Waterford Arms and embellished the premises with the Waterford escutcheon.

A street conjurer who talked to Henry Mayhew remembered the Marquis at Mother Emerson's with affection:

> I've seen him buy a pipe of port, and draw tumblers of it for anybody that came in, for his great delight was to make people drunk. He says to Mrs. Emerson, 'How much do you want for that port, mother?' and then he wrote a cheque for the amount and had it tapped. He was a good-natured fellow . . . if he played any tricks on you he'd always square up . . . I've seen him do some wonderful things.
>
> I've seen him jump into an old woman's crockery-ware basket while she was carrying it along, and smash everything. Sometimes he'd get seven or eight cabs and put a lot of fiddlers and other musicians on the roof, and fill 'em with anybody that liked, and then go off in procession round the streets, he driving the first cab as fast as he could, and bands playing as loud as possible. It's wonderful the games he'd be up to. But he always paid handsomely for whatever damages he did. If he swept all the glasses off the counter, there was the money to make them good again.

The Marquis was succeeded by his brother, a rural dean, of more decorous habits, but whose son, Lord Charles Beresford, inherited the Marquis's boisterous ways. Lord Charles was a playmate of the Duke of Edinburgh, Queen Victoria's second son (whom he was privileged to call 'darling Matilda') and of the Prince of Wales. The villainous but informative author of *Things I Shouldn't Tell*, Julian Osgood Field, expatriate American, man-about-town and swindler, describes him as 'the ringleader of a very silly, not to say offensive, clique of practical jokers':

One of their favourite pastimes would be to pretend at a country house to retire early, and then when the ladies began to ascend the stairs to go to their rooms, they would be pelted with all kinds of articles of a more or less intimate, personal or domestic character: socks, pants, jerseys, pyjamas, would come floating down from above; brushes, combs, boots, etc., etc., come rattling about. On one memorable occasion poor Christopher Sykes was a victim of such horseplay.

'Poor Christopher Sykes', brother of the eccentric Sir Tatton, a wealthy, good-natured hanger-on of the Prince of Wales, was the victim of 'horse-play' on many occasions. His Royal Highness was an inveterate practical joker, and Sykes, with his passionate love of royalty, a God-given target. On the 'memorable occasion', Sykes was invited up north to meet the Prince, and was received with an exceptional cordiality which concealed the fact that 'Tum-Tum', as the Prince was known to his intimates, and Charles Beresford had arranged a whimsical reception for him:

The following morning, very early, almost at dawn, Charles Beresford rushed into his bedroom very excited and said: 'I say, Sykes, get up at once, Tum-Tum wants to see you directly minute' (a favourite expression of his) 'so hustle, old cock – perhaps the Crown's in danger!' Then he retired. Up jumped Christopher and dashed to the door, plunging into his dressing-gown as he went, but as he left the room he tripped over a cord put there on purpose, and fell over heels into a big bath-tub of cold water!

Despite such incidents, Sykes's devotion to the Prince was indestructible. There was another 'memorable occasion' when both were supping at the Marlborough Club. The Prince, in a whimsical moment, slowly emptied a glass of brandy over Sykes's head. Sykes remained silent and impassive as the brandy trickled down his face and into his golden beard, making no attempt to mop it up. Then, after a pause, he leant towards the Prince and said without emotion, 'As Your Royal Highness pleases.' The clubmen thought this indescribably funny. 'The whole room burst into violent paroxysms of laughter, and no one laughed more heartily,

and certainly not more loudly, than the Prince,' writes the contemporary
Christopher Sykes. And he relates the sequel to the Prince's inspired
jape:

> The Prince flattered himself that he had made a discovery . . . he had
> lighted on the greatest comic act of his time . . . he had it again, he had it
> unnumbered times, he had it to the end . . . In place of the glass, a full
> bottle was substituted, and another royal discovery was that even
> funnier effects could be conjured by pouring the precious liquid not on
> his hair, but down his friend's neck . . . Amid screams of sycophantic
> laughter, the Prince invented an entirely new diversion. Christopher was
> hurled underneath the billiard-table while the Prince and the faithful
> courtiers prevented his escape by spearing at him with billiard cues. And
> there were further elaborations of the sousing theme. Watering cans
> were introduced into Christopher's bedroom and his couch sprinkled
> by the royal hand. New parlour games were evolved from the Prince's
> simple but inventive mind: while smoking a cigar he would invite
> Christopher to gaze into his eyes in order to see the smoke coming out
> of them, and while Christopher was thus obediently engaged, the Prince
> would thrust the burning end on his friend's unguarded hand . . .
> Christopher (an inviscerate snob) remained the statuesque figure . . .
> His hat would be knocked off, the cigar applied to him, the soda-water
> pumped over his head, and he would incline and murmur, 'As Your
> Royal Highness pleases.'

III

While the Heir to the Throne enjoyed such rugged buffooneries, it is not
surprising that a similarly playful spirit sometimes animated even his lowly
subjects. One such manifestation was noted in *The Times* index for 1863
under the heading:

Wilton, Elizabeth and another, for giving a Black Beetle Pie to a Neighbour.

The 'another' was Joseph Newlett, Mrs Wilton's late coachman, and
the 'Neighbour' was Edward Gardiner, in service of Mr Newell, a
gentleman. Mrs Wilton was charged with 'causing to be taken by Edward
Gardiner certain noxious things with intent to aggrieve and annoy him'.
Mr Gardiner had reason to be aggrieved and annoyed. He told the court
that while he was washing his master's carriage the defendant Newlett
leaned over the wall and handed him what appeared to be a nice pie. He
placed it on a shelf and as soon as he had done with the carriage, he ate
part of it; he felt the taste queer and on looking at it found it full of black
beetles. He was obliged to go to a chemist's and get an emetic, and could
eat nothing till the next day. When he called next door, Mrs Wilton told

him she would send for the police if he annoyed her. Newlett asked him to have a beer. He refused and took the pie to the police-station.

Sergeant Hammond, 10 P, took up the narrative. He said when the pie was brought to the station-house, it had so strong a smell he had to throw it out of the window. Some days later, Mrs Wilton drove to the station-house with Newlett, both having received summonses. Newlett said he did no more than what his mistress told him. His mistress said she had made the pie for a 'lark'. Dr Odling gave details of the ingredients of the pie. It contained, as well as a generous filling of black beetles, 120 grains of gamboge, double the quantity fatal to human life. (Gamboge, a gum resin from Siam, is today used as a pigment, but the Victorians believed it had therapeutic qualities. It was the principal ingredient of Morrison's Pills, whose inventor, James Morrison, made a fortune.) Sergeant Hammond, recalled, said Mrs Wilton had called at the Brixton station and presented him with a pie which contained black beetles and cockroaches.

The evidence revealed that Mrs Wilton's idiosyncrasies were not confined to pie-making. She had a habit of inviting a German band to play in the forecourt of her house, a practice not always appreciated by her neighbours.

James Painting, Mr Newell's coachman, said he had been sent by his master to Mrs Wilton to request that the music might cease because there was illness in the Newell home. She refused. Mr Newell then ordered the band to remove. Upon this, Mrs Wilton called Mr Newell a dirty old scoundrel and vagabond and ordered the band into her house, where it played till one o'clock in the morning. 'I have heard travelling bands playing several times at Mrs Wilton's house till one in the morning,' he said.

Edward Gardiner, recalled, said: 'I took two or three mouthfuls of the pie before I discovered what it really was. I ate two or three mouthfuls of the paste before I saw the beetles. I found there was a bad taste, but knowing that the things at gentlefolk's tables are very different from what we poor people have, I did not particularly notice them.'

The magistrate, Mr Norton, said he did not want to hear any more evidence. 'I do hope that the defendant will leave off these practical jokes and when her neighbour is in sickness and when he requests her not to have brass music, she will not cause annoyance to him,' he said. But he found that Mrs Wilton did not intend to injure Gardiner. If anything like malice had been shown, the case would have been different. She was discharged. Edward Gardiner must have come to the conclusion that words like 'injure' and 'malice', when used by gentlefolk, were 'very different' from the same words used by poor people.

IV

In May 1863 Mr E. T. Smith, the enterprising manager of Her Majesty's and Drury Lane theatres and the proprietor of Cremorne Gardens, wrote a monitory letter to *The Times*, which was published under the heading: *'Gents' at Cremorne*. Cremorne Gardens, a glittering complex of flowers, trees, ferneries, statues, sideshows, temples, kiosks, arbours, fountains, dance-floors and gas-lights, covering about twelve acres along the Thames just west of Battersea Bridge, were London's most popular pleasure-grounds, especially after ten o'clock. 'Until that hour,' wrote Daniel Joseph Kirwan, the London correspondent of the New York *World*, 'the middle class of London citizens, shopkeepers, tradesmen, and clerks, and their wives and sweethearts, have possession of the Gardens; but at that hour they leave the place, and from thence until one or two o'clock in the morning, Cremorne is in the possession of Lost Women and their males and abettors.'

It was the behaviour of some of these males – members of the 'upper class', as he put it – that led Mr Smith to write to *The Times*: 'A visit to the Derby or the Oaks is, with the class to which I allude, considered as nothing unless wound up by a row at Cremorne,' he wrote, 'and a row at Cremorne generally comprised the insulting of such visitors as appear incapable of protecting themselves; exciting others, assaulting the police, punching the heads of unoffending waiters. . . . On Tuesday and Friday last a number of gentlemen on their return from the races, thought proper to wind up their day's sport in this manner.' Mr Smith warned the gentry that he intended to invoke the police to protect his customers from their high spirits. 'I am willing on all occasions to make every allowance for fair fun and frolic, but beyond that I will not go,' he declared firmly.

The sequel was the appearance in a London court of six young men, John Birkett, Joseph Edward Saville, Robert Shawcross, Charles M'Dougal, Charles Mott, and Reginald Herbert, charged on twenty-four indictments arising out of a visit to Cremorne. They were described by Mr Sleigh, opening the case for the Crown, as gentlemen of fortune, position and unblemished honour who moved 'in a very superior position in society'. Mr Shawcross was 'a gentleman holding a very high position in life in Manchester'. Mr Saville was an ensign in the 34th Regiment of Foot, under orders to go to India, to help civilize the lesser breeds out there. The exalted social status of the young men was reflected by the formidable battery of expensive counsel deployed in their defence. It included Mr Huddlestone, Q.C., Mr Hawkins, Q.C., and Mr Digby Seymour.

One of the indictments charged the defendants with 'committing an assault by force of arms and in warlike array'. When Mr Hawkins objected to this phrase, he was told by the Bench that it was 'the old form', to which Mr Hawkins replied caustically, 'No doubt it is a very old form applied to very young men.' The warlike activities of the very young men were described in detail by many witnesses. Mr Sleigh, in his opening address, explained that 'persons in a station of society that might have known better' were in a habit of going to Cremorne during Derby week and creating

Cremorne Gardens, 1851.

scenes of disorder. This year, after a preliminary skirmish a couple of days before, a scene of 'riot, confusion, destruction of property and injury' had taken place on the Oaks day, 'which would have been a disgrace to a savage land'. There were about two thousand people in the gardens, dancing, drinking, promenading – and, of course, though Mr Sleigh did not say so, shopping for whores – when the riot began, at about one o'clock in the morning. Mr Herbert, Mr Birkett and Mr Saville were in the crowded 'circular bar': a shrill whistle sounded, upon which Herbert and his companions rushed among the crowd, shouting 'Now for a jolly lark!', 'Come on boys!' 'Go it boys!' 'Here's plenty of brandy and soda', 'Now, boys, for a jolly spree!', and other stirring cries. There was immediately a rush for the bar, in which the other defendants, then unknown to the three organizers of the *divertissement*, joined. 'They then commenced a riot,' the prosecutor explained, 'mingling with it shouts, hissings and other noises, and a scene of terrible confusion ensued.' Glasses, bottles and decanters were swept from the counter, six dozen flower-pots thrown in all directions, chairs pushed over, windows smashed, and gas glasses broken. Mr Smith estimated the damage at two hundred pounds.

To the accompaniment of 'hallooing and cat-calling' the jolly spreers then began striking people with sticks, knocking their hats off, and bonneting them. (To 'bonnet', in the Victorian idiom, meant not to place a bonnet on a person's head, but to smash his hat down over his eyes.) Mr George Forrest, a dealer in silks, satins and laces, who was drinking in the circular bar with the wife of a friend, had his coat torn into about thirty pieces. His companion, and many other women, were violently pushed around. When the police endeavoured to quell the spreers, loud cries of 'To the rescue!' rang out and Mr M'Dougal struck several policemen on the head with his umbrella. The bar had by then been closed, but the fighting M'Dougal, brandishing his umbrella, cried above the din, 'Burst the door open! We want more lush!'

The jury, impressed by the arguments of the defence, found that the young men were guilty of riotous proceedings, but that they did not go to Cremorne with riotous intent. They were fined sums varying from £10 to £50, and bound over in substantial bonds to keep the peace for twelve months. As they left the court, they were loudly cheered by the crowd outside.

A writer in *The Day's Doings* gives a lively picture of Cremorne on Derby night, 1871:

It is getting later and later, and every minute fresh arrivals are pouring in. I can almost hear above the hum and roar, the sound of the cabs and broughams (crestless these, and jobbed as a rule) rolling over the crisp gravel, and putting down their fair burdens at the glowing gate. It is a late night here – the gardens will be open till three, my refreshing companion has told me – and thus Cremorne is acting as a focus, so to speak, and centralising all the scattered rays of revelry of the metropolis. The 'Holborn' is shut, so is the 'Argyll' and the uniformed giants of the 'Alhambra' have closed its Moorish portals long ago. The theatres are all out, the 'Market' is thinking of turning off its lights, and even 'gay' London would be thinking of going to bed in the ordinary course of events. But the Derby day is not an ordinary day; nor is the Derby night as other nights; and Cremorne, reinforced by contingents from the giddy 'west' is preparing to make a regular night of it. Preparing, did I say? It *is* making a night of it. Don't tell me that we English have no notion of fun – that we are slow, elephantine, dull, crass, stupid, heavy and all the rest of it. I ask you to look round. Is there no gaiety, no sprightliness, no *abandon*, no *chic*, no grace, no merriment here? Isn't it a gay scene, I ask you? Isn't there something almost indescribably exciting in the whole aspect of the place? Did you ever see so many pretty girls before? What a chance for studying dresses; for seeing ravishing toilettes, for wondering at astonishing *chevelures*. Verily, these ladies of the 'Half world' know how to make a sensation. Tonight, brigaded, as it were, for a grand field-day, one cannot be but surprised at their numbers. Recollect they have mustered from all parts of the metropolis; from the shady groves of the Evangelist's Wood, from stuccoed Pimlico, from Formosan Fulham, from breezy Battersea, from the streets adjacent to the road of Tottenham-court. [St John's Wood was known in smart circles as 'The Grove of the Evangelist'. Many of its inhabitants were mistresses or harlots. 'Formosa' was the harlot-heroine of a very successful melodrama by Dion Boucicault. She lived in a luxurious Fulham villa.] Rank and file, officers and generals all are here. Generals, said I? Isn't there just before me at this very moment the greatest of them all? Old fogey as I may be, I am not blind. I can recognise likeness; and having studied her *carte* on scores of windows for the last three years, I know at once that the girl yonder, the centre of an admiring group, is none other than Mabel Grey. I wonder if she knows that she and her doings have been the town-talk for seasons – that she, a *quondam* draper's assistant in an Oxford shop, has been talked of more than a royal princess, or even a favourite for the Derby. She must have known that her photograph has been a feature of our shop-windows; that she has hung side by side with statesmen, generals, and bishops and that American newspapers have sent over irrepressible correspondents to interview her.

Whether or not he interviewed her, Mr Kirwan wrote of Mabel Grey (*née* Annie King) with enthusiasm in his book about London in the 'sixties, *Palace and Hovel*. A London police-inspector pointed her out to Mr Kirwan at Goodwood as she lounged in a handsome barouche, drawn by four grey horses, with two of her professional companions, 'Baby' Hamilton and Alice Gordon. 'That's her, Sir, as is sitting in the front seat with a plate of chicken in her lap, with the golden butterflies in her lace bonnet, and the splendid diamond cross hanging from her neck – that's the gal with the blue eyes and auburn hair.' Mr Kirwan continues:

That woman with the sunny smile, laying back in the drag, toying with her fan – Mabel Grey – was, five years ago, a wretchedly-paid working girl, who eked out an existence as a shoe-binder, in a shop in Oxford street, London, on a pittance of seven shillings a week. Now, the diamonds on her fingers would purchase a comfortable villa, and around her throat, which is white as alabaster, is a necklace of pearls, that cost the Prince of Wales five thousand pounds, it is said. She rides every day in Rotten Row, the famous ride and fashionable drive in Hyde Park, and her skirts often touch the garments of the Princess of Wales as they pass each other in the crowded Row. And certainly the Princess has no reason to look kindly at Mabel Grey. Mother of five children, and daughter of the Vikings, with clear unsullied Norse blood in her veins, she may well question herself, when alone, 'Why did I marry a profligate and a blackguard?'

Mabel Grey is the original of Boucicault's 'Formosa', and it was she who gave a name to Dan Godfrey's famous 'Mabel Waltz.' Godfrey is the leader of the Guards' band, and the musician thought it would be received as a delicate compliment by his aristocratic patrons, to call a delicious piece of dance music by the Christian name of the chief of England's Hetairae. In every shop-window the features of Mabel Grey are flaunted at one along with the portraits of Nilsson, Patti, the Queen, the Princess of Wales, and other virtuous and good women. You may meet her . . . at the Opera, at the Chiswick Flower Show, at Kensington Gardens, and other fashionable resorts, mingling unrebuked among the noblest ladies in the land. She has a sumptuous villa at St. John's Wood . . . and in her stables are constantly kept twelve to fifteen blooded animals for the saddle or for driving – these horses being the gifts of her numerous aristocratic admirers. At Ascot she induced the Prince of Wales to bet on a certain horse, whereby he lost the nice little sum of £20,000.

And it is this bold, brazen, and bad woman, who divides the heart of the Prince of Wales with the Princess Alexandra, his lawful wife and mother of his children, the other half being owned by Mabel Grey, together with his pocket book, which he is most apt to keep closed to all others.

Not even the august columns of *The Times* were immune from practical jokers. Sir William Hardman tells of the advertisement that appeared in *The Times* on 28 February 1863, when London was agog with the wedding of the Prince of Wales to Princess Alexandra.

ROYAL PROCESSION. First floor, with two large widows, to be let, in the best part of Cockspur Street, with entrance accessible behind. For cards, apply to Mr. Lindley, No. 10 Catherine Street, Strand W.C.

The address was that of a brothel, and, Hardman wrote, 'the whole affair is a hoax played off successfully upon *The Times*, which leading journal is in an unapproachable rage in consequence.'

The rage of the leading journal was even more intense on 23 January 1882, when this paragraph appeared in a five-column report of a speech delivered by the Home Secretary, Sir William Harcourt, at Burton-on-Trent:

> I saw in a Tory journal the other day a note of alarm, in which they said, 'Why, if a tenant-farmer is elected for the North Riding of Yorkshire the farmers will be a political power who will have to be reckoned with.' The speaker then said he felt inclined for a bit of fucking. 'I think that is very likely. (Laughter) But I think it is rather an extraordinary thing that the Tory party have not found that out before.'

'No pains have been spared by the management of this journal to discover the author of a gross outrage committed by the interpolation of a line in the speech of Sir William Harcourt reported in our issue of Monday

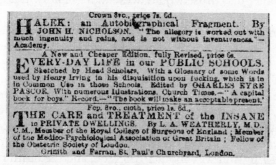

'EVERY-DAY LIFE in our PUBLIC SCHOOLS . . .— A joke played on *The Times*, 12 June 1882.

last,' thundered The Thunderer. 'This malicious fabrication was surreptitiously introduced shortly before the paper went to press. The matter is now under legal investigation, and it is hoped that the perpetrator of the outrage will be brought to punishment.'

Six months later, undeterred by these fearsome warnings, the Demon Joker struck again. Under the classification 'New Books and Editions', this advertisement appeared in *The Times* of 12 June 1882:

> A New and Cheaper Edition, fully revised, price 6s. EVERY-DAY LIFE in our PUBLIC SCHOOLS. Sketched by Head Scholars. With a Glossary of some Words used by Henry Irving in his disquisition upon fucking, which is in Common Use in these Schools. Edited by CHARLES EYRE PASCOE. With numerous illustrations. Church Times – 'A capital book for boys.' Record – 'This book will make an acceptable present.'

XI

Trading in Death

I

In 1841 an imaginative artisan employed at a glass factory at Mexborough near Doncaster manufactured a coffin of clear glass, a quarter of an inch thick and six foot two inches long, with ornaments of blue glass. He bequeathed it to a cousin in Guy's Hospital in trust, so that his cousin could see whether his corpse would decay more rapidly in it than in wood or lead.

The Victorian preoccupation with death – which has been compared with our present-day preoccupation with sex – had many extraordinary manifestations, but none more macabre than the publication of a periodical catering almost exclusively to this strange appetite. It was titled *Death Warrant*. The first issue appeared in January 1844, and may have been the last; the British Museum has no other copy. But the cult of death continued, manifested most spectacularly in the popular passion for elaborate funerals. *Death Warrant* estimated the annual cost of funerals, when the population of England was about 16,000,000, and the death rate 21·55 per thousand, at £4,871,493. Current prices ranged from £100 for a gentleman to fifteen shillings for a pauper. Mrs S. Peel, in *Early Victorian England, 1830–1865*, quotes even higher figures – £1,000 to £1,500 for a nobleman, £250 for a gentleman, £60 to £100 for an upper tradesman and describes the grisly paraphernalia of a Victorian funeral: the four black-plumed horses, the hearse glittering with golden skulls and lacquered cherubs, the hired mutes and mourners, sometimes too drunk to walk. 'An official estimate reckoned that £5,000,000 a year was spent on funerals, of which £4,000,000 went on silk scarves and brass nails, feathers for the horses, gin for the mutes and satin for the worms'.

Punch in 1849 had a poem about 'The Jolly Undertakers':

> *In these hard times, with all around*
> *For bare subsistence striving,*
> *We in employment still abound,*
> *Are prosperous and thriving,*
> *The shoemaker's and the tailor's trade,*
> *The Butcher's and baker's trade,*
> *Will kick the beam, together weigh'd*
> *Against the Undertaker's.*

Chorus
Yes, my hearties, we're the parties
  Who are money-makers;
Gaily working, smiling, smirking,
  Jolly Undertakers.

We envy not the Lawyer's place,
  However large his fee, Sirs;
Our friend, the Doctor, by his case,
  Gets less a deal than we, Sirs,
Oh! we're the lads to make you pay,
  To charge through thick and thin, Sirs;
Yes, we're the boys that know the way,
  And time to stick it in, Sirs.

    Chorus – Yes, my hearties, etc.,

With grief we find the party wild
  With whom we have transaction
A widow who has lost her child,
  Nigh driven to distraction;
A gent, who's ramping raving mad,
  Because his wife's departed:
An orphan, or a mourning dad,
  And either broken-hearted.

    Chorus – Yes, my hearties, etc.,

When tears the choking utterance drown,
  When sighs convulse the bosom,
That's just the time when we comes down
  On customers – and does 'em.
'Bout items folks just then are not
  Parti'lar to a shade, Sir,
We strikes 'em while their grief is hot,
  That's how our money's made, Sirs.

    Chorus – Yes, my hearties, etc.

II

A gentleman might be buried for as little as £250. But in 1852 it cost the British nation £80,000 – say £400,000 in today's money – to bury

Death Warrant.

No. I. | SATURDAY, JANUARY 20, 1844. | PRICE 1½d.

A REPRINTED RECORD OF FACTS—COMPILED FROM AUTHENTIC SOURCES;

Of the most dreadful Battles by Sea and Land ; Horrible and Mysterious Murders, Suicides, Plagues, Pestilences, Famines, Earthquakes, Storms' Shipwrecks, Conflagrations, Death-Beds, and every other appalling Calamity incidental to the life of Man ; forming

THE MOST COMPREHENSIVE COLLECTION OF GRAPHIC AND GLOWING NARRATIVES

Of Wonderful Discoveries, Thrilling Adventures, Scenes of Love in the Court, Camp, and Cottage, Curious Anecdotes, Conspiracies, Trials, Prophetic Warnings," and Sublime Descriptions, exceeding in intensity of agonizing Interest any Work ever published—showing how Man is dazzled and betrayed by the Vanities of the World, and that the real occurrence of this Life far surpass, in an extraordinary degree, any Events which can possibly be depicted in the pages of Fiction and Romance.

"THE DEATH WARRANT" will achieve for the People a Grand Moral Lesson, it will inevitably strike Terror into the Hearts and Minds of Thousands, and bring back to their Memories the too often forgotten but solemn admonition

"IN THE MIDST OF LIFE WE ARE IN DEATH."

A CHECK TO PRIDE AND VANITY.

SPECULUM MISERIÆ ET FRAGILITATIS HUMANÆ

HODIE MIHI CRAS TIBI

My turn To-day, To-morrow yours also.

CONTENTS.

ENGRAVINGS.

EXECUTION OF KING CHARLES—HORRORS OF WAR—GRAVE-DIGGERS PLAYING AT SKITTLES IN ST. ANNE'S CHURCHYARD, SOHO—HOPE LEADING DESPAIR FROM THE CHAMBER OF HORRORS.

OFFICE, 113, STRAND.

Wellington, who was not only a gentleman, but a duke and a field-marshal. Only one member of the House of Commons, Mr Samuel Carter, the member for Tavistock, objected to the vote for this amount, and he found it very difficult to get a hearing. (He had previously upset the House by calling a National Funeral a 'National Folly'.) Shouting above the uproar, Mr Carter said he thought the sum of £80,000 was 'greatly too much'. The vote was agreed to almost without discussion. In the same session a vote of £10,000 for a national art gallery in Edinburgh was rejected.

Dickens agreed with Mr Carter. He was horrified by the pomp and extravagance of the funeral, and the hysteria that accompanied it. 'The whole public has gone mad about the funeral of the Duke,' he wrote to his philanthropic friend Miss Burdett Coutts. 'I think it a grievous thing, a lapse into barbarous practices ... a pernicious corruption of the popular mind just beginning to awaken from the long dream of inconsistencies, monstrosities, horrors and ruinous expenses that has beset all classes of society in connection with death. I shall try and present the case in *House-hold Words*; at present I might as well whistle into the sea.'

Trading in Death, a sardonic attack on England's extravagant and ostentatious funerals, appeared in *Household Words*, Dickens's 'gentle mouthpiece of reform', at the end of November. Dickens denounced the 'unmeaning mummeries, dishonest debt, and profuse waste' associated with funerals, and the competition for 'superior gentility' ... 'the gentility being estimated by the amount of ghastly folly in which the undertaker was permitted to run riot'. No class escaped. The very poor had been forced to form clubs to defray the ruinous cost of funerals. Many of these clubs were conducted by designing villains. They were 'innumerable harpies who possessed no Funeral furniture whatever, but who formed a long file of middlemen between the chief mourner and the real tradesmen, and who hired out the trappings from one to another – passing them on like water-buckets at a fire – every one of them charging enormous percentages on his share of the black job.'

Turning to the State funeral 'in miscalled "honour" of the late Duke of Wellington', Dickens deplored not only the monstrous extravagance of the funeral itself, but the 'general trading spirit which it had awakened, quoting typical advertisements from *The Times*:

First, of seats and refreshments. Passing over that desirable first-floor where a party could be accommodated with 'the use of a piano'; and merely glancing at the decorous daily announcement of 'The Duke of Wellington Funeral Wine', which was in such high demand that immediate orders were necessary; and also 'The Duke of Wellington Funeral Cake', which 'delicious article' could only be had of such a baker; and likewise 'The Funeral Life Preserver', which could only be had of such a tailor; and further 'the celebrated lemon biscuits', at one and fourpence per pound, which were considered by the manufacturer as the only infallible assuagers of the national grief; let us pass in review some of the more eligible opportunities the public had of profiting by the occasion . . .

FUNERAL, including Beds the night previous – To be LET, a second floor, of three rooms, two windows, having a good view of the procession. Terms including refreshment, 10 guineas. Single places, including bed and breakfast, from 15s.

SEATS and WINDOWS to be LET, in the best part of the STRAND, a few doors from Coutts's banking-house. First floor windows, £8 each, second floor, £5.10s each; third floor, £3.10s each; two plate-glass shop windows, £7 each.

The DUKE'S FUNERAL – Terms very moderate – Two FIRST FLOOR ROOMS, with balcony and private entrance out of the Strand. The larger room capable of holding 15 persons. The small room to be let for eight guineas.

THE DUKE'S FUNERAL – To be LET, a SHOP WINDOW, with seats erected for about 30 for 25 guineas. Also a Furnished First Floor, with two large windows. One of the best views in the whole range from Temple-Bar to St. Paul's. Price 35 guineas. A few single seats one guinea each.

FUNERAL of the Late DUKE of WELLINGTON – To be Let, in the best part of the Strand, a SECOND FLOOR for £10; a Third Floor £7.10, containing two windows in each; front seats in shop, at one guinea.

The DUKE'S FUNERAL – To be LET, for 25 guineas to a genteel family, in one of the most commanding situations in the line of route, a FIRST FLOOR, with safe balcony, and ante-room. Will accommodate 20 persons, with an uninterrupted and extensive view for all. For a family of less number a reduction will be made. Every accommodation will be afforded.

But above all let us not forget the

NOTICE TO CLERGYMEN – T.C. Fleet-street, has reserved for clergymen exclusively, *upon condition only that they appear in their surplices,* FOUR FRONT SEATS at £1 each; four second tier at 15s. each; four third tier, at 12/6d; four fourth tier at 10s; four fifth tier at 7/6d; and four sixth tier, at 5s. All the other seats are respectively 40s, 30s, 15s, 10s.

The anxiety of this enterprising tradesman to get up a reverend tableau in his shop window of four-and-twenty clergyman all on six rows, is particularly commendable, and appears to us to shed a remarkable grace on the solemnity.

Dickens concluded by expressing the hope – a vain hope, it proved – that 'State funerals in this land went down to their tomb, most fitly, in the tasteless and tawdry Car that nodded and shook through the streets of London on the eighteenth of November, eighteen hundred and fifty-two'.

The *Illustrated London News* accompanied its full-page illustration of the 'tasteless and tawdry Car' with the 'Official Account' of it.

The Lord Chamberlain having requested the Superintendents of the Department of Practical Art to suggest a suitable design for the Car, the following are the arrangements which were approved of by her Majesty. The leading idea adopted has been to obtain soldier-like simplicity, with grandeur, solemnity, and reality. Whatever there is – coffin, bier, trophies and metal carriage, are all real, and everything in the nature of a sham has been eschewed. The dimensions have been controlled by the height and width of Temple-bar, which will not admit anything much higher than 17 feet.

The Car, with its various equipments, consists of four stages or com-partments. 1. The coffin was the principal object on the Car; at the summit uncovered, having simply the usual military accoutrements, cap, sword etc., upon it. To shelter the coffin and pall from rain, a small canopy of rich tissue, formed of a pattern suggested by Indian embroi-dery, was supported by halberds. The tissue consisted of silver and silk, woven by Messrs. Keith, of Spitalfields; and at the corners of the halberds were hung chaplets of real laurel. The canopy has been omitted in our representation, by the wish of Professor Semper.
2. The bier was covered with a black velvet pall, diapered alternately with the Duke's crest and Field-Marshal's *bâtons* across, worked in silver, and having rich silver lace fringe of laurel leaves, with the legend 'Blessed are the dead which die in the Lord.' The frieze was embroidered under Mr. Hudson's direction, and worked partly by students of the Female School of Ornamental Art.
3. The platform of the Car is of an architectural treatment, gilt, on which are inscribed the names of the Duke's victories. The construction and modelling were executed by Mr. Jackson, of Rathbone-place. In the centre, at the four sides, are military trophies of modern arms, helmets, guns, flags, and drums, being real implements furnished by the Board of Ordnance.

The whole was placed on a carriage richly ornamented by bronze, about 20 feet long and 11 feet wide.

The *Illustrated London News* was also critical of the commercial exploitation of the funeral. 'The love of gain', it moralized, 'may often be traced through the flimsy veil of sorrow,' and it pointed to many such instances, 'with mild reproof':

Funeral car of the Duke of Wellington.

A few ingenious traders provided for outward show of grief by 'crepe hatbands'; and others, after sympathisingly referring to the public sympathy and patriotic respect, ventured to suggest, as 'the appropriate indicator of public appreciation', 'a new sort of mourning for the occasion'; the advertisers adding, that they 'are in no way desirous of making this a business affair!' In this class we find 'a mourning head dress, suitable for wearing in the Cathedral', and for open air seats – the gear being warm, protecting the throat, and not impeding the view as would a bonnet. Nor was the hair itself forgotten; for the proprietors of the 'incomparable Huile Macassar,' indulged in a sort of historical retrospect, associating their own brilliancy with the glories of the Great Hero. Next, a tailor's firm recommended every one to be provided with a life-preserver, on the 18th; and the proprietor of a bath establishment delicately suggested that 'the luxury of a warm bath will be appreciated by those who have witnessed the Duke's funeral.'

Science was oddly pressed into the aid of the public appreciation of the Pageant, by a few opticians advertising their wares: as 'portable, perspective glasses, for viewing objects within the distance of a mile, so extensively patronized on this occasion,' etc. Another glass 'will surprisingly assist the sight in viewing the procession.' Another announces 'the Best View of the Funeral' for 12s 6d can be obtained by purchasing a glass, 'which will bring out, in a clear and distinct manner, the features of the great men and the most minute objects present on that memorable occasion. . . .'

We now approach a more censurable mode of 'watching the turn of the market,' by the raking up of *relics* and *memorials* of the Great Duke, and advertising them for sale to the highest bidder: though, in some cases, the strange proceeding is qualified by the owner providing that the sums realised shall be appropriated to charitable purposes. First on our list is a 'genuine and unique relic of the late Duke of Wellington – A lady will dispose of a Lock of his Grace's Hair, which can be guaranteed; the date of its being cut, and circumstances of possession, will be imparted to the purchaser. The Owner would not like to part with it under 50 guineas; but is open to a liberal offer.' Again: 'Memento of the late Duke of Wellington – To be disposed of, a Lock of the late illustrious Duke's Hair. Can be guaranteed. The highest offer will be accepted.' Next: 'A valuable relic of the late Duke of Wellington – A lady having in her possession a quantity of the late illustrious Duke's Hair, cut in 1841, is willing to part with a portion of the same for £25. Satisfactory proof will be given of its identity, and of how it came into the owner's possession.' Again: 'A Lock of Hair of the late Duke of Wellington to be disposed of, now in the possession of a widow lady. Cut off the morning the Queen was crowned,' etc., Next: 'The Greatest Relic of the Age – A Lock of the Mane of the Horse the late Duke rode in the Battle of Waterloo. Cut off by the Duchess. The property of a private individual. The most indisputable evidence given of its genuineness. It being supposed that this will, in all probability, be the only piece offered to public competition, the advertiser declines naming a price, but the most liberal offer will be accepted within a week,' etc. Again: 'For sale, a Waistcoat, in good preservation, worn by his Grace some years back, which can be well authenticated as such.' But, more reprehensible, is the following piece of cupidity, from *The Times* of 19th (we omit the name): 'Relic of the Duke of Wellington for sale – The son of the late ——, of Reading, the well-known haircutter, to his Grace the Duke of Wellington at Strathfieldsaye, has a small quantity of Hair, that his father cut from the Duke's head, which he is willing to dispose of. Any one desirous of possessing such a relic of England's Hero, are requested to make their offer for same,' etc. In *The Times* of 21st, also is offered 'a small portion of the Duke's Hair to be disposed of', 'with irrefragable testimony,' etc.

The traffic in autographs has considerably revived since the death of the Duke, for whose letters very large sums have been demanded. *The Times* of Nov. 10 contains thirteen advertisements of these relics for sale: the price asked for a letter, with seal and post-mark, written in 1828, is 20 guineas; of another 15 lines, with envelope, date 1844, £10; but, in the next advertisement, an autograph note, with stamped envelope and seal, is offered for 30 shillings.

A singular memento of the Duke has been preserved, under the following circumstances, and is offered for sale by advertisement in the *Times* of Nov. 12. Several years since, there was published in Italian an ode on the death of Napoleon by Manzoni, which was translated into French by one Angini, of Venice. It appears that the Duke was one day reading a copy of this work in passing through Kent. His Grace, we dare say, was not much struck with its merit, for he tore it to pieces, and threw it out of the carriage window. A gentleman on the road side picked up the fragments, and here they are, offered as a memento of his Grace, – an appropriation never dreamt of by the great Hero.

Dickens remembered the traders in death when he inveighed against the grisly mummery of plumes and mourning-rings, cloaks and crape, in *Great Expectations* (1860–61) and again when he wrote his will in 1869, a year before his death:

> I emphatically direct that I be buried in an inexpensive, unostentatious, and strictly private manner; that no public announcement be made of the time or place of my burial; that at the utmost not more than three plain mourning coaches be employed; and that those who attend my funeral wear no scarf, cloak, black bow, long hat-band or other absurdity ... I conjure my friends on no account to make me the subjects of any monument, memorial, or testimonial whatever.

Despite this emphatic direction, he was buried in Westminster Abbey, and his admirers have set up memorials of him in many parts of London.

Another writer who rejected the funeral trappings of his time was the Rev. Charles Dodgson, who died in 1898, leaving a paper dated June 1873 marked 'Directions regarding my funeral, etc.' in which he had written:

> I request of those who arrange for my funeral that no Pall may be employed and that no hat-bands or scarfs may be worn, at the Funeral or given to any one. Also that it may be a walking funeral, unless the distance or other cause should make that arrangement inconvenient. Also that the Coffin may be quite plain and simple, and that there be not

an inner coffin unless that may be necessary for some reason other than custom.

And generally I request that all the deals be simple and inexpensive, avoiding all things which are done merely for show, and retaining only what is, in the judgment of those who arrange my Funeral requisite for its decent and reverent performance.

I further request that no plumes may be carried, either on the hearse, or on the horses, if there be horses. Also that the Coffin be not black, nor covered with cloth.

Also that there be no expensive monument. I should prefer a small plain head-stone. . . .

Except for the 'small plain head-stone' – for which a monument of three steps surmounted by a marble cross was substituted – Dodgson's instructions were carried out exactly.

III

'The funeral arrangements are usually left in the great measure to the undertaker employed,' said Ward and Lock's *Home Book,* published in the eighteen-seventies as a companion volume to *Mrs. Beeton's Book of Household Management.* 'Everything should be quiet and void of senseless parade, and in this regard it is very satisfactory to see that an improved public taste is leading to the gradual but sure abolition of much of the absurd and ostentatious pageantry which upholders were – and are – so fond of introducing into a ceremonial which can hardly be too simple.' But the procedure which the *Home Book* recommends, despite the improvement in public taste, is still far from simple:

FIRST DUTIES UPON THE OCCASION OF A DEATH IN THE FAMILY

The first sign to the outer world that one of a certain home circle is 'smitten by the common stroke of death,' is the closing of the blinds at the windows of the house and the non-appearance in public of the female members of the family. The next step of the head of the family, or whoever stands in that place for the occasion, is the ordering of the coffin, sending notes to all relations and particular friends apprising them of the mournful intelligence, and despatching obituary notices to the newspapers, which must be prepaid according to the tariff of the different journals . . .

The FUNERAL. The relatives and friends invited arrive at the house at the time appointed (generally in the morning), and being assembled in the library, or other suitable room are each provided by the undertaker with a hatband, scarf, and pair of gloves. Ladies do not usually follow, but there are frequent exceptions to the rule. When they do so, they do not leave their own rooms until the procession is about to start, when they proceed at once to the mourning coach or coaches provided for them. In the order of procession, both to the church or cemetery and in the ground, the nearest relative follows next to the hearse or the coffin, and the others according to their nearness of kindred to the deceased. The empty broughams, etc., of acquaintances, sent out of compliment, come of course last in the cortège . . .

MOURNING. Ladies if chief mourners wear dresses made of stuff and crape only, and gentlemen black suits and neckties, a crape scarf worn across one shoulder and crape hatband. Those not related to the deceased wear black with moderate-sized hatband and black gloves.

XII

The Democracy of Drink

I

Drink, like sex, is a great leveller. The three nations which made up Victorian England were united at least in a democracy of drunkenness. In 1860 a gloomy statistician pointed out that while the country had a licensed victualler to every 202 of the population, there was only a parish church to every 1,384.

Gin was the anaesthetic of the working-class. Its introduction into England from Holland in 1735 was described by the historian W. H. Lecky as more momentous an event than any in the purely political or

DISGRACEFUL SCENE IN THE STREETS OF BIRMINGHAM.—UPROARIOUS CONDUCT OF DRUNKEN WOMEN.

military annals of the country. It was originally sold by apothecaries as a diuretic, but within a generation it had converted the English masses into a spirit-, as well as a beer-drinking people. Henry Fielding, towards the middle of the eighteenth century, said it formed the 'principal diet' of more than a hundred thousand Londoners. This was the London of Hogarth's horrifying 'Gin Lane', with the inscription over a gin-shop door: 'Drunk for a penny. Dead drunk for Twopence. Clean Straw for Nothing.'

A century later, as the cheapest spirit, gin was still responsible for most of the drunkenness in England. In the 1870s it cost 8d. a pint; rum was a little dearer, brandy and whisky half as dear again. Beer was from 1½d. to 3d. a pint. Temperance societies fought to stem the flow of ardent liquors. At the annual meeting of the United Kingdom Alliance in 1870 Sir William Lawson, M.P., suggested that England should not send out its idle workers to the colonies, but its 150,000 publicans, who were responsible for the prevailing misery of the masses. Also on the platform was the Baboo Keshub Chunder Sen of Calcutta, who declared impassionedly that the English, 'besides giving India the steam-engine and the telegraph, and enlightening the mind so as to receive *Shakespeare* and *Milton*, had also given the inhabitants of India the brandy-bottle, which was becoming such a curse that the widows and orphans, who were desolated by its use, hated the Government which made that and opium the traffic by which it raised its revenues.'

At about the same time *The Days' Doings* reported on the 'Uproarious Conduct of Drunken Women' in the streets of Birmingham, and on the curious engine employed by the police to deal with them:

Swaying up and down this lane was a vast miscellaneous crowd, laughing and shouting in the most uproarious manner; and in front of this crowd, the foremost rank of which made a circle like a bull-ring, in all the stages of drunkenness – but chiefly in the most helpless stage – there were in the midst a number of respectably-dressed women, tumbling, shouting, gesticulating, in the wildest fashion conceivable . . . The drunken women squatted themselves on the pavement, and howling and laughing by turns, invited the officers 'to come on'; while the boys, delighted with this determined attitude, cheered for the 'ladies' and then called on the 'Bobby' to 'go in and win'! But the officer was equal to the occasion; he saw the situation, and beat a retreat through the crowd amid cries of 'He's gone for the carriage', 'He'll settle 'em.' The mirth went on increasing, a few only protesting that it was a glaring outrage, a public scandal and so on, but the majority considering it 'as good as a play . . .' . . . Presently five policemen were seen approaching at a quick pace, pushing a curious kind of brown wickerwork carriage, mounted on four strong low wheels – a sort of giant perambulator, so constructed that its occupant might recline at full length. The laughter with which this cumbrous vehicle was received was hearty and general. The police advanced into the yard, and soon reappeared with the corporation perambulator occupied by one of the lady bacchantes. From the momentary glance obtained in the surging mass of people who rushed after the perambulator, one plump-faced matron was seen stretched at full length, winking, smiling, nodding, and kissing her hand to her hel-

meted escort ... How this happened is thus explained:– There is a
public-house down Coach-yard, having an entrance from Bull-street,
where married women, in respectable circumstances, meet every
morning to drink, and occasionally get drunk, as they did on Tuesday.

If these are the habits of 'married women in respectable circumstances'

THE DERBY NIGHT AT CREMORNE – KEEPING IT UP.

we are rather curious as to the doings of those who are lower in the
social scale. Perambulators, with their infantile occupants, are not the
most delightful vehicles to encounter in crowded thoroughfares; but
the 'giant perambulator of wickerwork' must be an unmitigated
nuisance. Is it a sign of the times in Birmingham? If it is, it might be
worthy of inquiry as to how far certain other 'signs' are answerable for
the disgraceful necessity of keeping such a vehicle at the public charge.

II

The matrons of Birmingham were gin-drinkers. The matrons of Belgravia preferred sherry and champagne, or a curious confection made by soaking lump-sugar in eau-de-Cologne. While *The Days' Doings* was lashing one group of tipplers, the *Saturday Review* was concerned with the other. In an article titled 'Drawing-room Alcoholism' it deplored this as

an increasing evil under the sun, one of pressing importance, but so contrary to our English traditions, and our notion of the fitness of

From 'London Sketches' by E. G. Dalziel. 'Sunday Afternoon, 1 p.m. Waiting for the Public House to Open.'

things, that we are unwisely inclined to hush it up . . . Yet some sincere effort should be made to check habits which are notoriously on the increase, and which threaten to degrade women even of the well-born and educated classes . . . It would seem that our doctors are too professional, our clergymen not professional enough, for candour on this ugly topic.

The literature of Temperance societies and police reports does not affect the divinities of our Olympus, who hardly guess the striking resemblance between their nectar and the gin of the 'masses'. Yet something should be done to startle ignorant and well-meaning lady-tipplers

A QUIET FIZZ DINNER FOR TEN, AFTER THE GOLD CUP AT ASCOT

who do not imagine it possible that they should approach, and even rival, Irish biddies of St. Giles in their craving for and absorption of alcohol.

Vice in women, said the *Saturday Review*, was 'almost more fatal to social safety' than crime in men, for custom was more than law in the conduct of a people, and women, especially the women of the upper classes, had large control over custom:

The rich escape the publicity of their practices which befalls our poor ... but there is reason to believe that the frequent 'pick me up,' the midday and afternoon sherry or champagne, may have much to do with the pace at which young men and maidens, old men and children, Mayfair mothers and Belgravian beauties, are posting downhill.

The *Saturday Review* rather ungallantly added that women's brains were not their strongest point. They had plenty of imagination but not much will to spare, and were therefore specially liable to the depression which was aggravated by alcohol. Their demoralization was extremely rapid once they had taken to 'pegs' between meals. And they showed extraordinary craft in maintaining their supply:

The devices of lovers seem poor in comparison with the skill with which she will make raids on the cellar, supply herself with strong waters in perfume bottles, and establish relations with the nearest public-house. She will bribe, lie, and steal, sacrifice credit, position, and the affection of those dear to her, sooner than do without the stimulant for which her brain and whole system calls imperiously. And, poor wretch, though she has no illusion about the evil case she is in, she can't help herself when once she is alcoholized to a certain point. We could multiply stories of the shifts to which well fenced-in ladies have been reduced when in their own homes spirits were not easily attainable; how one took to stealing the spirits of wine used for lamps, and another employed an old clo' man to fetch her champagne. The strategy used to secure the private drams of London ladies would suffice to outwit Bismark, Von Moltke, and all their following, and would baffle an Asmodeus.

Equally ungallant was the *Saturday Review*'s confident statement that women seldom drank for the gratification of their palate. 'Good or bad wine, potato brandy, curaçao or gin will satisfy her if only her nervous organisation be sufficiently saturated.'

The daughters of these tipplers, said the *Saturday Review*, would be dependent for their 'go' in society on copious champagne and frequent sherry. They would join 'the increasing mob of fast girls', with all that was involved in that evil:

We are sensible of a distinct moral relaxation among women, and of a new sort of unwomanly recklessness in the presence of men. We complain of a prevalent coarseness even among the virtuous, not only of manner, but of imagination and pursuits, and we are sometimes tempted to prefer the age of Nell Gwynne or Madame de Pompadour to the actual confusion of daredevil women and unabashed spinsters. It would seem that alcohol has something to do with this disorder ...

Both the *Saturday Review* and *The Days' Doings* would no doubt have been interested in the letter which Mr Gladstone wrote to his wife in October 1864: 'Mrs Bruce says the Queen was not well; and it seems she drinks her claret strengthened, I should have thought spoiled, with whisky.'

XIII

Children for Sale

I

One night in June 1886 a short man with a reddish beard and piercing blue eyes stood in the room of a notorious brothel in Poland Street, Soho, looking at a young girl who lay on a bed around which lingered the sickly smell of chloroform. He was William Stead, the thirty-seven-year-old son of a Yorkshire Congregational Minister and the editor of the influential London evening paper, the *Pall Mall Gazette*. The tableau was equivocal, but Mr Stead's intentions were not only honourable, but messianic. To understand what the famous editor was doing in the infamous house, it is necessary to go back to 1881, when a Committee of the House of Lords sat for many days listening to evidence about the export of English girls to foreign brothels and the prevalence of child prostitution in London.

In 1880 Mr Benjamin Scott, Chamberlain of the City of London, had set up a Committee for the Suppression of Foreign Traffic in English Girls – a traffic that dated back at least to the middle of the century. (A letter to *The Times* in the early 'fifties mentioned a two-way traffic in English and German girls, who were exchanged in batches.) Scott and his helpers found that men in London were selling English girls to brothels in Holland and Belgium. He presented a report to the Foreign Secretary, Lord Granville, who commissioned Mr Thomas William Snagge, a London barrister, to collect more evidence in Brussels. Snagge confirmed and amplified Mr Scott's findings. The problem was referred to the Under-Secretary of the Home Office, Lord Dalhousie, but there was no law on the statute-books to deal with the traffic, and Dalhousie set up a committee to inquire into ways of suppressing it.

As a result of Snagge's investigations, two Englishmen and a woman were sent to prison by a Belgian court on a charge of '*excitation à la débauche d'une fille mineure*'. These three had been the principal London exporters of girls since 1877, but before then Snagge reported that the leading merchant – or, in the language of the trade, *placeur* – was a Dutchman called Klyberg, who operated from premises in Dean Street, Soho. He had been dealing in girls for about twelve years when he was extradited and sentenced to two years' imprisonment after Dutch police, inspecting brothels in Amsterdam and the Hague, found many business letters he had written to brothel-keepers. Klyberg was an industrious and persuasive correspondent.

One of his typical sales-letters, sent from London in April 1876, read:

My dear Xavier:
I have several beauties, . . . let me know whether they will do for you at No. 4, or for Simon . . . Answer please by return post if you will send somebody over to London to take them.

A week or so later, he wrote:

My dear Xavier:
Mr. Citron has told me that you require two pretty English girls. I have the very thing for you . . .

Klyberg's scale of charges was rigid and explicit: '150 francs (£1) per package [per *colis*]' f.o.b. London, or 300 francs, delivered at Ostend. He always advised his clients to save forwarding charges by collecting the 'packages' in London. In one letter to 'dear Xavier' he shows a curious fastidiousness:

Monsieur Lemoine has written to me on behalf of Quoilin who is willing to pay me 300 francs per package, I have replied that I do not transact business with such *canaille*.

But this prejudice against dealing with *canaille* did not last long. Soon after, he writes to 'My dear Quoilin':

I have a fine, tall, dark girl, beautiful teeth, fine bust, in a word a handsome woman and a good girl . . . I have also a tall fair girl . . . It is cheaper to come and collect the packages than to have them forwarded. It costs half the price that you pay in your own house.

When the fair *colis* remained unsold, Klyberg sent Quoilin a more compelling description:

I do not wish you to miss this fine opportunity. One does not find such a package every 6 months. There is no comparison with the other fair girl who is at the Hague . . . My wife has examined her. She is quite healthy, well clad, silk dress, very lady-like [*très distinguée*], in a word, the very thing for you . . . It is a find [*une trouvaille*] so answer my telegram at once.

These transactions were completely out of the jurisdiction of the English courts, while the *placeur* protected himself from French and Belgian law by buying from Somerset House, for three shillings and sevenpence each, false certificates of birth for his 'parcels'. As Klyberg wrote to one of his clients: 'There is no danger. They can do nothing to you in London.'

Mr Snagge continued his investigations and was the first witness called before the House of Lords Committee, which was under the chairmanship of Earl Cairns, 'the first lawyer of his time', and included other distinguished judges. Cairns, despite a crowded career in law and politics, remained all his life an Evangelical Sunday school teacher. Other members of the Committee were the Marquis of Salisbury and the Bishop of London. They listened patiently as Mr Snagge related, sometimes in clinical and horrible detail, the practices of the *placeurs*, and read candid statements from English girls who had been their victims. The inquiry then shifted to the even more unpleasant subject of child prostitution in London, which the Lords were told had greatly increased in recent years.

The most important witness to this was Mr (afterwards Sir Charles) Howard Vincent, Director of Criminal Investigations at Scotland Yard, who expressed the opinion that 'juvenile' prostitution prevailed in London to an extent unequalled in any European city. He explained that the existing laws gave no protection to girls over the age of thirteen, and mentioned houses 'in many parts of London' where people would procure 'without difficulty whatever . . . children without number at 14, 15, and 16 years of age'. Children as young as this were openly soliciting in the Haymarket, Waterloo Place, and Piccadilly. He was keenly questioned about the deficiency of the law:

Q. With regard to children of this age, or any age, who are soliciting prostitution in the streets, the police have no power at all?
A. No power whatever.
Q. Only to keep order?
A. Only to keep order – and the consequence is that the state of affairs is such that from four o'clock, or . . . from 3 o'clock, in the afternoon, it is impossible for any respectable woman to walk from the top of Haymarket to Wellington Street, Strand. From 3 and 4 o'clock in the afternoon Villiers Street and Charing Cross Station and the Strand, are crowded with prostitutes openly soliciting in the broad daylight.

Mr Howard Vincent said that, according to a recent calculation, at half past twelve at night there were five hundred prostitutes between Piccadilly Circus and the bottom of Waterloo Place – a distance of 440 yards. 'A boy must be a paragon of virtue,' he said, 'who, at 16 or 17, can walk from 11 o'clock at night till half past 12 in the morning, from the top of Haymarket to the top of Grosvenor Place, without being solicited to such an enormous extent, that he is almost certain to fall. . . . There is scarcely a senior boy at Eton, a cadet at Sandhurst, or a subaltern in the army, who will not agree with me as to the enormous danger. . . .'

Questioned again about child prostitution, he repeated emphatically that 'the prostitution of very young children' was 'peculiar to London as compared with towns on the Continent' and that 'the defect of the law in England . . . as compared with the laws of other countries' was responsible.

Mr Howard Vincent was supported by Superintendent Joseph Henry Dunlap, who had been in charge of the C Division of the Metropolitan Police – the St James's District – for thirteen years. Superintendent Dunlap, quoting first-hand knowledge, said he would be 'within the bounds of prudence in saying that "juvenile" in his division referred to child prostitutes of 12 years'. He told the Committee of a recent visit to a brothel in Windmill Street, where he had executed a warrant. The brothel was above a saddler's shop, and had three rooms. In each of these rooms he found 'an elderly gentleman' in bed with two children 'who laughed and joked with him'. The girls cheerfully explained the economics of the triangular arrangement. Each girl received six shillings from the gentleman, who also paid his host six shillings for the use of the bed. If only one girl was provided, the room charge was reduced to four shillings, but on the occasion of the Superintendent's visit, each of the three gentlemen had booked in at the two-girl rate of eighteen shillings, *tout compris.*

Superintendent Dunlap said the prostitution of these very young children was a new thing to him. It had developed within the last two years. He mentioned a case that had occurred that morning:

> We had two lads charged at my station with attempting to steal from a carriage in Bond Street, and saw the 'Dialonians' [residents of Seven Dials] as they are called amongst us, waiting round the Station for the police van to come. Among them was a little child who had high boots buttoned halfway up her legs; she had very short petticoats, her hair was down her back, and she wore a tight-fitting polonaise . . . Her fingers were covered with rings . . . I went outside and endeavoured to get into conversation with her. She said she was waiting to see her man go down . . . I should say her age was not above 13.

Other witnesses told even more horrible stories of child prostitution. A gaol chaplain said many girls began to sell themselves at the age of seven or eight.

'Nothing more cruel, appalling or detestable could be found in the history of crime all over the world,' was Lord Shaftesbury's comment. But the British public, though still capable of weeping over the plight of little girls in three-volume novels, seemed curiously unmoved by the Committee's report on the traffic in living girls. Nor was a greater concern apparent at Westminster. The Committee recommended strengthening the law to deal with the traffic, specifically by raising the age of consent from thirteen to sixteen, by allowing children under eight to give evidence, and by making procuring an indictable offence. But it was two years before

H

Gladstone's ministry introduced a bill along these lines, and though this was twice passed by the Lords, it was talked out, counted out, and blocked out in the House of Commons, session after session. The determined opposition to it derived from many sources. There were old-world individualists, champions of *laissez-faire*, in sex as well as in commerce, who thought the bill an impertinent and fanatical intrusion on the private lives of English gentlemen; liberals who feared that raising the age of consent would encourage blackmail and extortion; radicals who argued that Parliament should remedy the conditions that bred child prostitution rather than make a hopeless attempt to suppress it; and, according to some students of the period, a little group of wicked men who had a financial interest in bawdy-houses.

While the Lords were hearing these reports on the melancholy state of London's morals, correspondents to *The Times* were lamenting about the annual saturnalia of the Kentish hop-pickers. Maidstone, it seemed was the centre of some rather uninhibited revels. Its high street was 'thronged with drunken men and women' and the side streets and alleys 'blocked with human beings prostrated with drink'. *The Times* in a judicial summing-up described the hop-pickers as 'men women and young children, who live together, drink together and sleep together without any of the separation, order or decency observed in the lowest stages of civilised society'.

> Hop-gardens themselves are admirably adapted to the game of hide-and-seek. They are equivalent to the woods, the groves, and the hangings in which in every age the wildest orgies have been celebrated. 20, or 30,000 people living for weeks in rather worse than a state of nature is a trifle to our statesmen and philanthropists.

II

The Criminal Law Amendment Bill, introduced again in the spring of 1885, was talked out in the House of Commons on 22 May. Next day Mr Benjamin Scott, now an old man of seventy-five, called at the office of the *Pall Mall Gazette* 'in great distress' and asked to see the editor. Stead, who had come to London from nine years' editorship of the Darlington *Northern Echo* was a brilliant, imaginative, courageous journalist, but a narrow-minded, egocentric, and emotionally unbalanced man. He had a quench-less Puritan zeal to regenerate the world and was quite sure the Lord had appointed him to the task, but he was not so sure how he was expected to go about it. (He once wrote that God seized him 'by the back of the neck and the seat of the breeches' to go forth and do His bidding.) George Bernard Shaw, a contributor to the *Pall Mall Gazette*, found him a 'stu-

THE
DARKEST ✠ ENGLAND
GAZETTE.

The Official Newspaper of the Social Operations of The Salvation Army.

INTERNATIONAL HEADQUARTERS. [Registered at the G.P.O. as a Newspaper.] 101, QUEEN VICTORIA STREET, E.C.

No. 9. | LONDON, SATURDAY, AUG. 26, 1893. | Price, One Penny.

THE MIDNIGHT INFAMIES OF PICCADILLY.
A WHIRLPOOL OF INIQUITY AND SHAME.

pendously ignorant person whose indignations did him credit but with whom a cultured mind could make no contact'. He seems to have been without humour, though his telegraphic address was 'Vatican, London'.

By his middle twenties, Stead had lost faith in republicanism, democracy, international arbitration, land reform, 'the regenerating power of education, of legislation, of almost everything except God's spirit'. He retained, of course, his belief in the importance of his message, which at this time had something to do with England's duty to civilize the 'weaker, more degraded nations of the earth'. Later, he discovered that his mandate was to be a 'Christ in politics' and to organize 'Government by Journalism'.

To a missionary in search of a mission, Mr Benjamin Scott, on this bright May morning, must have come like an appointed messenger of the Lord – even if what he told Stead about life in London was a bit hard to reconcile with England's divine role as the universal dispenser of civilization.

Scott said that for six years the horrors of the traffic in girls had been with him every waking minute, and now, for the third time, the bill was lost. 'Can you not do anything about it?' he asked Stead. 'You are the only man in the country who can save it. Will you try?'

A fellow worker on Scott's committee, Mrs Josephine Butler, repeated the appeal. Mrs Butler, wife of a canon of Winchester Cathedral, was the remarkable woman who for sixteen years had fought for the repeal of the Contagious Diseases Acts under which prostitutes in eleven English garrison towns had to submit to registration and medical examination.

Stead went to Scotland Yard and asked Howard Vincent if it was true that 'unwilling virgins' were being 'purveyed and procured to rich men at so much a head by brothel-keepers?'

'Certainly,' Vincent replied.

'Why, the very thought is enough to raise hell.'

'It is true and although it ought to raise hell it does not even rouse the neighbours.'

'Then *I* will raise hell!' said Stead.

He told Benjamin Scott and Mrs Butler how he proposed to do it. To convince the Government that it was necessary to put through the long-delayed bill he would himself buy a young girl, ostensibly for seduction, and publish the naked facts of the transaction in the *Pall Mall Gazette*. Mrs Butler enthusiastically agreed to help. She conducted a House of Rest – 'Hope Cottage' – for fallen women at Winchester. Among them was Mrs Rebecca Jarrett, who, in her own words, had been seduced as a child of fifteen by a 'person of position' and 'thrown aside'. For many years, she had kept 'gay houses' in London, Bristol and Manchester, with interludes of repentance and honest work. During one of these she had worked as an ironer at Claridge's for less than two pounds a month. Mrs Butler sent Mrs

Jarrett to see Stead, who questioned her about the *modus operandi* of brothel-keepers. She gave him details 'of a very ghastly character' and told him it was 'quite an ordinary thing' for a customer to order young virgins, confessing that she had herself procured many. Stead told her that if she had done this, she ought to be 'damned and hanged'. Alternatively, she could make reparation by helping him to expose the traffic.

'Will you go and buy for me one, two, or more girls who are in stock and who will probably be sold to someone else if you do not buy them?' Stead asked. He himself would play the part of the male customer 'in every detail short of actually consummating the crime'. At first Mrs Jarrett demurred, but Stead was 'as ruthless as death', and forced her to agree. He discussed his plan with many eminent people. Cardinal Manning, the Bishop of London, Dr Temple, and Bramwell Booth, chief of staff of the Salvation Army, approved of it. The Archbishop of Canterbury sympathized with Stead's motive, but shuddered at his method. And Howard Vincent warned him, as an experienced police officer, of the danger of the consequences. But Stead now had a clamant and irresistible message; the Lord had seized him firmly by the breeches.

Mrs Jarrett, once persuaded, went about her task with enthusiasm and expertise. To give colour to her assumed role of procuress, she took lodgings in Albany street, apparently a good trade address, from which she explored her old haunts in Whitechapel. But no girl was immediately available there, so she took her problem to Mrs Broughton, a former workmate at Claridge's, who lived at Lisson Grove.

When Mr Broughton was out of earshot, Mrs Jarrett came straight to the point.

'Nancy, do you know what I have come up for?'

'No.'

'I have a gentleman at my house who wants a girl. She must be pure. If you will help me to get one I will pay you for your trouble.'

While Mrs Broughton was considering, a young girl passed through the passage. Mrs Jarrett asked how old she was. Mrs Broughton said 'about sixteen'. Mrs Jarrett said that was too old. She wanted one between thirteen and fourteen. Mrs Broughton then remembered that her neighbour, Mrs Armstrong, had a daughter of thirteen, Eliza. She would introduce Mrs Jarrett to her. It is impossible to say what now took place. According to Mrs Jarrett's first story, which Stead and his friends accepted, Mrs Armstrong handed over her daughter, believing she was going to a brothel, after receiving a sovereign deposit, with the promise of two more when the girl's virginity was certified; Mrs Broughton, as the broker, received two pounds. Mr Armstrong, a former soldier turned chimney-sweep, who was drunk during the discussions, thought his daughter was going into a 'situation' and took no interest in the transaction. Later,

when Eliza had become a national sensation, Mrs Armstrong claimed that
she, like her husband, believed her daughter was going into service.
Possibly her memory, too, was blurred by alcohol. On the day when Eliza
was handed over Mr Armstrong had come home drunk and knocked her
down because she wanted to go to a funeral. She then got drunk and was
picked up in the street by the police.

Benjamin Scott had introduced Stead to a former Greek war correspondent called Sampson Jacques, one of the investigators for Mr Scott's
Committee. Jacques told Stead of a French midwife, Madame Mourey,
who was employed by fashionable London brothel-keepers to certify the
virginity of young girls. Her fee for this service was one guinea. On
Derby Day, Stead instructed Jacques to engage Madame Mourey for the
following evening: 'I told him', Stead said, 'to represent himself as the
cousin of a rich American, I being that American, who had a taste for little
girls'. It was probably the patriot in Stead that dictated the change of
nationality. Madame Mourey, in accepting the commission, offered
Jacques, on behalf of his 'rich cousin', friendly advice. She said she was in
the habit of certifying children for a one-armed gentleman, a valuable
client. She advised Mr Jacques to do as her one-armed client did – to go
down to Whitechapel, when girls were at their dinner hour, or at night,
and pick up a girl for himself. It was 'quickest and easiest'. Madame
Mourey also mentioned that she supplied drugs to the one-armed gentleman, for the purpose of lessening the resistance of his girls.

Eliza, equipped with a new dress, was taken by Mrs Jarrett to Albany
Street, where she and her hostess drank beer. Soon after, Stead arrived and
asked Eliza if she went to school. She said 'Yes'. Stead asked what school?
'The Board School.' Did she go to Sunday school? 'Yes, to Harrow Road
Sunday school in the morning and afternoon and the Richmond Street
school on Sunday nights.'

The purpose of these questions was obscure, and the conversation soon
flagged. Mrs Jarrett proposed that Eliza should have her hair cut short,
with a 'Piccadilly fringe' over the forehead, but Eliza refused. Mrs
Jarrett then took her to Madame Mourey's residence in Milton Street,
where Jacques was waiting. Here she was 'indecently examined' by
Madame Mourey, whom she described to Mrs Jarrett as a 'nasty woman'.
Mrs Jarrett then took her to the Poland Street brothel and told her to get
into bed. Mrs Jarrett lay down beside her, and gave her a chloroform-
soaked handkerchief, telling her to take a 'good sniff'. Eliza did not inhale
deeply, and was conscious when Stead came into the room. She called
out: 'There is a man in the room.' Mrs Jarrett said there was not. When
Eliza persisted, Mrs Jarrett told her to get up 'as there were too many men
in the house'. It was now after midnight. Mrs Jarrett and Eliza dressed,
and drove to a house in Nottingham Place, where Dr Haywood Smith,

of Harley Street, examined Eliza, and certified that she was still virgin. About 3 a.m. Eliza was driven in a cab to a Salvation Army home in the country, and then taken to Paris, where she stayed in the care of the Army for some months.

She seems to have accepted her unusual experiences with equanimity. From Paris she wrote an affectionate letter to Mrs Jarrett which finished with this verse:

> *As I was lying in my bed,*
> *Some little thoughts came into my head,*
> *I thought of one, I thought of two,*
> *But most of all, I thought of you.*

III

Stead now set up a 'Secret Commission' to collect more facts about the sale of young girls to brothels. 'With the aid of a few faithful friends,' he said, 'I went disguised to the lowest haunts of criminal vice and obtained only too ample proof of the reality and extent of the evils.' Stead's crusading zeal was admirable, but he was not the ideal investigator. Like every fanatical Puritan, he was obsessed with sex. Havelock Ellis recalled that whenever he and Stead met, sex was the main topic of conversation; Ellis thought Stead's 'repressive sexuality ... was the motive force of many of his activities'. Stead and his helpers used assumed names when they visited brothels, and to perfect his disguise, Stead, a lifelong teetotaller and non-smoker, bravely participated in the traditional man-about-town ritual of champagne and cigars. This must have been somewhat of an ordeal, but it is doubtful if he found all his experiences as an investigator quite as unpleasant; for example, he describes a scene at a procuress's when a young girl was made to go through 'all sorts of movements' to display her marketable qualities.

Valuable material for a social history of the 'eighties is preserved in Stead's voluminous notes of his conversations with madams and procuresses. Some of this was used, discreetly disguised, in his *Pall Mall Gazette* articles, but much remains unpublished. 'Carroty Kate', in three pages of disclosures, gave Stead the names of many well-known 'old gentlemen', including an earl, who were regular buyers of little girls, and he was told of an elegant brothel in St John's Wood patronized by a prince (unidentified) and by cabinet ministers. When this was mentioned in the House of Commons, a Conservative member was happy to point out that the cabinet ministers were Liberals. It was a period when, by the dual morality of the Victorians, the brothel was still 'respectable'. J. W. Robertson Scott, in his biography of the *Pall Mall Gazette*, recalls the death in a London brothel of a Judge of the High Court. A few years before there had been a scandal when Inspector Minahan claimed he had been dismissed from the London police force for reporting that Mrs Jeffries's house in Chelsea was 'a brothel for the nobility'.

By the end of June Stead and his 'Secret Commission' had amassed enough material to launch the campaign in the *Pall Mall Gazette*. Sitting up all night with a wet towel round his forehead, he dictated to three short-hand writers the first of four articles on 'The Maiden Tribute to Modern Babylon'. It is apparent from the febrile excitement of his prose that the towel dried long before the articles were finished. Under the heading 'A Child of Thirteen Bought for Five Pounds', Stead told the story of Eliza Armstrong, whom he called 'Lily', with no surname, and giving no hint that the transaction had been fabricated. In a leader accompanying the first article, he wrote:

> The report of our Secret Commission will be read today with a shudder-ing horror that will thrill throughout the world. After this awful picture of the crimes committed, as it were under the very aegis of the law, has been fully unfolded . . . we need not doubt that the House of Commons will find time to raise the age during which English girls are protected from inexpiable wrong.

Stead did not overestimate the effect of the articles, nor understate the horrors they exposed. He wrote of Madame Jeffries 'patching up' virgins for aristocratic clients, of fourteen-year-old-girls in a Half Moon Street brothel being tied hand and foot to the four corners of a bed for the convenience of idiosyncratic patrons, of a West End villa with thickly padded rooms in which, he was assured, 'you can gloat over the cries of the girls with the certainty that no one will hear them besides yourself'. He described a visit to a house in Marylebone Road when a procuress had arranged to deliver five virgins to him in a batch. It was all very business-like. The girls were examined for virginity, and signed papers agreeing to their seduction.

Similar disclosures had been made to the House of Lords Committee five years before without much effect. But there was a big difference between the sober phrases of a judicial report, buried inconspicuously in *The Times*, and the flamboyant prose of an emotional journalist, flaunted in the *Pall Mall Gazette* day after day. England reacted convulsively to Stead's articles. In Lord Snell's words, she was 'stripped naked and shamed before the world, and she did not like it. Such things might happen on the wicked Continent but that anyone should say that these occurred in Pimlico, under the very shadow of the home of "our dear Queen", was an indefensible and wanton outrage.'

In what Snell describes as 'the savage cry of resentment against the man who had exposed the loathsome traffic', port-swilling patriots, uncharitable men of letters, and indignant brothel-keepers were curiously united: 'The music halls inflamed the tempers of their patrons with patriotic guff accompanied with as much lubricity as could be safely introduced into rhyme and gesture.' And Robertson Scott writes of the 'shocking way in which men of some literary eminence ranged themselves against Stead'. Among them were Edmund Gosse, who wrote 'sanctimoniously' to Robert Louis Stevenson of Stead's 'spurious revelations', and W. E. Henley, who referred to the Lord's messenger as 'Bed-Stead'. Gosse, apparently, had not heard of the report of the Dalhousie committee.

For the most part, the London press, Liberal and Conservative alike, joined in a chorus of execration. Editors took the view that the crimes Stead had exposed were to be preferred to the crime of exposing them. 'A plague worse than any Egyptian plague has visited the homes of England,' said the *Weekly Times*. Every boy and girl in England would be 'tainted by the disgusting pabulum'. Another paper protested against the streets 'being turned into a market for literature which appeals to the lascivious curiosity of every casual passer-by and excites the latent pruriency of a half-educated crowd'. Some members of this crowd demonstrated angrily, it is not clear against what, unless it was the difficulty of buying copies of the paper, outside the *Pall Mall Gazette* offices in Northumberland Street, breaking a few windows in their excitement. An eye-witness said the scene had not been equalled in London since the office of *Bell's Life* was besieged after the famous Sayers–Heenan prize-fight in 1860. It was two days before Scotland Yard acknowledged Stead's request for police protection. Meanwhile, among the hundreds of congratulatory letters he received was an offer from 'a pretty good heavy-weight' of a body-guard of boxers, professional and amateur.

Later the London press became more sympathetic. A notable exception was the *Evening News*, which Frank Harris was editing. Why this indomitable lecher should have attacked Stead is puzzling, unless he was personally interested in maintaining the supply of young virgins. Some months after the revelations he wrote:

The hideous narratives of obscene practices which Stead professed to have revealed were based merely on gossip he had picked up from prostitutes when wandering about brothels 'in a state of intense mental excitement' and obfuscation due to unwonted indulgence in champagne and cigars.

W. H. Smith & Sons banned the *Pall Mall Gazette* from their bookstalls, and George Bernard Shaw offered to take as many copies as he could carry and peddle them in the streets. Mr Cavendish Bentinck, one of the most tenacious opponents of the Criminal Law Amendment Bill in its many presentations, asked the Home Secretary whether any means existed 'of subjecting the author and publishers of these objectionable publications to criminal proceedings'. The Home Secretary replied politely that the publication of obscene matter could be prosecuted by indictment in the usual way. But the only action taken was against eleven newsboys who were charged with causing obstruction and selling copies of a paper containing indecent literature – the *Pall Mall Gazette*. The Lord Mayor of London, before whom they appeared, said the editor of the paper had been 'influenced by high and honourable views'.

Letters of congratulations poured in to Stead's office from many important people, including Lord Shaftesbury, Lord Dalhousie, Dr Clifford, Canon Wilberforce, Mr Spurgeon, Professor Sylvanus Thompson, and Mr Ernest Hart, editor of the *British Medical Journal*. Mr Hart, in a powerful editorial, acclaimed Stead's social surgery: 'Desperate diseases need strong remedies.' The *Pall Mall Gazette* had applied the knife 'publicly, red-hot, and with an unsparing hand'.

On a hot Saturday afternoon at the end of August more than 250,000 people took part in a febrile demonstration in Hyde Park. A huge crowd of men and women streamed along Piccadilly to the park, bearing a white banner inscribed 'Honour to the *Pall Mall Gazette*'. Many carried white roses, symbols of purity. Stead rode among them in a wagon, acknowledging the shouts of 'Long life to Stead'. In the park, speeches went on for hours till the 'citizens of London' in a mighty resolution, declared 'their shame and indignation with regard to the evils' Stead had exposed. Among the citizens were unrepentant prostitutes who found the occasion favourable to trade, and energetic hawkers offering copies of a pornographic magazine called *The Devil*, the cover of which displayed three very buxom girls in tights.

The Ministry, in Stead's words, 'capitulated to the storm'. His first article had appeared on 6 July and three days later, while the series was still running, the Criminal Law Amendment Act was again introduced in the House of Commons; next day, amid cheers, it passed the second reading. Cynics attributed this haste to a paragraph in Stead's article of 9 July :

> We challenge prosecution ... We are prepared, if we are driven to it, to prove our statements, prove them to the hilt, although in order to do so it may be necessary to subpoena as witnesses all those who are alluded to in our enquiries, either on proof of our *bona fides*, or as to the truth of our statements, from the Archbishop of Canterbury to Mrs Jeffries, and from the Prince of Wales down to the Minotaur of London.

The Minotaur was Stead's label for the man whom he believed to be the mastermind of London iniquity, a sort of Professor Moriarty of the virgin market. There was no evidence that he existed outside of Stead's perfervid imagination.

Early in August the bill, amended and in some ways strengthened, passed the House of Lords, though in both Houses there was still eloquent opposition to it. The debates reflected the traditional Tory reluctance to have sin confused with crime, and many members seemed more anxious to gaol Stead than to gaol the men and women who trafficked in little girls. Mr Cavendish Bentinck, perhaps the most dogged opponent of the bill, attacked the Government for allowing such an 'abominable paper' as the *Pall Mall Gazette* to be sold on the streets. 'When I was at public school, he said, 'if I had been found with a copy of such a paper in my pocket, I would have been soundly flogged.' The Secretary of State, Sir Assheton Cross, assured the House that eminent lawyers, including the Lord Chamberlain, had advised the Government that it would be unwise to take action against the paper. Mr Thorold Rogers said there were two ways of treating the subject dealt with in the *Pall Mall Gazette* – one was the language of the Old Testament, the other was the language of M. Zola. He did not make it clear whether Stead's language was Mosaic or Zola-esque. Mr Warton thought it was 'sentimental inflammatory language written with a spice to make it as attractive as such vile filth could be made'. He denounced the Bill as a 'tissue of nonsense promoted by ill-conditioned Democrats and Salvationist sentimentalists' to set class against class.

Mr Broadhurst, apparently an ill-conditioned Democrat, suggested tracing the evil of child prostitution back to its sources, which included herding whole families together 'in a manner worse than the beasts of the field'. Standing on Westminster Bridge in the morning did not move Mr Broadhurst to a mood of sonnet-writing rapture similar to Wordsworth's:

Let anyone stand on Westminster, Waterloo, Blackfriars, or London Bridges any morning and watch the continuous stream of girls crossing from the southern side of the river to the City and the West End to labour to their utmost capacity for a mere pittance insufficient to maintain them in the decencies of life. Very many of them were poorly clad and hungry, and he asked if it was within human nature to expect that those poor wretches should withstand the temptations which wealth offered them on their return journey every evening?

The impish and wealthy radical Henry Labouchere made two notable contributions to the debate. He told the House that he believed there were more brothels on the property of the Dean of Christchurch than on any other property in London – another member had estimated the total number in London at between 6,000 and 10,000 – and he introduced almost unnoticed, at the committee stage, a quite irrelevant amendment that has had far-reaching consequences. It made acts of indecency between males, even when performed in private between consenting adults, a

serious offence. Labouchere's amendment was introduced in the small
hours of the night, and the few members who were present and awake
accepted it without discussion and apparently without realizing what it
meant.

The frankness of some of the speeches in Parliament displeased London
editors. 'What will become of those hot thoughts, those morbid imagina-
tions, those foul memories, which the reading or hearing of these addresses
leave behind it?' asked the *Spectator*. 'The mischief done to purity of
thought . . . will infinitely outweigh the blow struck against impurity of
action.' And *The Times* wrote coldly of the 'intemperate and discreditable'
agitation.

When the amended bill was sent back to the Lords for approval, Earl
Beauchamp moved its acceptance with a worldly lack of enthusiasm. He
said he was not one who believed that the morals of people could be very
much influenced by legislation. 'An Act of Parliament', he declared,
'would not make those chaste and moral who were unchaste and immoral.'
However, no one would rejoice more than he if the bill produced the
results hoped for. And he pointed out with asperity that for two years the
House of Commons had not even found time to consider the bill though
in each of those years it had found time to pass bills against pigeon-
shooting.

At the end of July, while the bill was still being debated, a committee
which included the Archbishop of Canterbury, Cardinal Manning, the
Bishop of London and Mr John Morley sat for several days in the Venetian
Parlour of the Mansion House to investigate the truth of Stead's statements. After questioning Mrs Broughton, Mrs Armstrong and other
witnesses, the committee announced that the articles in the *Pall Mall
Gazette* were, taken as a whole, 'substantially true'. This finding provoked a
fresh tirade from press and politicians. In the House of Commons, Mr
Staveley Hill declared: 'A filthy editor of a filthy production had no right
to make gross charges against Englishmen occupying exalted positions in
Church and State and then go skulking before four or five men who were
as unfit to try the case as they would be to try a domestic cat.' Nor was the
Saturday Review more respectful: 'The sitting of the Commission was a
scandal, its decision a farce . . . There was indeed one serious thing about
it. It has given the PRIMATE of England and the Bishop of London an
opportunity of making themselves ridiculous.'

Mrs Booth wrote to Queen Victoria and asked her to express sympathy
with the campaign. Her Majesty replied, very properly, through the
Dowager Marchioness of Ely, that though she felt deeply on the subject
she had been advised that it would not be desirable for her to express any
opinion on a matter before Parliament. How deeply she felt is a matter of
conjecture. As E. F. Benson, son of the Primate who sat on the Mansion

House Committee, says, 'To the end of her life, Queen Victoria knew almost nothing of the working class and its sufferings.'

Up to the time of the meeting of the Mansion House Committee Mrs Armstrong had expressed no curiosity about the whereabouts of her daughter. But, questioned by the august members of the Committee, she burst into tears and said she wanted her child back. Her neighbours, it seems, had identified 'Lily', and were taunting her with having sold her daughter. 'I went in to Mrs Broughton's . . .' she afterwards explained, 'and said "What a dreadful thing that is in the *Gazette*. I am all of a tremble."' Mrs Armstrong took her troubles to the police, protesting that she had only let her daughter leave home to become a servant girl, a statement incapable of proof or disproof, and Mr Armstrong swore, quite truly, that he had never consented to her leaving home at all.

There was, as Stead put it, 'a good deal of fuss in the hostile papers', to which he replied publicly and proudly that he had abducted Eliza, and that she was very well cared for. As she was still being held incommunicado in Paris, and her mother had demanded her return, the police had little option but to charge Stead and his colleagues with abduction. Stead, of course, at once saw himself as the martyred messiah: 'The opponents of the reform which the *Pall Mall* had forced upon the Government and the House of Commons exulted over the chance which this case afforded them of dealing what they believed would be a fatal blow at the man who had defeated them,' he wrote later. He was more factual when he said the trial created 'almost as much sensation as the original publication'. With him in the dock at the Old Bailey, charged with abduction, were Mr Bramwell Booth (General Booth's son), Jacques, Rebecca Jarrett, Madame Mourey and Madame Coombe – a wealthy widow Salvationist who had taken charge of Eliza in Paris.

IV

A public defence fund – £6,000 in one of Stead's accounts, £10,000 in another – was quickly raised, and a battery of eminent counsel, among them Sir Charles Russell, afterwards Lord Chief Justice, retained. Stead, however, conducted his own defence. The Old Bailey was too good a pulpit to be missed. The Archbishop of Canterbury, Cardinal Manning, Bishop Temple, John Morley, Arthur Balfour and Mr Labouchere were subpoenaed to prove the purity of Stead's motives, a proof that was quite irrelevant. Stead, in fact, had no chance of being acquitted for he had admitted, 'in the clearest possible terms', that he had taken Eliza away, certainly without her father's consent, nor could he prove that he had the consent of her mother. He afterwards claimed that if he had asked Mrs Armstrong to produce her marriage lines, the case would have collapsed, because Eliza was born out of wedlock; Sir Charles Russell had prevented him, saying, 'I will never be a party to such a license of cross-examination.' But even if Stead had beaten the charge of abduction, he must have been convicted on the second indictment of 'unlawfully assaulting' Eliza, or 'causing her to be indecently assaulted'.

The case was the first of any importance heard under the New Criminal Law Amendment Act which Stead had forced through Parliament, and it was the first time in an English court that the accused were able to give evidence in their own defence. Stead delivered impassioned homilies from the dock. 'There are', he announced confidently, 'between 50,000 and 60,000 lost girls on the London streets now, and if you think that that great multitude of our fallen sisters got there without the intervention of any go-betweens . . . you are muchly mistaken.' He said there were 10,000 little girls living by prostitution, and mentioned one brothel staffed by forty children.

Cardinal Manning was excused from appearing because he had a cold, but the Archbishop of Canterbury answered his subpoena and was given a seat on the bench alongside Mr Justice Lopez. His honour decided, however, that His Grace could not speak to any relevant facts on the question of the alleged abduction, Mr Stead's intention having nothing to do with the case. 'The only question,' he told Stead, 'is whether in carrying out your good motives you did not overstep the law'.

This in fact was the only thing to be decided, and it was silly for Stead, or his admirers, to claim that he was unfairly convicted. (Stead said the animus of the judge in his summing-up was 'undisguised', and Mr J. W. Robertson Scott, sixty-seven years later, wrote of the 'glaring injustice' of the trial.) In his summing-up, which took an entire day, Mr Justice Lopez told the jury not to be prejudiced against Stead because of the 'disgusting and filthy articles' emanating from the *Pall Mall Gazette* offices – 'articles so filthy and disgusting that one cannot help fearing they may have suggested to the minds of innocent women and children the existence of wickedness which had never occurred to their minds before'.

But 'the law cannot be broken to promote any good or supposed good', he reminded the jury, and 'the sanctity of private life cannot be invaded for the furtherance of the views of an individual who believes that the end justifies the means'.

Jacques, Bramwell Booth and Madame Coombe were acquitted on the abduction charge and Rebecca Jarrett and Stead convicted; the jury adding a rider that Stead had been deceived by his agents. They recommended him to mercy and recorded their appreciation of the services he had rendered the nation. Next day, the defendants and Madame Mourey were found guilty on the second charge, of indecent assault.

The name of England has been blackened before the world [said *The Times*]. The continent had grinned with jealous delight at the hypocritical monsters of 'vice' revealed by the Commission; and now the microscopic eye of the law court has been turned full upon one of the most important pieces of evidence, and it has been found to be false and baseless.

It is a matter of rejoicing that a test case has shown that one of the gravest charges against the English populace – the charge of selling their children for infamous purposes cannot be substantiated.

The test case had shown nothing of the sort. It had shown that Stead had broken the law by taking Eliza Armstrong away without her putative father's consent, that Eliza had, technically, been indecently assaulted, and that, as Mr Justice Lopez put it, the law could not be broken 'to promote any good or supposed good'.

V

The continent, particularly France, continued to grin 'with jealous delight'. A book exposing the 'seamy side of social life' in the European capitals, by Juliette Adam, with a chapter on London based on the Stead disclosures, had a wide circulation. This French exploitation of English vice enraged Swinburne, and inspired some savage 'Rondeaux Parisiens'. He also addressed some uncomplimentary verses to Stead and Booth. In one ballade he conferred the title of 'Marquis' on Stead, a delicate allusion to Swinburne's spiritual mentor, the Marquis of Sade.

Here is part of it:

THE MARQUIS OF STEAD

Knaves, kidnappers, forgers and strumpets,
    Thieves, penitents, panders and saints,
They have scared with the blast of their trumpets,
    Poor truth till the heart in her faints.
Till, conscious how foul and accurst is
    The brood that in Grubstreet is bred,
She can hardly be sure if the worst is
    The Marquis of Stead.

Obscenity, falsehood, monstrosity,
    Foamed forth from the lips of the beast,
Whose genius, not grown to precocity,
    Suborned not the press and the priest.

But Archbishops and Cardinals, hoary
   In honour – what prayers have they said?
'God bless and receive into glory
   The Marquis of Stead!'

He has erred – we can hardly deny it:
   It is painful to say he has erred.
Though a lie may be hardly a lie, it
   Is at least an inaccurate word.
Who cares though the mob have its fill of
   Rant, falsehood, and poison for bread,
If it brings but in grist to the mill of
   The Marquis of Stead.

His motives we all must applaud – he
   Endured for the holiest of frauds
To tipple in houses called – gaudy
   With – ladies, whose titles were gauds.
His motives, his deeds, are not plainer!
   Truth smiled at beholding abed
As drunk as a – total abstainer
   The Marquis of Stead.

Not as drunk as a lord, nor as vicious,
   This truth is the plainest of truths
And the savour thereof as delicious
   As the reek and the roar of the Booths –
The Booths of the fair of salvation
   Whom devils and decency dread
Who salute with obscene salutation
   The Marquis of Stead.

VI

Stead was sentenced to three months' imprisonment, dating from the opening of the Sessions, an actual sentence of two months and seven days. Madame Mourey and Mrs Jarrett each received six months, and Jacques one month. Bernard Shaw and many other of his supporters were shaken to learn that the Eliza case was a 'put-up job'. After that, said Shaw, no one ever trusted Stead: 'We all felt that if ever a man deserved six months' imprisonment, Stead deserved it for such a betrayal of our confidence in him.'

Stead enjoyed his imprisonment even more than he had enjoyed his trial. For three days he wore a yellow convict dress, bespattered with broad arrows, and picked oakum in Coldbath gaol. Then, at the direction of the Home Secretary, he was transferred to Holloway as a first-class misdemeanant. He occupied a cosy room, comfortably furnished with bed, writing-desk, easy chairs, rug, gas ring and tea-kettle, for which he paid six shillings a week, including room service. He was well supplied with food, fruit and flowers. Pots of lily-of-the-valley, tulips and cyclamen decorated his retreat, and a fire blazed cheerfully in the hearth. He was allowed visitors every day. Members of the *Pall Mall Gazette* staff called regularly, and among distinguished pilgrims to what Stead called 'the pleasantest of little rooms imaginable' was Cardinal Manning. Stead found his 'cell' an ideal editorial office. He received his newspapers every morning at a quarter-past seven, and a messenger called for his 'copy' at ten. 'I do not think that I have ever been in better spirits in my life or enjoyed existence more intensely than in these two months,' he wrote. He wanted all his friends to know how 'jolly' he was. 'There is nothing like being in gaol for getting rid of bores and getting on with work.'

It was certainly not so jolly for Madame Mourey, who died in gaol, and it is not known how much Stead's other helpers enjoyed their imprisonment. But two, at least, in the cosy tradition of the Victorian novelist, lived happily ever after.

Rebecca Jarrett, who had been a very bad witness at the trial, contradicting herself and lying glibly, returned to her good works with the Salvation Army, and lived to her eighties, 'loved and esteemed by those around her', and little Eliza married happily and became 'the proud and happy mother of a family of six'.

To Stead, 10 November, the day of his conviction, was always the 'Red Letter Day' of his life. He celebrated its anniversary each year by coming to work (by train from Wimbledon, over Waterloo Bridge, to the Strand) in his prison clothes – the yellow jacket with broad arrows, the peaked cap, the round badge inscribed R$\frac{2}{7}$. Few Londoners could have realized that this earnest, hurrying little man who looked like an escaped convict was a special messenger of the Lord.

Stead continued to carry out his Master's instructions, though they remained confused, till he disappeared with the *Titanic* in April 1912.

VII

Stead's spectacular campaign may have diminished child prostitution in England, but the brisk traffic in women continued. London, and particularly Piccadilly Circus, remained a busy market-place of sex. In 1898 members of the Salvation Army, with a heroism matching Stead's, boldly investigated the nightly traffic in the Circus, and the fashionable streets

around it. Their vivid report on Piccadilly's 'Midnight Infamies' was
published in the Army's official newspaper, *The Darkest England Gazette*.
Here are extracts from it:

What Monte Carlo is to Continental gambling, what the Epsom
Saturnalia is to horse-racing, such is Piccadilly to the immorality of the
greatest city the world has known. It is the 'blue ribbon' of prostitution
to be 'on the streets' there . . . the high-priced and haughty importations
of Paris and Amsterdam agree on this, that Piccadilly is the goal of the
fallen woman . . . hundreds of women, primed with brandy and
absinthe, their silks and laces fluttering in the night air, ply their trade
regularly from the early hours of the evening until two or three the next
morning . . . Between twelve and one the pandemonium is at its height.
Cabs by the score are prowling about, to pick up the couples who
continually make their arrangements and drive off. The cabbies are
worldly wise, they quietly pull up by the likely-looking pairs.

Just before midnight the great music halls, The Empire, The Pavilion
and Alhambra, close, and the supper-rooms, pubs and pavements are
crowded with people. Gradually the decent people withdraw; they catch
the last 'bus. Piccadilly assumes its darkest aspect, especially when the
pubs and restaurants close. Just opposite that splendid building, so
richly fitted up, glowing with the light and glitter of gold and colours
reflected in the mirrors of the *buffet*. This is the St. James's Restaurant.
At twenty-five minutes past twelve a gay crowd emerges; no less than
twenty-five of them are evidently prostitutes; some are with men, but
most are alone. One is splendidly dressed in some creamy cloth. She
walks with a regal air; others are in pink, sea green or blue, but all in the
height of fashion, with a certain suggestive Parisian voluptousness
superadded. The street is thronged; one can only press through with
difficulty.

There is little blasphemy, but filthy shouts and invitations and
actions to any extent, revolting and pitiful. Another swell gin-palace
belches forth its quota of fallen men and fallen women to the awful
scene.

Twenty-seven more women glittering in long-trained satins and
muslins, set off with rose sprays, delicate feather-tufts and modern frills,
rush from another stained-glassed, electric-lighted pub. Many of the
men are intoxicated, and bands of youths, well-dressed, and evidently
sprigs of the aristocracy, who might be Eton or Harrow boys, are
engaged in disgusting conversations with ghastly French procuresses,
who, sure of their prey, are describing the dreadful delights in store.
Everything is a roar and whirl of noise and immoral traffic. The police
do their best to keep order, but of what avail are their efforts? They can

but utter an occasional 'move on'. They are apparently helpless to stop, and are contented to regulate matters. They practically become the priests and servants of the black Goddess Prostitution. The whole scene – the pathetic dreadfulness of unsexed woman and devil-possessed man, the oaths, the filth, the palatial streets and Circus turned into a hell for the time being – is appalling! It is Walpurgis night. Mephistopheles, in his red cloak and feather, would complete the scene. It is horrible!

The men are as bad as the women, or worse. On every hand are bloated and leering visages, marked with drink and vice. See them lounging about the Circus corners, going off arm in arm with a Lois or Cressida, or leaning against a shop-front, and engaging in a beastly conversation, larded with oaths and horrid anecdotes, with a Phryne in pink satin and roses.

Or, a hansom drives up, the cab touter rushes to throw back the door. Out jumps a swell in evening dress and opera hat, who, after critically surveying the crowd of stylish and handsome women who bid for his custom, selects his preference, nods to her and they drive off to some shady house off Shaftesbury Avenue or King's Road, Chelsea. So the traffic goes on, until by degrees the crowd thins. The higher-class women who have failed for tonight, drive home in cabs, and the streets are left to a few dozen stragglers, who, hungry and weary, wait about to make some stray drunkard or late bird their prey, committing the most flagrant immoralities in the yards and doorways of the streets, and then with difficulty plodding off to a cheap lodging-house, to gain a few hours' rest before renewing their traffic the following night.

Whilst Piccadilly Circus is the root of the cancer, its branches spread therefrom in all directions. Right up Regent Street, for a considerable distance, the market is carried on. Scarcely a shop but has in front of it several couples coming to terms. Up Piccadilly towards the Park, things are busy as on the Circus itself. . . . At Prince's Street corner alone thirteen women (mostly French) are making night hideous; the principal girl, in a low cut violet velvet dress, flourishes a gilt fan, and dances to and fro. There are, of course, brothels innumerable. They are not difficult to find. Any of the women almost will give you her card . . .

The relations of our Rescue workers to the Piccadilly women are such that we have not the least difficulty in saying how the vice victims reach the Piccadilly abyss. Many are domestic servants, housemaids who have attracted the attention and satanic designs of the 'son of the house', of a swellish visitor, or, very frequently, of the master himself . . .

The large and increasing percentage of foreigners is a strong feature. The fallen Englishwoman is bad enough when primed with drink, but the Frenchwoman adds to the native British horrors a certain cold-blooded Parisian *diablerie* that is specially revolting . . .

The evil, as represented in the foreign woman, is particularly formidable. Thoroughly conversant with all the medical dodges of Continental brothels, she is often an adept at evading the physical difficulties and results of the situation. The result is, instead of dying in a few months of a loathsome disease or from bodily wreck, she survives, takes rooms near Piccadilly, rises to a brass plate, even, with the inscription, 'Madame de Pompadour, dressmaker,' gets hold of several young girls, initiates them into the dreadful mysteries of harlotry and walks them into Piccadilly with the air of a driving-master exercising horses.

Many more come driven by hunger and the sweater's whip. Many a bright girl works at a City neck-tie or mantle factory, barely able to eke out a scanty existence on starvation pay. Chronic hunger is her continual companion. Disease, death, dog her footsteps. By the most arduous labours she fails to support herself. An introduction to high-class Piccadilly whoredom is more than she can resist. From starvation to seeming luxury, from rags and dirt to glittering dresses and freedom from the dull grind of work! She looks, hesitates, leaps into the vortex, and is lost.

So they come from all over the country, betrayed, invited, lured, entranced, to swell the high tide in Piccadilly . . .

There is no gainsaying these facts. The evidence is overwhelming. We saw and heard, the other night, solicitations by the score. Several of our staff were repeatedly tackled. The police simply stood by. In one side street was a most sickening spectacle. A tall English girl stood in a doorway, arranging her clothes, with the help of another girl, in a most indecent and abominable manner, cursing, swearing and shouting. Meanwhile, two police constables and a sergeant stood looking on as if it were the most common-place sight in the world, whilst a little lower down the same thoroughfare further abominations were being practised.

Select Bibliography

Apart from these books, principal sources were the files of *The Times*, the *Illustrated London News*, the *Saturday Review* and many fugitive nineteenth-century English weeklies.

Acton, William. *The Functions and Disorders of the Reproductive Organs*
Bassett, A. Tilney (Ed.). *Gladstone to his Wife*
Benson, E. F. *As We Were*
Bloch, Iwan. *A History of English Sexual Morals*
Croft-Cooke, Rupert. *Feasting with Panthers*
Drummond, J. C. *The Englishman's Food*
Ellis, S. M. (Ed.). *The Hardman Papers*
Fiedler, Leslie A., *Love and Death in the American Novel*
Forster, J. *Life of Charles Dickens*
Gorer, Geoffrey. *The Americans*
Griffiths, Major. *Chronicles of Newgate*
Hennessy, James Pope-. *Monckton Milnes: the Flight of Youth*
Hudson, Derek. *Lewis Carroll*
Kellett, E. E. *Aspects of History*
Kirwan, Daniel Joseph. *Palace and Hovel*
Kingsmill, Hugh (pseud.). *After Puritanism*
Koestler, Arthur and Rolphe, C. H. *Hanged by the Neck*
Lennon, F. B. *Lewis Carroll*
Leslie, Shane. *Film of Memory*
Lindsay, Jack. *Charles Dickens*
McCabe, Joseph. *Social Record of Christianity*
Mayhew, Henry. *London Labour and the London Poor*
My Secret Life. (Anon.)
McCarthy, Justin. *A History of Our Own Times*
Nevill, Ralph. *Unconventional Memories*
Newsome, David. *History of Wellington College*
Oman, Sir Charles. *Memoirs of Victorian Oxford and of Some Early Years*
Peel, S. *Early Victorian England, 1830–1865*
Pisanus Fraxi (Henry S. Ashbee). *Notes on Curious and Uncommon Books*
Renier, G. J. *The English: Are they Human?*
Salt, Henry. *Memories of Bygone Eton*
Straus, Ralph. *Sala: The Portrait of An Eminent Victorian*
Sykes, Christopher. *Four Studies in Loyalty*

Taylor, Shepherd T. *Diary of A Medical Student*

Thompson, Anthony F. *The English Schoolroom*

Thomson, David. *England in the Nineteenth Century*

Toynbee, William. *The Diaries of William Charles Macready, 1833–1851*

Trevelyan, G. M. *English Social History*

Weldon, E. C. *Recollections*

Wingfield-Stratford, E. *Before the Lamps Went Out: The Victorian Tragedy*

Woodward, E. L. *The Age of Reform 1815–1870*

Woolf, Virginia. *Roger Fry*

Young, G. M. *Victorian England*

Index